PREPARATION FOR TRANSLATION

by Milton G. Crane, M.D.

(Third Edition)

TEACH Services, Inc.
PUBLISHING
www.TEACHServices.com

World rights reserved. This book or any portion thereof may not be copied or reproduced in any form or manner whatever, except as provided by law, without the written permission of the publisher, except by a reviewer who may quote brief passages in a review.

This book was written to provide truthful information in regard to the subject matter covered. The author assumes full responsibility for the accuracy of all facts and quotations as cited in this book. The opinions expressed in this book are the author's personal views and interpretation of the Bible, Spirit of Prophecy, and/or contemporary authors and do not necessarily reflect those of TEACH Services, Inc.

This book is sold with the understanding that the publisher is not engaged in giving spiritual, legal, medical, or other professional advice. If authoritative advice is needed, the reader should seek the counsel of a competent professional

Copyright © 2008 TEACH Services, Inc.
ISBN-13: 978-0-945383-33-8
Library of Congress Control Number: 88-50091

Published by

www.TEACHServices.com

TABLE OF CONTENTS

Forgiveness By Faith–Obedience By Faith 1
Set This Aside For Holy Use 7
The Way To Our Inheritance Unveiled By The Sanctuary 13
How The Law Helps Grace 29
Power To Think And To Do 33
The Record Of Your Life 39
A Special Look At The Record 45
Guilt 50
Character 54
Pictures In The Halls Of Memory 59
The Subtle Change Of The Mind 64
Temptation Without—answering Chord Within 69
Righteousness 75
The Ministry Of The Spirit 82
Perfection Versus Maturation And The Nature Of Humanity 87
The Humanity Of Christ And The Perfecting Of Humanity 92
Gold And Silver And Precious Stones 106
He Was Rejected 111
Vital Lessons From The 1888 Experience 115
The Purpose Of The Health Message 132
The Role Of Cholesterol And "Free Fat" In Disease? 137
Other Ways "free Fat" Cause Disease 140
God's True Remedies = The Secret Of Success 146
The Benefits Of God's True Remedies 152
Development Of The "omega" Of Deception 164
Will The Real Omega Please Stand Up And Be Identified! 167
The Modern-day Inroads Of Pantheism 168
Some Theories And Manifestations Of Pantheism 171
Pantheistic Concepts Stealthily Enter The Church 186
Those Dramatic Changes In Europe - The Pantheism Component 191
Tidings Out Of The East And Of The North 202
The Final Movements Will Be Rapid Ones 209
God's Harvest Sequence 216
Conclusion And Appeal 220

TO THE READER

This booklet is about **your** preparation for translation. It is about **your** plans to live without a mediator after probation closes. It is about overcoming temptation **now** in anticipation of those events. It is about God's plans for the renewing of **your** mind through the ministry of Jesus.

Much that is discussed herein is about future events. Some may say, why be so concerned about insight into future events? One answer to that can be found on page 594 of the book *Great Controversy* by Ellen White. "The events connected with the close of probation and the work of preparation for the time of trouble are clearly presented. But multitudes have no more understanding of these important truths than if they had never been revealed." On that page the author of those words also indicated that those truths have been revealed to us as clearly as Jesus foretold to His disciples the events connected with His death and resurrection. Why were the disciples not waiting at the sepulcher on that eventful first day morning? Their preconceived ideas and their concern as to who was to be the top man interfered with their ability to hear and believe what He said about His time of trouble and resurrection. But the Pharisees remembered and made plans to care for the situation just in case He would arise.

We have been informed that the last righteous generation will spend a certain period of time on the earth without a mediator after probation closes. After Jesus throws down His censer, will there be forgiveness for sins available to anyone thereafter? Can the righteous go to the Father and ask for removal of guilt of a known or an unknown sin then? If they cannot, then they will live without committing a known or unknown sin. Do God's people really have enough faith in God's keeping power to believe that they, with the assistance of God, can live without sinning for a period of time on this earth? Jesus asked this question, "Nevertheless, when the Son of man cometh, shall He find faith on the earth" (Luke 18:8)? A knowledge of **how** to cooperate with God for purity of heart and **how** to develop a righteous character are questions not to be postponed to some future time without running the risk of being counted with the five foolish virgins of Matthew 25.

My reasons for writing this are fourfold. First, I desire to inform others, as best I can express, of my thoughts and the insights that I have obtained by prayerful study. Second, writing these considerations on paper helps me to consolidate and clarify the concepts in my own mind. Third, some of my readers may mention where they differ with me, if they do. By reasoning together from the Scriptures, we both can be "hewed and squared for the building" by the prophets (EW71). Fourth, I find that after I have tried to give to others what I have learned, then I, in turn, receive more understanding.

We do not have to understand all truth to be saved or, for that matter, to be effective witnesses. Where we disagree, let us discuss, study, and pray for more insight.

Truth, like a gem, has many facets. Precious stones of truth are to be identified and polished to reveal their luster in the world of deceptions. Truths of Scripture can also be likened to parts of a puzzle. There are some statements of Inspiration that are a bit perplexing. In some instances it may not be readily apparent how some statements fit into the overall picture. As we try to locate their place, we may have to lay some aside until more pieces are in place, and the relationship of the parts become evident. Certainly, we should guard against trimming or distorting a concept in order to fit it into a preconceived spot. When we do that, eventually we will need to reshape other truths to finish the picture; but the final result does not quite look right.

If the reader will accept two main premises that are presented in these chapters, perhaps it would be safe to wait for further insight on other points. It would seem to me that in order to be prepared for the investigative judgment and the troubles to follow, we must be found doing two things:

1) Searching our souls and praying for purity of heart (see PK59l). We must be found examining ourselves to see that we have such a hatred of sin and a love for God and His ways that we want to be His servant in all things at all times forever. Also, we must repent of all our sins.

2) Striving to be under the control of the Holy Spirit at all times so that we may overcome temptations and trials and fulfill our opportunities to be of service to God. In other words, we are to develop the habit of calling to God in the name of Christ for the desire and power to be obedient moment by moment, at the time of need. In this way we have a religion of experience, a settling into the truth. **We know by experience that with God working in us to will and to do we can overcome every temptation every**

time, and we know that if we try in our own power we will fail. Then, in the time of trouble, we merely continue to keep the heart perfect toward God and continue to request Divine power to stand for God "though the heavens fall."

A note about the references:—In some instances the texts that are given refer to direct quotations or to concepts that I have paraphrased. In other instances one or more references are given to substantiate a conclusion based upon a comparison of the several references. In other words, in some circumstances we may arrive at conclusions through sanctified reasoning by studying a combination of texts. There are many places in which several additional references could have been added, but they were omitted for sake of brevity. It is hoped that the reader will be stimulated by this book to further study and meditation.

Although the references in this book are predominantly from the writings of E. G. White, they are consistent with Biblical teaching. This study is primarily designed for Seventh-day Adventist Bible students. Certain subjects need to be explored in depth. The writings of the Spirit of prophecy, the "lesser light," give me clearer insight into the Scriptures, the "greater light," since many key words dealing with the mind such as habits, character, propensities, etc. do not appear directly in the Bible. By the help of the Lord's messenger we can better understand the meaning of the symbols, parables, and illustrations on these and other topics in the Scriptures.

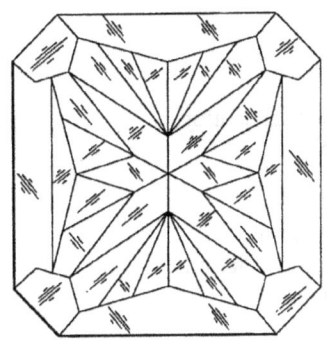 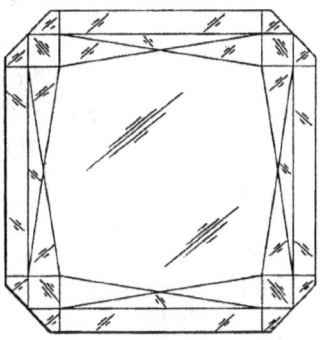

Truth, like a gem, has many facets

KEY TO ABBREVIATIONS TO WRITINGS OF ELLEN G. WHITE

AA	The Acts of the Apostles
AH	The Adventist Home
1-7BC	The Seventh-day Adventist Bible Commentary, Vols. 1-7.
CDF	Counsels on Diet and Foods
CG	Child Guidance
CH	Counsels on Health
COL	Christ's Object Lessons
CPT	Counsels to Parents, Teachers, and Students
CW	Counsels to Writers and Editors
DA	The Desire of Ages
ED	Education
Ev	Evangelism
EW	Early Writings (1945)
FCE	Fundamentals of Christian Education
GC	Great Controversy (1939)
GW	Gospel Workers
HP	In Heavenly Places
LS	Life Sketches of Ellen G. White
MB	Thoughts from the Mount of Blessing (1956)
MH	The Ministry of Healing
MLT	My Life Today
MM	Medical Ministry
MS	Manuscript
MYP	Messages to Young People
OHC	Our High Calling
PK	Prophets and Kings
PP	Patriarchs and Prophets
RH	Review and Herald
SC	Steps to Christ (1956)
SD	Sons and Daughters of God
1-4SG	Spiritual Gifts, Volumes 1 to 4
SL	The Sanctified Life
1-3SM	Selected Messages, Books 1 to 3
SOC	The Sufferings of Christ
SpT	Special Testimonies
SR	The Story of Redemption
ST	The Signs of the Times
1-9T	Testimonies, Volumes 1 to 9
Te	Temperance
TM	Testimonies to Ministers and Gospel Workers

Chapter 1

FORGIVENESS BY FAITH–OBEDIENCE BY FAITH

In recent years there has been a renewed interest in the events that happened in our church around the time of 1888 as portrayed by the writings of Ellen White, Elders A. T. Jones and E. J. Waggoner. It is not my intention in this presentation to go into this subject except for one aspect. I wish to discuss the relationship of faith and works, or the application of the **imputed** and **imparted** righteousness of Christ.

In 1882, God impressed Ellen White to make a renewed emphasis on the teachings of righteousness by faith (5T84, 217-235; 1SM350). Her messages were even more imperative in 1887 (see A.G. Daniells, *Christ Our Righteousness*, R&H Publishing Co., p. 28-34). Elders Waggoner and Jones also gave this message,

> "Justification through faith in the Surety; it invited the people to receive the righteousness of Christ, which is made manifest in obedience to all the commandments of God" (TM92).

Some may say that the message brought at that time was not rejected. The answer to that, however, is too plain to be mistaken. Some accepted the message correctly, but **far too many** rejected the message for God to do what He desired to do (TM89-98; 1SM234-5). Two quotations are presented here in this connection.

> "Some of our brethren are not receiving the message of God upon this subject [justification by faith]. They appear to

be anxious that none of our ministers shall depart from their former manner of teaching the good old doctrines" (RH04-01-90).

"For nearly two years we have been urging the people to come up and accept the light and the truth concerning the righteousness of Christ, and they do not know whether to come and take hold of this precious truth or not" (RH03-11-90).

Perhaps the rejection of this truth at that time was comparable to the situation when the children of Israel were to go into Canaan the first time. When God desired to take them into the land of promise, **they** decided to send spies to see if **He** could do it (PP387; GC457). Because of the report of the ten, **too many of them** lost faith and murmured. God changed His plans. Then, in rebellion, they tried to go into Canaan in their own wisdom and strength but failed.

God could not lead them into that Canaan until He had a **people**, not just a few, who (a) believed that **they were unable** to enter **in their own strength alone** and (b) believed that they could overcome every enemy if they depended upon God's plans and called upon Him for power in the struggle.

God did not design that ancient Israel should wander for forty years in the desert. Nor did He intend that modern Israel should be in this world for so long after 1844 (1SM68-69). In that connection four things, - unbelief, worldliness, unconsecration, and strife among His professed people are listed as causes for the delay.

We are directed to the messages of the three angels of Revelation 14 and to the sanctuary service for understanding as were His followers in 1844 (1SM67; GC424-5). We would do well to evaluate the situation and try to determine humbly, without prejudice, under the guidance of the Holy Spirit, just what God wanted His people to understand in 1844 and 1888, for it must have been most significant truth for the closing work on the earth.

A letter from E. G. White to Elder A. T. Jones dated 1893 introduces one facet of truth revolving around righteousness by faith that needs consideration (1SM377-82). It has to do with the relationship between faith and works, a topic of key importance. In that letter she warned Elder Jones against presenting the subject of faith and the imputed righteousness of Christ in such a way that his listeners would think that, "works amounted to nothing, that there were no conditions." She pointed out that there were conditions and that cooperative works (man working while depending upon the power of Christ) amounts to a great deal in the eyes of God.

She said even though, "You look in reality upon these subjects as I do, yet you make these subjects, through your expressions, confusing to minds" (1SM378).

It would appear from the foregoing statement that the complete message of righteousness by faith encompassed more than justification (forgiveness) by faith, and that the relationship of works to faith needed to be presented clearly.

Our enemy wants desperately to confuse Bible doctrines. He has an enduring hatred of Christ since first he rebelled with pride and jealousy. He turned against the authority of **Christ** initially (PP40). He says that man cannot keep the law of God (DA761). To his way of thinking the law of God is faulty and needs to be changed (PP69). It is he that originated the fundamentals of existentialism and the "new morality." Since early in the rebellion, his philosophy has been "love" God and do as you please (GC495, 499, 555). He has originated many ideas which may be used to rationalize away disobedience. We see examples of this in the common things of life as well as in the spiritual realm.

In the small Adventist city where I once lived there were traffic laws. There was the usual 35 mile per hour speed limit and the requirement that the vehicles stop when pedestrians were in the cross walk. If you were to ask the citizens of that town, drivers and nondrivers, both would most likely concede that those were good laws for the busy thoroughfare. And yet, when I walked in the town and crossed into the central area, I was fearful for my safety on occasions, more fearful than when in larger cities nearby where traffic was better policed. Glaring in "righteous" indignation at the driver who barely missed me did not seem to help. The driver appeared to feel that he had done his duty if he missed me.

Is it possible that Adventists are keener and more expert drivers because of healthful living? Has our affluence given us better automobiles with better braking devices than those of other drivers? Perhaps we are afraid of being called "legalists" if we keep the letter of the law. No, I doubt that these are conscious reasons. We have been subtly influenced by the world to a new way to look at law. Here are some of them.

If a law is too strict, perhaps it was designed for those inferior to you in driving prowess. You are the exception and hence do not need to keep that law. It is now all right to do a deed contrary to law so long as no one gets hurt. It is all right to go against the rules if you can get by without getting caught. For some, the concept of "keeping" the law goes something like this,–Once you acknowledge that the law is good, you may drive your car at your preferred speed and come within inches of a pedestrian and still be guiltless. After all, it is the "spirit" of the law that counts (cf DA309.6)!

Our enemy is especially active in distorting the perspective of church members. Satan professes belief in the cross. After all, Calvary is history. Symbols of it adorn apostate and true churches alike. Satan wants to join the Christian churches. He has his priestly confessional in some churches. Ellen White in vision saw a representation of Satan endeavoring to carry on the work of Christ in the first apartment of the heavenly sanctuary after the services had been moved into the second apartment in 1844 (EW55, 261). Satan now concedes that God can forgive. He even offers "victory" power (EW56). But, when it comes to real obedience to God, there he draws the line.

> "Obedience or disobedience is the question to be decided by the whole world." (DA763).

The teachings of apostate Protestantism separate obedience from love. Obedience to the ten commandments is made part of the Old Covenant and is nailed to the cross. Love is identified with the New Covenant and kept. The Christian who accepts this philosophy now looks to himself rather than to the law of God for guidance in right doing. They say, "If you love God, you will **naturally** do what He wants you to do." But this is risky business. My **natural** tendencies are wrong. What I do seems right in my own eyes. Love without communication is blind. It takes careful, prayerful study of God's word to know what He wants.

This can be illustrated by an incident from our family. On the morning after our wedding, my new bride got up early to prepare an extra special breakfast for her husband. In the process she darkened the toast a bit too much. Since I desired to be a loving dutiful husband, I complimented her on the wonderful breakfast. For many months thereafter I always got nearly black toast for breakfast. One day, a young couple, close friends of ours, came to stay overnight with us. The next morning I overheard my wife say to the friend who was helping her in the kitchen, "Be sure to toast some of the slices quite well. Milton likes his toast dark." I then understood why my toast was always so black while hers was so light in color. All those months I had eaten black toast rather than hurt her feelings, and she had been sure to make them that way because she loved me. She had never asked me what my preference was. By then the honeymoon was over, and we knew how to communicate without running the risk of devastating each other. It pays to ask what our loved one wants.

By means of various rationalized attitudes we, as a people, have been swerved from strict obedience. The subtle tactics of criticism by mislabeling have been used against us. Because of our desire to do God's will conscientiously, we have been accused of being "legalists." Certain of our protestant friends have branded us such for years. To avoid that label we tend to shy away from the teaching of obedience by faith. We make ourselves emphatically clear that we believe in "justification by faith alone," but our voice becomes weak when we get to the topic of works for God.

Are works to be done without faith? Has God said, "Friend, you are now forgiven; go [in your own strength] and sin no more"?

Is it not the genius of the Remnant Church to define the difference between **legalism** and **loving obedience**, and place the latter into its rightful place of **righteousness by faith in action**?

God says that man, with Christ's help, can render loving obedience (MH180). God plans one last demonstration of His redeeming-keeping power. He wants a group about whom He can say, "Here are they that keep the commandments of God, and the faith of Jesus" (Rev. 14:12). He plans that the last generation will live on the earth for a period of time after probation closes without sinning, prepared by the daily mediation of Jesus and His final atonement (EW253, 251, 280), and kept as Jesus was kept by the **enabling grace** of God (AA56; GC641).

Jesus carried out His part in the plan of salvation "to the letter and in the spirit of the law" (RH07-28-74). Should we do less in our role, in the sphere of our influence, here **in the strength of the Lord**? Is it not our duty as God's ambassadors to present both **forgiveness** by faith - **a free gift** - as well as **obedience** by faith in God's power - **a free gift** - so that the world can plainly see God's plan? Christ is the source of both imparted and imputed righteousness, and we need both for salvation.

The laws of God are not restrictive commandments, but positive promises. Christ invites us to search out His promises, claim them by prayer, believe that we receive them because "He is faithful that promised," and then thank Him (Matt. 7:7-11; Heb. 10:23). The same law that says, "Thou shalt not steal," also says, you can own and control property under God. The same law that says, "Thou shalt not commit adultery;" also says, you may choose a mate, set up a home, and no one has the right to intrude into your marital relationship. When God says, "Despondency is sinful and unreasonable" (PK164), He is saying to us that we have the right to call to Him for deliverance from the "Slough of Despond." "All power, all wisdom, are at our command. We have only to ask" (MH514). When we ask in faith according to his promises, He imparts the Holy Spirit, the fruit of which is joy (Gal 5:22). Sadness leaves us.

The law contains the promises which we may claim from our Father in the name of the loving Lawgiver (Deut 33:2, 3). "The great sin of the Jews was their rejection of Christ; the great sin of the Christian world would be their rejection of the law of God, the foundation of His government in heaven and earth" (GC22).

The Jews took great pains to fulfill the law, but they rejected the Saviour. Many professed Christians "accept Christ;" but when you mention the law, there is suddenly an icy silence. The law was done away with, so they say, at the cross.

It is not God who disparages works of righteousness (1SM381). "He [Satan] is constantly seeking occasion against those who are trying to obey God. Even their best and most acceptable services he seeks to make appear corrupt. By countless devices, the most subtle and the most cruel, he endeavors to secure their condemnation" (5T471). Shall we not counteract these activities by encouraging our fellow Christians in their good works? "And to esteem them [labourers among you] very highly in love for their work's sake" (1 Thess 5:13).

"In as much as ye have done it...."

Jesus

Chapter 2

SET THIS ASIDE FOR HOLY USE

In the previous chapter we have considered the importance of works. But before righteous works commence, certain preliminary changes must be made in us. Full surrender, total consecration of our body, mind, and soul must be made to our Ruler and to the government of heaven. Full surrender results in pardon.

The term "surrender" is used because we are rebels, but there is a connotation to that word that does not apply in the Christian sense. In some minds surrender may portray a dejected, forlorn individual who walks with mournful and labored gait. The mental picture is of a poor soul, almost exhausted, clothed in tattered remnants of his former uniform, housed in a concentration camp, awaiting deliverance by his former ruler.

When we surrender to Christ and consecrate ourselves to His service, we give up the old (DA172.4). We **defect**, if you please, from the old ways and pledge allegiance to God's government. Christ gives the "prisoner" of His love a new uniform, His robe of righteousness. He is now made an ambassador for the greatest Ruler in the Universe.

When the prodigal son came within reach of the father, He covered the son with His own robe, the imputed robe of righteousness. But the father does another thing. He says, "Bring forth the best robe, and put it on him; and put a ring on his hand..." (Luke 15:22; COL203-4). In other words, after the **imputed** covering robe, the Father **imparts** a robe that is woven in the loom of heaven. It is the son's robe to wear because it comes through the combined efforts, the choice of the son and the power of the Father, which produces obedience (Ed249.5). Clothed in this robe the son now chooses to let the Father work in Him from a new matine. No longer does he work for hope of a reward or to secure his inheritance. These are figts not something to be earned.

The term "sanctification" seems to be used in more than one sense by the prophets under inspiration. The word embodies a gem of truth with several facets. Facets of truth can be found and polished by searching for definitions of the specific words or terms in the Bible and Spirit of Prophecy. Whenever you read statements like, "Sanctification is the work of a lifetime" (1SM317), you may know that that word is there being defined.

The above definition of sanctification is perhaps the one most widely remembered by Seventh-day Adventists. Many who believe that definition seem to hold the concept that a person is to struggle diligently along day after day, year after year, working away at getting sanctified; and finally, at the very end, he makes it. Let us examine this concept in the light of other statements which define sanctification.

In Leviticus 20:7, 8 we read of a two-fold function that is needed for sanctification of an object or a person. "Sanctify yourselves, therefore, and be ye holy¤. I am the Lord which sanctify you."

These two verses tell us that sanctification is something that a person does **and** God does. Man's part is to set himself apart for holy use just as the articles of the sanctuary were set aside for holy use. When he does this, following the order of God, the Lord also sets the person aside for holy use. The person is then sanctified. The promise of the Lord can then be fulfilled. "And ye shall keep my statutes and do them" (Lev 20:8). In his common labor, as well as in his spiritual activities, man is to be in God's service at all time, just as Jesus was (DA74.9; 2SM163.9). On the other hand, a person who is not set aside for holy use (not sanctified) might be good and kind, but he is not in the service of the King (GC509.5; MB94.6).

Outside our kitchen door there is a bowl for dog and cat food. It is made of sturdy stainless steel. It could serve a better purpose, but under present circumstances it is not suitable for human use. If it is to be given a better role, it must be cleansed and set aside for new duties. It must be soaped, scrubbed, sterilized inside and out, and set aside for the new use. After this is done, it would be suitable for use by the family.

Of course, at any time someone may take it and use it again to feed the pets. If this should happen, it would not be suitable for human use until it had been recleansed.

The apostle Paul writes about vessels "in the great house" that may be purged and "sanctified, meet for the master's use" (2 Tim. 2:20, 21). When we dedicate our all to Christ and are set aside for heaven's service, we are sanctified. When temptations come from the old man of sin within or from the devil from without, we can say, "By the grace of God I am set aside for holy use. How can I indulge in that sin and dishonor my Master? Give me strength Lord, and I shall overcome." God would have us maintain this attitude of sanctification at all times (Ev702).

The **setting of ourselves aside for holy use** is a daily work (SL92.5). We are not once saved, always saved. This relationship must be diligently sought after as long as this life shall last (SL10.5). If we give it up, we must be reclaimed by the Master.

We rest in this promise. "When we surrender ourselves wholly [physically, mentally, and morally] to God, and fully believe, the blood of Christ cleanses from all sin. The conscience can be freed from condemnation. Through faith in His blood, all may be made perfect in Christ Jesus. Thank God that we are not dealing with impossibilities. We may claim sanctification" (2SM32.9).

But the definition of sanctification does not end there. There is another facet to it. We are informed that, "The work of sanctification is progressive" and that sanctification is not an instantaneous work (GC470.2; SL10.5). It is not enough to "only believe" (GC471.8). God's agencies must add the Christian graces with our earnest cooperation (SL90.7 to 93.7).

Coming back to the analogy of the "vessel" that was cleansed and set aside for holy use, we would see that it is not enough for Jesus to do that and set us up on a shelf as a decoration. He uses us. He puts us into His service by His grace.

Full surrender with repentance, dedication of ourselves to God is the first step (1SM366.4). When I do this in all sincerity, I am pardoned perfectly. He writes His law in my heart, and I love to do His will. He proceeds to put His law in my mind and help me keep it as I study and meditate upon His word guided by the Holy Spirit.

Even with this provision I still have two important problems. My heart has to be kept perfect toward God (COL50.9; DA324), and I need to have my wrong habits and my misinformation about God revealed to me. The true hidden motives of my heart must be revealed to me. God has promised to tell me "as much as I can remember and perform" with His help as we walk together. (DA313).

Even though I am converted and set aside for holy use, there are things that I think and do that are not right in the sight of God. Whether I recognize them or not, they need to be forgiven. Furthermore, the motive of love may not always be supreme with my actions (1SM366-7; SC34). The phrase "Please Be Patient, God Is Not Through With Me Yet," describes my condition.

The Psalmist says, "Thy way, O God, is in the sanctuary." (Ps 77:13). In the daily service of the sanctuary in the court, there were four basic types of sacrifices made: the sin offering, the burnt offering of consecration, the meal (meat) offering, and the thank offering.

For the sin offering, the sinner brought a lamb, confessed his sin with his hands on the head of the offering. The priest stretched the lamb's head toward the ark. The sinner cut the lambs throat. The priest caught the blood in a basin and sprinkled some of it around the altar of incense. In some instances he placed some of the blood on the horns of the altar of incense or the horns of the altar of burnt offering. The sprinkling in the holy place represented that the guilt of sin had been transferred to the sanctuary. The blood on the horns of the altars was to remind the sinner that sin cost the life of the Saviour and that there was power available to keep one from sinning. The body of that lamb was taken outside the camp and burned.

For the burnt offering of consecration, the lamb was brought in by the offerer. With his hands on the lamb, he confessed that he was a sinner. The priest pointed the head of the lamb toward the ark. The offerer cut the lamb's throat, the priest caught the blood in a basin and poured it out at the base of the altar of burnt offering. The body of the lamb was skinned, cut in pieces, washed at the laver, and arranged to look like the animal on the altar of burnt offering, and then burned. It was in this service that the person was represented as giving up his old ways and putting all of himself on the altar after being washed by the "water of life" (Titus 3:5; John 4:14).

This is the aspect of sanctification in which one sets himself aside for holy use and God sets the person aside for holy use. But sanctification also includes the work of our Saviour in us as portrayed by the daily service at the altar of incense which results in obedience by faith in the health reform, mental renewal, and spiritual realm (SL7, 10, 25; GC469-73).

In the sanctuary service, twice daily, morning and evening, a lamb was offered and kept burning continually (Ex. 29:38-42; PP352; Lev. 6:12, 13). Incense twice daily and the continual presence of the shewbread and burning incense signified the ever present ministration of Christ for forgiveness of our sins (PP352-3). This daily service, or the "continual" atonement, makes provisions for the pardon by the merits of Christ for unrecognized sins, the sins of ignorance, for those who are "in Christ Jesus" (Rom. 8:1).

When the person was convicted of a sin of ignorance, and it became recognized, then a separate offering, a "sin of ignorance offering" was made (Lev. 4:1-35).

Willful transgression of a sin placed the sinner without this relationship. He was "outside the city of refuge." To reestablish this relationship a "trespass offering" was needed (Lev. 6:1-7). Beyond that, there were "high-handed" presumptuous sins for which there was no sacrifice (Num. 15:30; DA322; PP405).

Thus, the sanctuary service teaches us that Christ by His life of obedience has obtained the right to offer the incense of His life and by His death offer His blood (1) for the continual remission of sins of which we are unaware, (2) for special forgiveness when we finally are convicted of these sins of ignorance, and (3) for forgiveness of known trespasses (DA762; 1SM337, 367; PP353). It is eloquently phrased in the paragraph below.

> "The religious services, the prayers, the praise, the penitent confession of sin ascend from the true believers as incense to the heavenly sanctuary, but passing through the corrupt channels of humanity, they are so defiled that unless purified by blood, they can never be of value with God. They ascend not in spotless purity, and unless the Intercessor, who is at God's right hand, presents and purifies all by His righteousness, it is not acceptable to God. All incense from earthly tabernacles must be moist with the cleansing drops of the blood of Christ. He holds before the Father the censer of His own merits, in which there is no taint of earthly corruption. He gathers into this censer the prayers, the praise, and the confession of His people, and with these He puts His own spotless righteousness. Then, perfumed with the merits of Christ's propitiation, the incense comes up

before God wholly and entirely acceptable. Then gracious answers are returned" (1SM344).

There are some, however, who are wanting to impute **imparted** righteousness. They want to take the obedience of Christ and substitute His obedience for our obedience in such a way that no obedience by faith in the power of God is required of us. Statements are made such as this, "The perfection that is required of us to go through the time of trouble is **not** the perfection of character but a perfection of repentance." **But, such a concept would only prepare us to be in the "foolish virgin" group.**

Perfect repentance is necessary, but God's plan of salvation promises more for His people for the great time of trouble. Ellen White warns us away from that as follows: "The opposite [from trusting in keeping the law in our own strength concept] and no less dangerous error is that belief in Christ releases men from keeping the law of God; that since by faith alone we become partakers of the grace of Christ, our works have nothing to do with our redemption" (SC60).

True obedience becomes the fruit of faith (SC61). It is the gift of obedience by the power of the indwelling Holy Spirit. Satan refuses to acknowledge that such obedience is possible prior of the second coming of Christ. He does not want us to be ready for the close of probation (See GC489).

The daily services in the holy place teach us the second phase of sanctification. At the altar of incense, Christ offers our prayers up to the Father who then bestows knowledge of His will, the desire to His "will," and the power to perform each thought, word, and action according to do His "will." These repeated form the perfect character, our most valuable treasure from heaven.

Surrender prepares us to receive Christ's ministry. The cross of Christ has provided justification and all other benefits of the atoning sacrifice as a free gift and made provisions whereby Jesus can lead us in our Christian walk in such a way that He separates us from our evil ways (DA311; 1SM312-3). Further than this, He can impart power to us to develop a righteous character in us (7BC943; AA531). "In order for man to retain justification, there must be continual obedience, through active, living faith that works by love and purifies the soul" (1SM366).

The great doctrine of the day of atonement teaches us that this ministry of justification continues until the sealing, until that "final atonement," until Christ throws down His censer and closes His priestly work. When the investigative judgment is over and probation is closed, no more sins known or unknown can be forgiven for anyone forever (7BC989; GC613-4; 2T355, 691). Yet imparted power for obedience is still available. God's people are kept from sinning completely as Christ was kept from sinning, by the enabling grace of God. (GC612; 641; AA56, 531).

"In all [the tabernacle service], God desired His people to read His purpose for the human soul" (Ed36).

"That temple, erected for the abode of the divine Presence, was designed to be an object lesson for Israel and for the world.... God designed that the temple at Jerusalem should be a continual witness to the high destiny open to every soul. But the Jews had not understood the significance of the building they regarded with so much pride.... In cleansing the temple from the world's buyers and sellers, Jesus announced His mission to cleanse the heart from the defilement of sin, – from the earthly desires, the selfish lusts, the evil habits, that corrupt the soul" (DA161).

Let us examine more deeply in the next chapter what our High Priest does in the heavenly sanctuary to prepare His people to stand, by His power, without a mediator after probation closes.

Chapter 3

THE WAY TO OUR INHERITANCE UNVEILED BY THE SANCTUARY

The Need for Word Definition: Why did God set up the sacrificial system? Why go to all that trouble, bloodshed of animals, expense and effort? The answer comes from the symbolic meaning of words and from their manipulation by the enemies of truth.

Several years ago it was my good fortune to hear a Wycliffe Translator relate experiences about translating the Bible in Central America. One of his colleagues had been given the responsibility to translate the New Testament into the language of an Indian tribe. There was one major hurdle; the tribe had no word for love.

How does one translate John 3:16 and like verses into such a language? The translator could have walked out and asked for a new assignment, but that was not his way. You see, he was faced with the same problem that God has had from the beginning of sin on this earth.

When Eve and Adam sinned, Christ "offered" to take their "guilt" and "punishment." This was all new to them. Heaven and earth needed a whole new set of words. New concepts must be explained.

The Wycliffe translator began his task. For months he lived with the tribe, getting acquainted. With every helpful act, every smiling deed of service, he was weaving a feeling of love within the hearts of the natives for his service. Then he asked them, "Do you know what I have done for you"? They had no word to describe what he had done. Oh, they knew the actions, the hauling of the wood, the water carrying, and the soothing of the fevered brow of the sick, etc. What they lacked was a word to express **why** he had done all that for them. He had given all, but had taken nothing. Together they coined a new word. That word became the symbol for *agape*, the love that expects nothing in return.

Before "the Word was made flesh and dwelt among us" God needed to define the attributes of His character. He chose the sacrificial system to begin to define the concepts of the plan of salvation and to show them what He is like. The altar of unhewn stones, the lamb, the wood, and the fire became the material tools to teach spiritual things.

But the plan of salvation called for a much larger vocabulary than could be defined by a lamb and an altar. Mankind must understand deeper insights into the plan of redemption, else how could they follow intelligently the sacrificial as well as the ministerial nature of Christ's work? The sanctuary service with its intricate specifications and details was, therefore, established in Israel. After Christ came and died, the blood of animals and the earthly priests had served their purpose. Those ceremonies had defined His mission well enough and could be laid aside. The Word had become flesh, and dwelt among us (John 1:14). Agape had been defined. Self-renouncing love and merciful justice had been spelled out for all to see.

Was the blood of sheep and calves and the priestly ministry in the tabernacle only for those before Christ?

Words change in their meaning. The definitions may be tampered with by men and by our enemy, the devil. For example the word "gay" has been ruined by its application to the homosexual. Yes, the words may vary, but the intricate services of the sanctuary still define the effect of sin on the person and present what Jesus must do as well as what we must do to be cleansed of sin.

When I was a child, the stories of the Bible came to life in the sandbox of our little Sabbath School. This was the highlight of the Sabbath School. The sanctuary is God's giant sandbox, as it were, to tell the story of redemption. May we never tire of the lessons that it teaches!

There are multiple lessons that we can see and various approaches that can be made to the sanctuary, but what is the central theme that God desires to teach us in the sanctuary. Let us simplify the ceremonies. Let us parallel them with the gospel story of salvation. Let us summon it to give us an understanding of what God will do through Christ and what we must do to be rid of the hold of sin in our lives and of the effects of sin in our past. Let us approach God in the sanctuary as a sinner had to day after day in Israel of old. Let the imagination, then, go back to the wilderness thirty-four centuries ago.

The Camp of Israel & the Court: In our imagination we find ourselves in the camp of Israel. We detect an aroma of sweet incense. As we search for the source, our attention is directed to an enclosure of white linen. We cannot see over the nine foot high curtain, but we can see the top of a black tent in the western half of the court. As we get closer, we smell also another aroma, that of blood and of burning flesh.

God's people are to be a part of that sweet incense of good deeds designed to attract sinners to God. The good deeds of the saints are to attract their neighbors and associates. They do not take credit to themselves but give glory to God, for it is He that is working in and through them. As we read, "But thanks be to God, who in Christ always leads us in triumph, and through us spreads the fragrance of the knowledge of him everywhere. For we are the aroma of Christ to God among those who are being saved and among those who are perishing..." (2 Cor. 2:14, 15 R.S.V.).

However, too many in the world detect the smell of blood and of sacrifice first, and these become an offense. The fear of sacrifice overpowers their desire to come to God. They see nothing beautiful as they stand outside the court. As we read, "...to one a fragrance from death, to the other a fragrance from life to life" (2 Cor. 2:16 R.S.V.)

The Veils: As we look at the court, we see an entrance on the east end of the court made of white linen interwoven with blue, purple, and scarlet threads and with gold embroidery. It measures 5 by 20 cubits. Two other veils of the same material serve as curtains for entrance into the two rooms of the sanctuary. They measure 10 by 10 cubits. Thus, all three are 100 square cubits. One opens the way into the court, the next one opens the way into the first apartment, and the third one opens the way into the most holy place, the second apartment of the sanctuary.

We read in Hebrews 10:20 that the veil represents the flesh of Jesus, His humanity. Jesus said, "I am the door" (John 10:9). "I am the good shepherd" (John 10:11). In olden times the shepherd laid down at night at the entrance of the sheepfold and slept there. No predator could enter, nor any sheep leave the fold without meeting

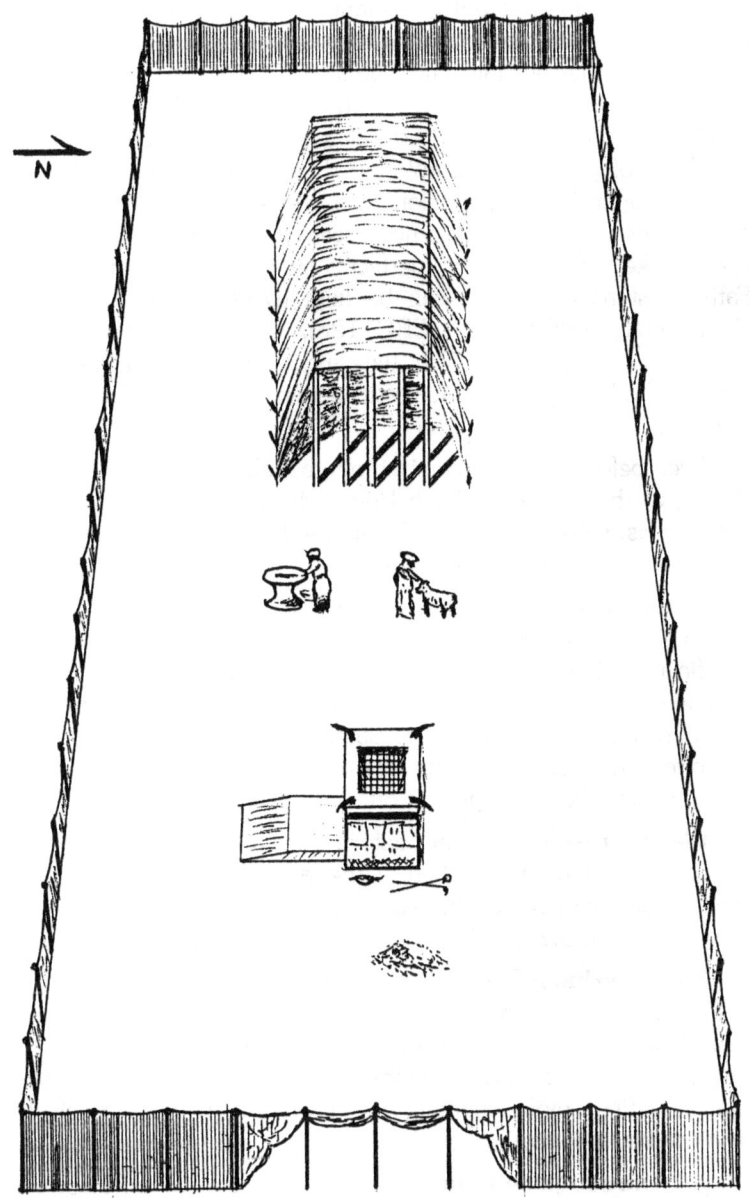

the shepherd first. Jesus said, "I am the way, the truth, and the life: no man cometh unto the Father, but by me" (John 14:6).

Our understanding of the humanity of Christ is very important to us. We shall study this further in a subsequent chapter, but for now let us realize that our faith must be in a Saviour who took upon His sinless nature our sinful physical nature with the infirmities, liabilities, conditions, and weaknesses of degenerate sinful flesh with the possibility of yielding to temptation. He was **not** exempt from our natural propensities and passions, but He had no evil propensities or passions within Him because not once did He participate in our sin. He was kept from sinning perfectly by the Holy Spirit from the Father just as you and I can be kept (DA49, 117; YI10-26-99; YI04-25-01; RH02-18-90; 5BC1128). Unless we believe in the Christ who came in **that** flesh, we cannot come to God through the veil that God has prepared for us to obtain entrance by faith into His presence.

Even before we have received any benefit of pardon or enabling power, we have such an High Priest who invites us to "come unto me" just as we are (Hebrews 8:1 and 4:15). He will receive us and adopt us into His family (Ephesian 1:4, 5; John 1:12, 13).

Within the Court Before the Tabernacle: When we enter the court, we see a brazen altar, the laver, and a stake to which the sacrificial lamb has been tied. As we study Exodus, Leviticus, and Numbers, we find a confusing array of ceremonies and sacrifices in the court. However, they can be classified into four basic categories,- sin offerings, burnt offerings for consecration, "meat" or meal offerings, and thank or "peace" offerings (see Lev. 7:37).

Washing At The Laver: Before we can perform the services in the court, we must be washed at the laver (Exodus 30:18-21). We need to be cleansed by the washing of regeneration by the Word (Titus 3:5; Eph. 5:26).

Sin Offerings: First, there are the offerings for sin, to remove guilt from the sinner and cleanse the heart. When we sin, we have guilt of sin, a mental record of love for that sin in the heart, and the knowledge of it recorded in the mind. In a study of Exodus 29:38-42 and the first nine chapters of Leviticus, we learn of four classifications of sins,–

(a) **Unrecognized sins**, sins that we are guilty of, but we are unaware that they are wrong in God's sight (Lev. 5:17).

(b) **"Sins of ignorance,"** sins that we had been unaware, but, when God convicts us that they are wrong, we turn from them (Lev. 4).

(c) **Known trespasses** (Lev. 6 & 7).

(d) **"Presumptuous sins,"** high-handed sins committed in self-declared rebellion against God (Num. 15:30).

The first classification of sin is **unrecognized sins**, sins which have not yet been brought to the knowledge of the sinner. He does not feel guilty; but, whether he is aware of it or not, in the eyes of God, he is guilty of the sin (Lev. 5:17). God does not reveal all that He might to us. He reveals as much as we can remember and perform (DA 313). God expects us to follow the leading of the Holy Spirit, and give up every idol as He reveals them to us as we travel life's path (Gal. 5:16-18; Hosea 4:17). We are to plead for purity of heart as well as for wisdom to know God's will (PK591; GC597-8). As the converted person trusts in the merits of the "daily sacrifice" of the continually burning lamb, the Lord imputes the guilt of these unrecognized sins to the sanctuary (Exodus 29:38-46; 2 Cor. 5:17-19).

The second classification of sin is the "**sin of ignorance**" (Lev. 4:1-35). These are sins that a person commits, but is unaware that they are wrong at the time. But, when he is finally convicted that they are wrong, at that point they are called the "sin of ignorance," and he has a special offering to bring to acknowledge that they are sins.

The third classification is known sin (Lev. 6:1-7). "Therefore to him that knoweth to do good, and doeth it not, to him it is sin" (James 4:17).

All of three classes of sins have to be dealt with before we can enter the holy place.

A righteous act consists of doing what God wants us to do, as He wants it done, from a motive of love, by the power of the Holy Spirit through a faith relationship with God through Christ. Basically, all sin is transgression of the law that specifies the action and/or transgression of the law of love that specifies the motive behind the action (1 John 3:4; Luke 11:42; Romans 13:10). We may sin by having the wrong motive or by disobeying God's will in regard to the act or by both a wrong act and a wrong motive. These separate us from God (Isaiah 59:2).

Both the proper motive as well as the knowledge to do right are promised in the everlasting covenant (Hebrews 8:10-12 LB). To be free of guilt, we place our hands on the head of the sin offering and confess all our sins, the recognized ones and acknowledge that we have unrecognized ones. And, as the priest stretches the neck of the lamb toward the Most Holy Place, we cut its throat. The priest catches the blood in a basin, takes it, and sprinkles it around the altar of incense within the Holy Place. For some sins, the blood is placed on the horns of the altar of incense and for others, on the horns of the altar of burnt offering (Lev. 4:7, 18, 25, 30). The fat of the lamb was burned on the altar of burnt offering, and the body was burned without the camp.

All of this has specific meanings. The Lamb of God, takes my guilt upon Himself, dies in my place, and with His blood He places my guilt on the sanctuary in heaven. The record of sin in my heart is covered by the blood until the "final atonement" of the yearly service. The guilt of sin is held in abeyance on the sanctuary until the final atonement. **Guilt is transferred, but is not cancelled nor blotted out** (GC418-21). As part of the cleansing of the saints and the sanctuary in heaven in the final atonement, He blots out the records of all the sins from my heart, and the guilt is transferred onto Satan.

The Burnt Offering: We also have access to the "burnt offering of consecration." For this, too, we perform the same confession of sins on the head of the sacrifice and then take its life. The animal is skinned and the body cut in pieces. These are washed at the laver, arranged to resemble the lamb on the altar of burnt offering, and burned (Leviticus 1).

What does this mean? This ceremony signifies that we have set ourselves aside (sanctified ourselves) for holy use. As it is written in Romans 12:1, "I beseech you, therefore, brethren, by the mercies of God, that you present your bodies a living sacrifice, holy, acceptable unto God,¤." After our guilt has been taken away and our records of sin are covered, our old ways of living are to be put away, "crucified with Christ," and laid away in a tomb (Romans 6:6). My Godless appetites, passions, and desires are to be dead and buried (Gal.5:24).

Our body temples are to be set aside for the good ways of God and "dead to sin" (Romans 6:11). No tobacco, no alcohol, no poisonous drugs, no harmful foods should enter the body temple. And what about the mental soul temple? We should no longer let anything such as trashy novels or filthy TV enter our minds through the senses or the imaginations and defile it (Isaiah 33:14,15; Psalm 119:37). We want the mind to be transformed by Christ's renewing ministry (Romans 12:2).

The concept of sanctification has a two-fold application. Once again let us look at the homely example of the stainless steel bowl for feeding the dog at our back door. At one time it was a good kitchen utensil. Before it can again be used in "the master's house," it needs to be thoroughly cleansed by soap and water, and sterilized by fire. But, unless it is set aside ("sanctified") for human use, it would again become unfit for use in the kitchen. Further, even though it were to be brought into the master's house, and set aside on a shelf, it would not be a productive utensil. The master of the house must put it to use. That use becomes a part and completes the "sanctification" of the vessel. In the sanctuary service, the cleansing is portrayed by the offering for sin and the washing at the laver while sanctification includes the consecration at the altar of burnt offering and the utilization of the vessel for service portrayed by Christ's work at the altar of incense.

The Meal (Meat) Offering: Next, a meal offering is to be performed. For this we take some flour with oil, frankincense, and salt and present it to the priest. Some of it is burned on the altar of burnt offering (Leviticus 2). This offering always accompanied the burnt offering (Num. 15:4). What is the significance of this offering? All of my earthly goods are set aside for holy use. We put our pocketbooks, as it were, on the altar. We consider ourselves to be merely stewards of God's funds in this life. If we place all on the altar, He has promised to reveal to us what and when we should use it for the cause of God (EW57).

The Peace Offering: We, next, present a peace offering by which we show thankfulness for being cleansed by the blood of the sin offering, by the water or life, and by the fire of the burnt offering (1 John 5:6; John 13:10; Psalm 107:22; 66:10-16). After that, by the virtues of Jesus we are invited to enter by faith through the veil and come to God in the Holy Place. If we are to be heard, we dare not omit the thanks and praise offering (5T317).

Washing At The Laver: Before we can enter the holy place for communion, we must be washed at the laver (Exodus 30:18-21). The "water of life," the joy and hope of the gospel, must be applied to us by the Priest (MH157).

Communion in the Holy Place: As we enter the sanctuary, we see on our left a seven-branched candlestick and on the right a table with the two stacks of the "bread of the presence," a flagon of grape juice, and some dishes (Ex. 25:23-9; see Num. 15:8-10 & Lev. 7). What do these symbols represent, and what does this part of the sanctuary illustrate and define?

I am indebted to my Arab friend, Elder Salim Elias, for insights into these customs related to the service in the holy place. The ancestors of Elder Elias were hosts to Paul when he spent those months in the wilderness (see Gal. 1:17, 18). From these customs we can see deeper meaning in the Passover service and the Lord's supper.

If a native Arab or Israeli invites you to eat with him, it means that he wants to be your friend. If you accept, it signifies that you want to be his friend. If, at the meal, he takes one of the small loaves of bread, breaks it, gives you some, and you both eat of it, that means that you are now "at one" with each other because you have partaken of the same nourishment. If, after the bread, he gives you some unfermented grape juice, it means that you are at peace with each other. Further than this, the host has committed himself and all that he has to defend you against your enemies. On the other hand, the serving of fermented wine meant war with one another.

As we look at the articles of furniture in the holy place, we see some symbols that seem to function as a unit for a meal, "a communion service," as it were. Who will be at the banquet? The Holy Spirit, represented by the golden candlestick, along with the Father and the Son, represented by the two stacks of bread, invite us to dine at their table to get acquainted with Them. Through this custom, it is as though God is saying, "We, the three Persons in the Godhead, want to be your Friends. Will you come and have communion with Us. Study the Scriptures in the light of the Holy Spirit as if you were there in the holy place."

The oil in the lamp represents the work of the Holy Spirit to enlighten our thinking and to give us spiritual insight (Zech. 4:1-6). Jesus said, "I am the bread of life." (John 6:35). By studying the life of Jesus, we will know what the members of the Godhead are like. "Man shall not live by bread alone, but by every word that proceedeth out of the mouth of God" (Matt. 4:4). The more that we study, the more we see the loving kindness, the gentleness, the meekness, the mercy of God. The more that we commune with the Father and the Son in the light of the Holy Spirit, the greater will be our admiration and love for Them. They will come into our hearts, and we will be at peace with Them. God places all the resources of heaven in the hands of Christ to save us from our enemies (DA57; Isaiah 49:25).

This is the invitation of Jesus. "Behold, I stand at the door and knock; if any one hears my voice and opens the door, I will come in to him and eat with him, and he with me" (Rev. 3:20 R.S.V.). Jesus knocks at the door of our hearts. He wants to be our friend and eat with us. We should let Him in immediately. Let Him walk down the corridors of the heart with the mind's eye in the light of the Holy Spirit. As we walk with Him, He will reveal some pictures on the halls of memory that we may wish to hide from Him. He says, "What shall we do with these"? If we love the pictures more than Jesus, He will have to leave them there. If we are wise, we will ask Him to remove the guilt, cover them with His robe of righteousness, and prepare to blot them out at the final atonement. Jesus will cleanse the soul temple just as He did the temple in Jerusalem. He will bring in love and healing. If we will let Him, He will examine all the halls of our memories with our mind's eye and cleanse out everything that would burn at the presence of God.

All this preparation in the court and at the table of communion, has been for a purpose. It is so that we can present a request "boldly unto the throne of grace" (Heb. 4:16) at the altar of incense. But, what should be our request? To understand this, we need the enlightenment that Paul can give us in his letter to the Hebrews.

Our Inheritance At The Place of Incense: As we examine Hebrews nine, we are struck with two things of special interest.

First, in his description of the sanctuary (Heb. 9:4, 5) Paul leaves out the altar of incense in the holy place or else associates it with the most holy place. Second, in verses 15-17 Paul presents the concept of an inheritance in the legal context of a last will and testament when he points out that a will is in full force only after the death of the testator. Proverbs 13:22 tells us that a good man leaves an inheritance to his children's children. Since we know that our Saviour is good, did He make out a will before He died? If so, what did He bequeath? Is it property or wealth? The apostles specifically state that we have an inheritance (Ephesians 1:9-14; 1 Peter 1:4, 5). Paul admonishes us to "Do not be foolish, but understand what the will of the Lord is" (Eph. 5:17).

The question is, what is the inheritance, and just how do we go about obtaining it?

In most countries a person claims the provisions of his inheritance by having the executor of the estate take the will to the designated court. Three things must be established. It must be shown that the last will and testament was truly that of the testator. There must be documented proof of the death of the testator. And, third, you must be the one specified in the will.

The Psalmist says that we are to take those Testimonies, the law, as our heritage (Psalm 119:111). Moses tells us about the occasion when the Father and the Son came with myriads of angels down to Mt. Sinai and gave the Ten Commandments and proclaimed them to be the inheritance of Israel (Deut. 33:2-4; Ev616). Paul clarifies this by stating that the inheritance is not based upon **our** keeping the law but upon the promises of what **God** will do for us. The law makes it legal for God to give us loving obedience (Gal. 3:18-29). These ten commandments embrace every moral principle enjoined in the Bible and embody the will (covenant) of God (MB46; PP372; SD56). Whatever God placed in the ark of the covenant with the great original in the sanctuary in heaven contains God's provisions for us.

What about the death of the Testator? Is there any doubt that Jesus actually died? Heaven made every effort to prove beyond a shadow of doubt that Jesus actually died. The Jewish requirement was that those who died had to be in the grave for parts of three days before they were legally dead. Jesus used this in the example of Lazarus to prove beyond question that He could raise the dead. Specifically, the circumstances around the death of Christ fulfilled this condition. His grave was sealed and guarded by His own enemies until the morning of the third day. God has given us additional proof that Christ was dead. Those familiar with physiology know that when blood stops flowing, the red blood cells settle and the clear, watery serum or plasma comes to the top within the space of an hour. When the spear pierced the side of Him that hung on the cross, it let forth both the red cells and the clear fluid. Our Lord had been dead long enough for the red cells to settle.

It is this blood with which Jesus, our Great High Priest, enters the holy places to perform the daily atonement for us (Hebrews 9:12). It is this blood with which He enters the Most Holy place to perform the final atonement for us and restore our inheritance (Hebrews 9:7).

Thus, by Christ's sacrificial death the will (His covenant) was established in full force. Nothing in it can be changed. No one can rearrange those commandments. They were written by the finger of God. No one can add a codicil. The seventh-day still remains the Sabbath. His will, expressed in the ten promises of the Ten

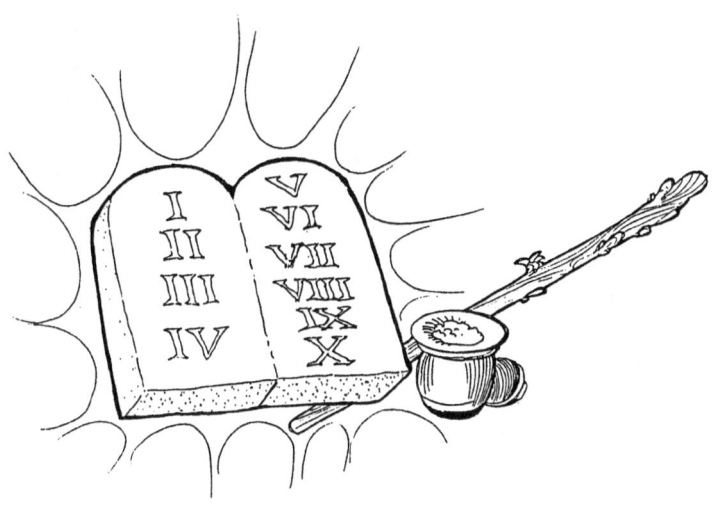

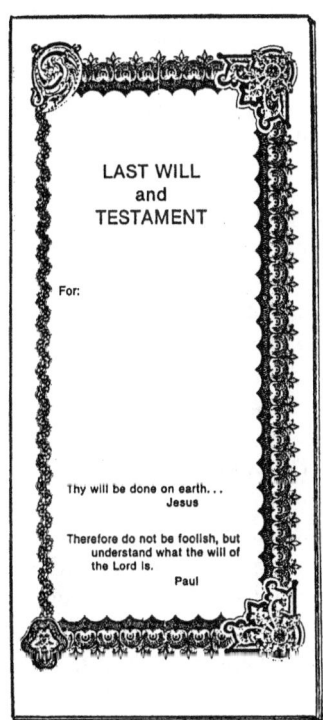

Commandments and placed in the "will" box, in the ark of the covenant in the sanctuary, was unalterably in full effect.

Who, on this earth, are entitled to this inheritance? If we are "born again," we are Christ's children and heirs according to the promise (John 3:3-5; Gal. 3:29). God makes us fit to be adopted and then adopts us (Ephesians 1:5-19; Ezekiel 16:2-14). If we so choose, we can be the children of God and entitled to this inheritance provided by heaven so long as we remain in the family. We may have the "earnest," the down payment, of our inheritance now (Eph. 1:14). We may obtain the benefits of the kingdom of grace now (Matt. 10:7), and have the promise of the kingdom of glory yet to come (1 Peter 1:4-7; Matt. 24:30, 31).

How do we go about getting our inheritance? Paul uses the sanctuary and its services as a "giant sandbox" to teach the concepts of "**covenant living**." By the word that the Apostle chose in Hebrews 9:4 that is translated as "censer," Paul brings to our attention the concept that the altar of incense, the veil, and the ark of the covenant are a functional unit. The word, "thumiasterion," could be translated "censer," "altar of incense," or "a place of incense." This is interesting in that the altar of incense was associated with the ark of the covenant in Solomon's temple, even though we know that the altar was in the holy place (See 1 Kings 6:16-23; Exodus 30:1-10).

How does our request get to the court in heaven? Through prayer to Jesus where He ministers we can come "boldly before the throne of grace." Jesus, our High Priest, has been designated to be the executor of His own estate (John 5:27). We can pray, "Heavenly Father, in the name of Jesus, I would like my inheritance." That prayer ascends to our High Priest at the altar of incense. The Holy Spirit bears witness that we are God's children and also intercedes for us there (Romans 8:16, 26, 27). Jesus adds the incense of His merits to our request (1SM344). In response, He might say, "Be specific, what do you want?" (Luke 11:9-13). I would reply, "In the name of Jesus, I would like to have no other gods before You. I would like to stop taking the name of the Lord in vain. I would like to remember the Sabbath day to keep it holy. I want to honor my father and mother. I would like to quit lying and stealing and coveting and committing adultery in my mind." Jesus takes that request to the Father on His throne between the cherubims. The Father looks at the mercy seat and at the law. His answer is, those requests are in the will. If he is "born again," you may give them to him. Jesus then

returns to us with the desire and the power to do all that we have asked for in the will.

Each item that is in the ark of the covenant represents some part of our inheritance. What else was in the ark ("the will box") in addition to the ten commandments? There was a golden pot of manna and Aaron's rod that budded. Why are they there? When God led the children of Israel in the wilderness, He wanted to establish their faith in Him that He would provide for their spiritual food as well as their physical food. He said, I want you to be vegetarians. I am going to give you some manna, some special food from heaven, which I will miraculously provide six mornings a week. Pick up your supply and make it into food along with the other plant foods that you can find in the wilderness.

We can go to the Executor of our inheritance and say, "Jesus, I would like to know what is right for me to eat, and I would like the desire and the power to control my appetite." Jesus will take that request to the Father; and, since it is according to God's will, Jesus will bring us the answer which includes control of our appetite. Here are some promises!

> "If thou wilt diligently hearken to the voice of the Lord they God, and wilt do that which is right in his sight,… and keep all his statutes, I will put none of these diseases upon thee, which I brought upon the Egyptians: for I am the Lord that healeth thee" (Exodus 15:26).

> "If our will and way are in accordance with God's will and way; if we do the pleasure of our Creator, He will keep the human organism in good condition, and restore the moral, mental, and physical powers, in order that He may work through us to His glory" (1BC1118).

We will need those promises because, "As we near the close of time, Satan's temptations to indulge appetite will be more powerful and more difficult to overcome" (CDF59).

Jesus showed that even when we are nearly dead from starvation and dehydration, as He was in the wilderness, the wisdom and power in the promised Word are strong enough to bring us forth more than conquerors.

What promises are included in the symbol of Aaron's rod in the ark? This was placed in the ark after the occasion when Korah, Dathan, and Abiram decided to take over the leadership of Israel. The promise is this. When things need to be changed at the head of the work, God will take care of it (5T80, Jere. 3:15; 23:14). I do not need to fret. I am to "sigh and cry" about the abominations that are done in the church. Aaron and others may make a golden calf. There may be lewd celebrations in the camp, but I do not need to follow a multitude to do evil. I should follow the example of the Levites and other loyal ones in Israel, and follow God even when the Aarons go astray. If the Aarons repent, He will be gracious and forgive them. In our time, what if there is heresy taught in the church? What if there are sexually immoral persons, i.e. homosexuals, etc., who want to belong to the church? My role is to cry aloud to those in my sphere of influence. It is not to call the church Babylon, and leave it. God will deal with the tares in the church. Soon, all too soon, persecution will come; and those who will not partake of Christ's ministry in the place of incense (the most Holy Place), will leave the church.

The "Yearly" Day-of-Atonement Service: All of the above services were done every day. But, there was also an additional part of our inheritance that is available when, what is called the "yearly," the day of atonement services were to be performed. A "final atonement" is described (PP357). All of that which was available in the daily was also available on the day of atonement along with the final examination of the records of sin in the hearts of God's people with the blotting out of these sins (GC480).

This is of special importance to those who will be translated without seeing death. Their "books" will be examined while they are still alive (GC425-30; GC480-89). As the Lord leads us to examine every record in the hall memory, we are to turn from every idol sin that may be there, let Him cover it up, and help us overcome that in the remaining time before our probation closes. The final atonement will include this investigation, the putting of the law in its entirety in the mind so that we will know exactly what the Lord would have us do, the writing of the law of love in our heart so that we will just love to do God's will in all things to glorify His name, the blotting out of the record of sin from the heart, and the full outpouring of the Holy Spirit. These are the advantages of the everlasting will-covenant (Heb. 8:10-12). The topic of the final atonement will be explored in more detail in other chapters of this book, but they are presented here to put them into the perspective of our inheritance.

When George Johnson was seventeen, his desire to be "free" caused him to leave his well-to-do family on their plantation in Charleston, South Carolina. He chose the hippy lifestyle, hitch-hiked west to San Francisco, and settled down on a "pad" in the Haight-Ashbury District.

One day, after three years of being totally immersed in the typical hippy lifestyle a friend looked up from his paper to tease him by saying, "I notice in the financial section of the San Francisco Examiner that multimillionaire, George Johnson, is dead."

George read the notice and exclaimed, "That's my dad." Then George got to thinking. "As much money as my father had, I know that he must have left me something." He decided to hitchhike back to Charleston.

He arrived back at the plantation about four days later, but no one was there. He went to the office of his father's attorney in downtown Charleston. The receptionist, who had worked at the office for about a year, was not prepared for his coming.

When George walked in with his shaggy beard, dirty hair, and clothed in his smelly, rumpled hippy garb, she recoiled and yelled out, "What do you want? Who are you? Do you have an appointment?" She was in a hurry to get him out of the office.

George reponded, "Is attorney Taylor here?"

The receptionist replied loudly, "Do you have an appointment?"

By this time the attorney came out of the back office to see what the commotion was about. He had known George since he was a baby; but it was difficult for him to recognize him. He looked at George and asked, "George, is that you?"

George affirmed, "Yes."

The attorney replied, "What do you want?"

George said, "I heard that my father died."

The lawyer interrupted by asking, "But what do you want?"

"I, ah, went out to the place..."

Again the lawyer interrupted by asking, "What do you want?"

"Well, I have been traveling four or five days now, and I am hungry."

Again came the question, "What do you want, George?"

He stammered, "Could I have a dollar to get a sandwich?"

The attorney reached in his pocket and gave him a dollar. Then George ventured, "I want to know, did my father leave me anything?"

Attorney Taylor explained, "George, I was just in the back office going over your father's will with your mother and your sister. Your father left thirty-eight million dollars in cash in a couple of banks in town plus a number of other holdings. The will said this, 'When you see my son, George, ask him what he wants. Give him the first thing that he asks for and nothing else.'"

What did George get? What could George have gotten? If George had studied the will, how much do you suppose he would have asked for?

What about you and the will of your heavenly Father. How much of it will you get?

(This story courtesy of Richard Bland of United Prison Ministry.)

When Bill was seventeen, he became involved in crime. After some time in a detention home, he lived aimlessly in rundown rooming houses in San Francisco. For fifteen years he contacted his mother and his sister only to threaten them. Although his mother and his sister were afraid of him, yet they loved him. They avoided him for their own safety.

In her will, the mother left half of her property to her son. The sister was too fearful to contact Bill herself, so she hired Wayne, an Heir Finder, to search out her brother for his part of the inheritance.

With the description of Bill and an old address supplied by Bill's sister and an aunt, Wayne began his search. The address was that of an old locked building, secretly used by various orientals and "street folk" as a resting place at night. None of the English-speaking dwellers knew of such a person who fit Bill's discription. With careful watching, Wayne never saw any one resembling Bill enter or leave that building.

After some searching and discussions with owners of delapidated rooming houses, Wayne finally found one who knew Bill. The problem was that she refused to help until she had payment of one of Bill's old debts. Wayne could not meet that demand. The funds were in the hands of the court.

Wayne went back to watching those who entered and left cheap rooming houses. Finally, Wayne found Bill. Very carefully, he explained to Bill that he had inherited some money. But, when Bill found out that the money was from the will of his mother, Bill refused to take the money.

"After all that I have done to my mother, I cannot accept that money. I have been so very mean to her. I have not spoken to my mother for nearly fifteen years. How can I, now, accept her loving gift?"

After much persuasion, Bill agreed to help him settle the inheritance records in the court. Bill's identity was confirmed by his aunt, and he received the money. But he wanted nothing to do with it. He put it into a bank and refused to take any of it.

Our heavenly Father has made out a will. He loves us with an undying love even while we are in rebellion and make threats against Him. He sent His Son, Jesus, to provide a ransom. Some feel that they are too wicked to be forgiven. But, if we refuse the gift, we make the will of God of noneffect. If we merely hide it in a vault, we are like the prisoner who has been pardoned by the governor, but refuses to accept the pardon.

What is **not** in the inheritance of God can be illustrated by an experience with a medical patient whom I shall call Ruth. In the course of the consultation, Ruth had stated that she no longer believed in prayer. When I inquired, "why," she stated, "God does not answer my prayers. I asked the Lord for $50,000., but He didn't give it to me."

My next question was, "What would you have done with the money"?

Ruth replied, "I would have gone to Las Vegas and had a high old time."

I then asked, "Do you suppose that the Lord wants you to go to Las Vegas and have a 'high old time'"?

"No, I guess not," was her answer.

I then was able to point out that God did answer her prayers, but she had asked for something that was not in the "will" of God (James 4:3).

God waits with loving arms to welcome home His children. He wants to give us the inheritance that He has reserved for us. Not the inheritance that we would squander on riotious living, but the inheritance that will glorify His name in the earth. He wants to strengthen our will power. We are to give our will to Him that we may receive it again, so linked in sympathy with Him that He can pour through us, "tides," not just a trickle, of His love and power (MB62;6T12).

God's People As Executors of the Heavenly Estate: We have been called to be ministers of this inheritance, executors of Christ's estate under Him, to those in our sphere of influence (2 Cor. 5:18; 1 Peter 2:5; Exodus 19:6).

"Those who are invested with Christ's Spirit are virtually clothed with priestly garments, and are placed on vantage ground, commissioned to minister to others. Christ puts into their hands a censer filled with the incense of His righteousness" (SpT, Series B, Nos. 2:28).

"He [Christ] told them that they were to be the executors of the will in which He bequeathed to the world the treasures of eternal life" (AA27).

Chapter 4

HOW THE LAW HELPS GRACE

In my medical office I see so many people with high blood pressure, heart trouble, or with a weight control problem who should change their living habits. They could avoid doctor bills and cut back on their medicines. Frequently, my patients who have already changed their diet and exercise pattern and are getting good results, wonder why more people are not interested in living as they should. What is the problem? The answer lies in our application of the key one of the "true remedies," –TRUST IN DIVINE POWER (MH127).

You see, we have good intentions; we make good resolutions; but what we lack is power working with our will to carry them through. All of our promises are like ropes of sand (SC47). We resolve to do this or that, but we fail; then we feel guilty; then we get discouraged; and then depression sets in. If, to a bit of remorse, we add some anxiety as to what sickness is likely to come upon us, we get mentally distraught.

The apostle Paul knew all about this. His description goes something like this in Romans 7. "I don't understand myself at all, for I really want to do what is right, but I can't. I do what I don't want to – what I hate. I know perfectly well that what I am doing is wrong, and my bad conscience proves that I agree with these laws I am breaking. But I can't help myself,... Oh, what a terrible predicament I'm in! Who will free me from my slavery to this deadly lower nature?" (Romans 7:15, 16, 24 LB).

This is the tragic cry of so many people. But, we must see that Paul's hope can be ours. "Who will free me from my slavery to this

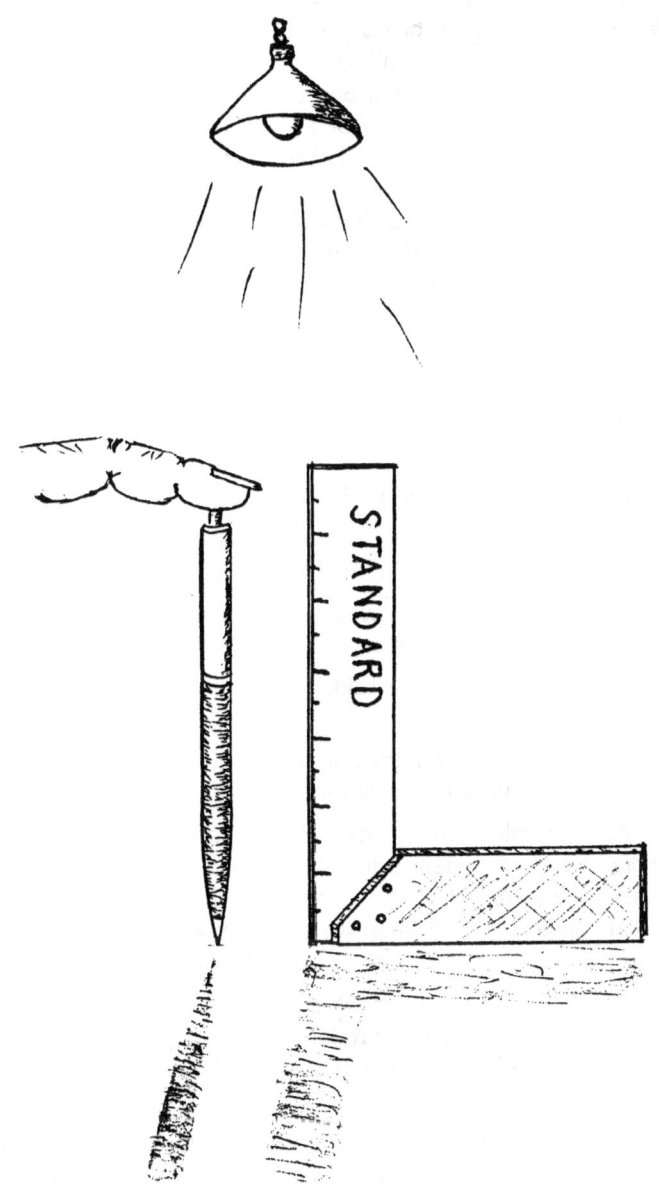

deadly lower nature? Thank God! It has been and will be done by Jesus Christ our Lord" (Romans 7:25, LB).

This reminds me of Pastor White, a Baptist minister, who was under my care for high blood pressure and anginal heart pain. The routine that I followed for all such patients after their initial workup was to instruct them in a diet and exercise program that would very effectively give them a return of a measure of their lost health. As was my custom, on each return visit of Pastor White to my office, I inquired about his diet and exercise pattern. I urged him to correct his diet. I reminded him that those chest pains that came on when he exerted himself would probably go away and that his blood pressure would quite likely remain normal without medicines if he would eat and exercise properly. I tried to picture to him how much better he would feel.

On one such return visit after about two years of this, He said, "Doc, I can do 'most every thing that you say, but I can't give up meat."

My reply was, "Pastor White, are you planning to go to heaven?"

He said, "Why, yes, of course! I'm a preacher."

I then asked, "What do you plan to eat there? You know that nothing will be killed in heaven."

After a long pause, he said, "Doc, you sure know how to hit hard!"

"Pastor," I said, "you are not getting the down payment of your inheritance from your heavenly Father yet."

From a simple sketch in my office, I introduced Pastor White to the concepts of "covenant living" as outlined in the previous chapter. I explained to him that the apostle Paul in the first chapter of Ephesians indicated that when we are adopted into God's family, we can go to Him through Christ for the "earnest" of our inheritance, which, among other things, is the self-control fruit of the Spirit.

We can illustrate this interrelationship between ourselves, God's law, and His enabling power by a simple ball-point pen, a carpenter's try square, and a light.

As we attempt by trial and error to make the ball-point pen stand on its tip, we notice that every time that we take our finger off the top, it falls down.

You see, I am like that pen, –dead in trespasses and sin. Jesus can take me, forgive me, lift me up, and stand me on my feet. But I will fall again unless the finger of God holds me up. My part is to be willing for Him to lift me up.

Romans 3:24 and 5:1 shows me that through forgiveness by grace, God lifts me up from the degradation of sin just as the pen was lifted up. Romans 5:2 shows me that through faith in Christ, I can obtain "enabling grace" and be kept upright by the finger of God just as the pen was held. So long as I am "willing to be made willing," God will work in me both to want to be upheld as well as to be kept upright (Phil. 2:12,13; MB142). How can I tell that I am upright? If I place this carpenter's try square next to the pen, I can tell whether I am upright or not. The law of God is like the try square. It does not hold me up, but it does tell me what position I am in, whether I am true to God's laws or not. I need something more. I need some light so see myself and the try square. I cannot see whether or not I am right with God unless I compare myself with the law of God in the light of the Holy Spirit. Finally, I need a firm foundation upon which to rest the pen and the try square. That foundation is Jesus, our dear Saviour. He is the Rock upon which we built our character. We are to let Jesus take us in His hand and use us to write loving deeds for the world to see (2 Corinthians 3:2).

We are to come to God through Jesus and let Him know that we love Him and want to obtain our inheritance which is the fruit of the workings of the Holy Spirit. We study God's laws with the guidance of the Holy Spirit because we consider them the blueprint for our lives. We submit ourselves completely to Him. God responds by working in us to be loving and kind. He works in us to control our appetites. We regain health to an extent such as we have never dreamed possible. We want Him to renew our minds to overcome every evil trait. The degree of recovery will look like a miracle to the worldling. When we do this, we want to point others to God. We want to point out how wonderful God is. These are the great principles of Trust In Divine Power. No longer do we trust in ourselves and what we can do. Our trust is to be in Jesus and what He can work out in us.

Chapter 5

POWER TO THINK AND TO DO

I never cease to be amazed at the accomplishments of God's creatures. Consider the marvels of the intricate web building instinct of the Miranda spider. How can it have such precision? What kind of nerve reflex circuits does nature's helicopter, the hummingbird, have which allows it to beat its wings at better than sixty times a second? Truly, all animate nature displays an intelligence that is a mystery (MH315.9).

We marvel at these; but, when God designed and formed the human brain and mind, He made something so intricate and so fantastic that adjectives seem too weak to describe it. "Every human being, created in the image of God, is endowed with a power akin to that of the Creator–individuality, power to think and to do" (Ed17.6).

Some time ago I rode with friends to the top of the Palm Springs Tramway. How did we get there? Someone had a vision of a cable car which could transport visitors two miles above the canyon floor, up over impossible terrain, to the mountain crest. Someone had to build the weight-bearing towers and call into use every degree of agility to anchor them on the rocky ledges. Still others considered the cables. The foundation of the upper part had to be anchored against the massive weight of inch-thick cables. Provisions had to be made to maintain the correct tension on the cables as the cars moved up and down. A special device had to be used to compensate for changes in length of the steel cords from desert daytime heat to the cool nighttime mountain breeze.

Cities hold few attractions for me, but how does man comprehend the plans and genius of builders of skyscrapers, or the hydroelectric dam with its giant dynamos which energizes entire states?

Have you ever watched a musician at a multirank organ? What powers of the mind allows one rapidly to read dots, lines, and words on a musical score and have that information relayed to the body, the fingers, and the feet to produce near flawless renditions of beautiful music page after page? Indeed, "We are God's workmanship and His word declare that we are 'fearfully and wonderfully made'" (FCE425.9).

But all the capabilities and powers of individuals to think and to do that we see now, we reckon as puny, indeed, in comparison with what God designed for humanity. We have been given some insight into this aspect of mankind when we read the comparison by Ellen White of the minds of the antediluvians with intellectual giants of our day.

"Notwithstanding the wickedness of the antediluvian world, that age was not, as has often been supposed, an era of ignorance and barbarism. The people were granted the opportunity of reaching a high standard of moral and intellectual attainment. They possessed great physical and mental strength, and their advantages for acquiring both religious and scientific knowledge were unrivaled. It is a mistake to suppose that because they lived to a great age their minds matured late; their mental powers were early developed, and those who cherished the fear of God and lived in harmony with His will continued to increase in knowledge and wisdom throughout their life. Could illustrious scholars of our time be placed in contrast with men of the same age who lived before the Flood, they would appears as greatly inferior in mental as in physical strength." (PP82-3).

"The antediluvians were without books, they had no written records; but with their great physical and mental vigor, they had strong memories, able to grasp and to retain that which was communicated to them, and in turn to transmit it **unimpaired** to their posterity" (PP83.7).

From the above information we can safely deduce that God designed the human mind to have strong reasoning powers and to be capable of remembering and recalling information **without**

mistakes indefinitely. In contrast, six thousand years of degeneration has damaged the finely designed brain and left the mind with many handicaps that the creator never intended to be present. The fact that it works so well after so much degradation indicates how strong was the original in the beginning.

The study of the mind is of special importance to the Christian. The mind is the source of actions (FCE426). It is the entity that develops character (4T606.8).

"He has prepared this living habitation for the mind; it is 'curiously wrought,' a temple which the Lord Himself has fitted up for the indwelling of His Holy Spirit. The mind controls the whole man. All our actions, good or bad, have their source in the mind. It is the mind that worships God, and allies us to heavenly beings. Yet many spend all their lives without becoming intelligent in regard to the casket that contains this treasure.

"All the physical organs are the servants of the mind, and the nerves are the messengers that transmit its orders to every part of the body, guiding the motions of the living machinery..." (FCE426).

The workings of the mind have been compared with functions of the body. Spiritually speaking, the mind feeds upon the Word of God which it receives through the senses (Deut. 8:2, 3). It receives "the water of life" from the life of Christ (DA195.4). The reception of the workings of the Holy Spirit on the mind is compared with the taking of a breath into the lungs (DA805.7). Prayer is compared with exhaling a breath (GW254.9).

We can perceive some of the attributes, faculties, and powers of the mind as they have been revealed to us by the writings of Inspiration. In addition to that, in so far as the observations are true, we can understand the mind by the intellectual discoveries of man, including our own personal experiences. The powers of the mind include perception, judgment, memory, and reasoning (3T33.1). Mental faculties include love, judgment, foresight, tact, and energy (5T457.9). These powers and faculties do not constitute character, but they are part of the working facility that develops character.

Let us examine the functioning capabilities of the mind under four major headings; (a) the "eye" (6T205.5) of the mind, (b) the will, (c) the heart, and (d) the memory. The chapter which follows will deal more directly with the memory. The first three will be considered briefly here to place them in perspective. In order to obtain a common working knowledge of the mind, we will need to illustrate or compare the various functioning entities with objects that are more familiar to us.

THE "MIND'S EYE": That aspect of the mind by which we are conscious of our surroundings, by which we perceive through the senses, can be likened to something, illustrated by the name "the eye of the mind," which traverses the electrical circuits of the mind. In Ephesians 1:18 we read about the need for the "eyes of your understanding" to be enlightened." The eye of the mind receives information from the senses,—sight, hearing, touch, taste, and other sensory nerve impulses,—and is conscious of them. It also can obtain information from the memory, previously recorded information within the brain. It may also originate a new idea by imagination. It is as though the mind's eye is constantly traversing the electrical circuits of the brain; and, as we shall study further, wherever it goes within the brain it leaves a track,—a memory pathway of all information received through the senses and all that is reasoned or imagined. As we shall see, the mind's eye records both feelings and thoughts, and these are kept in sequence.

It is as though while a person is alive, beginning even before birth, the mind's eye traverses the circuits of memory's halls; and, wherever it goes, it leaves a twin track recording of (a) what is discerned by the mind's eye and (b) how the individual feels about the thought under consideration (5T310.4; AH436; 5BC1085).

THE WILL: The mind's eye is under the control of the will. The will is the governing power (Ed289.2). It is the deciding power (SC47.6), the spring of man's actions. The will is to be under the control of reason (3T84.6; 5T310.2), of conscience (2T408.2; 3T84), and specifically under the control of the Holy Spirit (2T565.2; MH130.3). If the will is not decidedly under the control of the Holy Spirit, we may think that we are controlling our own will as we go about our daily life, but we are under Satan's control (DA324.5; DA466.4; TM79.9). **But there are some things that the will cannot do**.

"Education, culture, the exercise of the will, human effort, all have their proper sphere, but here [the changing of evil hearts] they are powerless. They may produce an outward correctness of behaviour [morality], but they cannot change the heart; they cannot purify the springs of life. There must be a power [Christ] working from within, a new life from above, before men can be changed from sin to holiness" (SC18.5).

It is crucial that we understand this point. In God's plan, we do **not** exert our will to do this good deed or that good deed directly. Rather we **will** (choose) to be under the control of God. When that situation prevails, God works in us and through us to accomplish His ways.

> "What you need to understand is the true force of the will. This is the governing power in the nature of man, the power of decision, or of choice. Everything depends on the right action of the will. The power of choice God has given to men; it is theirs to exercise. You cannot change your heart, you cannot of yourself give to God its affections; but you can *choose* to serve Him. You can give Him your will; He will then work in you to will and to do according to His good pleasure. Thus your whole nature will be brought under the control of the Spirit of Christ; your affections will be centered upon Him, your throughts will be in harmony with Him" (SC47.5).

In fact, we are to realize that we need even greater assistance to our will in spiritual matters than is generally thought. Ellen White says elsewhere,

> "Our will is not to be forced into co-operation with divine agencies, but it must be voluntarily submitted. Were it possible to force upon you with a hundredfold greater intensity the influence of the Spirit of God, it would not make you a Christian, a fit subject for heaven.... The will must be placed on the side of God's will. You are not able, of yourself, to bring your purposes and desires and inclinations into submission to the will of God; but if you are **'willing to be made willing**,' God will accomplish the work for you, even 'casting down imaginations, and every high thing that exalteth itself against the knowledge of God, and bringing into captivity every thought to the obedience of Christ.' 2 Corinthians 10:5. Then you will 'work out your own salvation with fear and trembling. For it is God which worketh in you both to will and to do of His good pleasure.' Phillipians 2:12, 13" (MB142.5 emphasis supplied).

When the mind is under the control of God it is energized by God to do good deeds (MH176.5). The will, unaided by divine power, is powerless against evil (MH429.2).

THE HEART: The heart has been compared to a garden (AH200-3). Ideas like plants may be sown in the heart (AH196.1). The heart is the citadel of man (5T536.7). It has a door (2T216-7), and a chamber (6T376.1). The heart is the source of complicated emotions and of feelings (4T85.4; 2T660.3). It is a source of imaginations (TM463.9). It has to do with our lusts, (DA161.5) and our intents and motives (4T583.9). God weighs the motives of the heart (3T370.2; 5T147.6).

Christ came to cleanse the heart from the defilement of sin, from earthly desires, evil lusts, and evil habits (DA161.5). He knocks at the door of the heart and wishes to come and search the chambers as with a lighted candle (2SM318.2). Our Saviour desires to give us a new heart. The new heart will, in turn, have its influence upon the entire being.

"When Jesus speaks of the new heart, He means the mind, the life, the whole being. To have a change of heart is to withdraw the affections from the world, and fasten them upon Christ. To have a new heart is to have a new mind, new purposes, new motives" (MYP72.2).

We began this chapter with wonder in regard to the mental and physical capabilities. Now we come to the question, what is it that determines the use of the works of men? The dynamos of Grand Coulee may be used to breed some plutonium. Shall we use it for the big bomb or to generate atomic energy? The computer may be programmed to land a module on the moon or to guide a death dealing missile. The computer has no spiritual values. Mankind without God would self-destruct.

Chapter 6

THE RECORD OF YOUR LIFE

Our family has a great appreciation for the beauties of our national parks, the deserts, and for the wild life that make those places their home. Before the energy crisis every weekend possible found us with our sleeping bags and camping gear on our way to some spot of beauty. It would be late Sunday night, near midnight, before we would be returning to our home in the busy megalopolis. The last portion of our trip was usually over the Angeles Crest Highway, an hour's drive over a well-kept but winding mountain road.

Usually as I drove along, all others in the car were asleep. To help the time to pass more speedily the radio would be tuned to our favorite good music station.

On one such return journey the radio was off, but I began to notice that I was recalling a musical rendition of a favorite symphony that I had heard broadcast on a previous trip down that same stretch of highway. As we wended our way over the mountain road, I was vividly recalling the musical performance in its full body as if it were sounding forth from the radio speaker. Even the station announcements with the commercial was recalled with clarity. After a while the necessity to give my undivided attention to driving interferred with my ability to recall the program, but the whole episode lasted well over twenty minutes. This experience clearly illustrated to me the unconscious strength of "association" thought pathways in the mind. On the prior trip the broadcast was associated with the driving. On the latter trip, driving the same road under similar conditions help recall the broadcast by mental association pathways.

Perhaps you have noticed remembrances return to your mind after watching a favorite TV program. Have you experienced the mental flashback of extremely impressive scenes for several hours after the last commercial? Murder mysteries or crime presentations are especially likely to intrude into our consciousness for hours after the program is over. Why does this happen?

How is it that we are able to remember? What happens within our brain that allows us to store information from the senses? Also, what influences our capability of recalling these past experiences?

Considerable study in the scientific world has been given to understand the memory and our ability to recall information that has been stored there. Even though many scientists hold to the "Theory of Actuality"[1] which proposes that a thought is not a state or thing but merely an event, other scientists realize that the mind does record information from the senses and imaginations and stores these for the entire life of the individual. Scientific observations have confirmed what is revealed to us in the Bible and in the writings of Ellen White about this aspect of the workings of the mind. Although God has not spoken to us about this in technical language, He has used the words with which we are familiar to convey an understanding of memory and the capabilities of the mind, particularly in the realm of what He has to do through Jesus to correct the effects of sin on the mind. We can faintly see what He is describing about remembrance and recall.

Some of the most fascinating reports of scientists in regard to the mental record have been made by Dr. Wilder Penfield, a neurosurgeon.[2] He has described observations of "the stream of consciousness in the brain record." In his discussion on the topic, he points out that there are two facets to the recording of memory within the brain. The hippocampus part of the brain has to do with preservation of recent events in the memory, whereas, long-term memory includes the functioning of additional parts of the brain. The elderly may have damage of blood vessels to one part of the brain and exhibit difficulty in recalling recent events from the damaged nerves. Yet they are able to remember information from the distant past. This suggests that the mental recordings of recent events are then organized in a more permanent memory bank.

Dr. Penfield's comments are interesting in light of the writings of Ellen White.

"He who has grown old in the service of God may find his mind a blank in regard to the things that are happening about him, and recent transactions may soon pass from his memory; but his mind is all awake to the scenes and transactions of his childhood" (SD78.5).

Doctor Penfield was able to demonstrate the preservation of memory in his patients. In this study his patients who underwent brain surgery were conscious during the operation under local anesthetic. This was the technique he used for he needed the patient's help in locating the focus of irritation in the brain that was causing their epilepsy.

As he searched the brain with his electrode, he found that when he applied a gentle electric stimulus into certain areas of the brain, the patient would be aware of experiences from his past life. We quote Dr. Penfield,

"While the surgeon's stimulating electrode is kept in place at some point in the temporal cortex, a steady stream of consciousness moves through the patient's mind. It is an awareness of things as they were in some previous strip of time. Action goes forward at the original tempo; he is aware of those things to which he paid attention then, and yet he is also aware of the present. When the electrode is withdrawn from the temporal cortex, the experiential review usually stops instantly. Often, when the electrode is placed at approximately the same spot a minute later, it happens that the stream of past consciousness is caused to flow again through the patient's mind, beginning at the same moment in past time."[2]

Doctor Penfield called this area, the "interpretive cortex". He observed that the patients could recall not only the scenes and what they had heard, but they also had recollection of feeling the emotions that had been experienced in times past.

A lawyer, Louis Nizer, has used both aspects of memory to help his clients recall particular events of their previous experience so that he could arrive at the best means to help his client on the witness stand. At the interview he would have his client recall all that they could remember of the original incident. In some places in the story the ability to recall the events or what was said was limited. He then used another trick to get crucial information. He asked the client to recall how he felt about what was said or done at the time that the original incident transpired. Very often that jogged the memory so that the patron was able to give the information needed to develop his case properly.[3]

Doctor Benjamin Libet, of the Mt. Zion Neurological Institute in San Francisco, has been able to document that the mind is capable of registering subliminal sensations. Such sensations are transmitted to the brain, but the duration of effect on the sensory nerve is too short to elicit conscious recognition of the experience. Brief as these are in duration, they still elicit activity and leave a record in the cerebral cortex.[4]

Such a possibility has been known from experiments by others. In one study the information was intermittently flashed on the screen during a movie in a theater to the effect that popcorn would be for sale in the lobby of the theater during intermission. Whenever this was done, even though the duration of the flash was too short to be consciously perceived by the audience, more than twice as many patrons as usual went to the popcorn machine during intermission.

What is the importance of memory? The answer is obvious. That stored information, when arranged as habits, permits us to perform many duties without being consciously involved in the process. It also helps us consciously perform our work and make decisions. Much of what we think, what we do, and our manner of response is based on the stored information. In some way, without taking the time to traverse each and every memory pathway consciously, the mind's eye is able to determine what is applicable in the mind on a certain subject and render a decision. That decision will of necessity be based upon the stored bits of information, the degree that this can be remembered unconsciously, and the amount of repression that has been given to the various unwanted information on the topic under consideration.

In the field of learning, repetition is important to us. Acts repeated make habits, and these take over much from the conscious activities of the mind. We learn and recall with greater ease the things that we love and enjoy. A student who dislikes his English teacher or the subject matter suffers the penalty of difficult learning in that material. The third truism of learning is that difficult items can be recalled with greater ease if they are consciously associated with more seasoned information or by the help of a mnemonic prompter.

Those tenets of learning should be contemplated in relation to our daily activities. If we feed the mind a diet of sensational or demoralizing literature, intoxicating amusements, and a dessert of TV cops and robbers, our responses to situations will be enfeebled and perverted to that extent (CW134; SD131; 6T194.2). This is the hazard of theaters; it is not the building nor its patrons! The mental pathways are packed with nonsense, trash, rubbish,—"hay" and "stubble",—if you please. We are impeded to that extent for, as the saying goes in computer lingo, "Garbage data in yields garbage results out."

The scientist may ask the question, "Are all the previous thoughts and experiences of a person recorded in the memory bank of the brain? Or is the mind like a sieve which sifts out the bad, lets it fall, and saves only the good?" God's revelation to us through the Bible and the Spirit of prophecy can answer these questions. The entire ceremony of the sanctuary was laid out, "to show them that they could not come in contact with sin without becoming polluted" (GC419.8). Sin leaves a scar on the mind here and a blot on the copy in heaven (OHC227). Every thought is a seed cast into the soil of the mind (4T366.2). Every thought, word, and deed of our lives will meet us again for angels are by our sides making a record of our words, deportment, and manner (5T466.3; DA302.5; PP218; CH416.2). The prophet Jeremiah stated, "The sin of Judah is written with a pen of iron, *and* with the point of a diamond; *it is* written upon the table of their heart and upon the horns of your altars" (Jere. 17:1).

It is the mental record of our life that indicates to us who we are. An amnesiac is one who cannot remember his past. Not only do we have a record in the brain here in this life, but God also keeps a record in the "books of heaven." It is as though an exact picture of our character with the thoughts and feelings is transferred as they occur to His giant "hall of records" above (MM184.4).

Does this not make sense? What would God have to keep a record of in order to make you or me again at the resurrection if we should die? Identical twins may look alike, but their thoughts are different! It is the memory of our feelings and thoughts in the past by which we know who we are. Jesus can make the same person again at the resurrection when He creates a new body with a new brain and imprints that mental record which He has preserved in heaven into the brain of the newly resurrected body and starts the thinking again (GC550.5).

The record of the wicked as well as the record of the righteous is kept in heaven (RH04-05-92). When the wicked are resurrected, they will continue their thinking in the same train of thought right where they left off at the time of their death (GC662.5, 664.4).

Character is the treasure, the great harvest, of life (MB90.3). "Death brings dissolution of the body, but makes no change in the character" (5T466.4). "It is the spiritual and moral character that is of value in the sight of Heaven, and that will survive the grave and be made glorious with immortality for the endless ages of eternity" (1SM259.1). As we form our character here, it is imprinted upon the books of heaven (CG562). God preserves it until the day of resurrection (6BC1093).

The emphasis of the prophets in reference to the memory is on moral and spiritual issues. It is important to understand, though, that in our daily lives there are common activities and thoughts which may or may not have moral significance (1SM38-39). These, as well as those of moral significance, are recorded. We, as individuals, have been given freedom to think and to do things within the guideline principles of God (GC285.4; cf. CT342.9; AA565). Adam was given talents and jurisdiction over this world under God (PP50.8). The moral law is in force at all times, but it may not be applicable in every situation. Let me illustrate it this way. If I decide to plant goldenrods in my flower bed, there may or may not be a moral principle involved. If my wife is allergic to goldenrods, and I, while knowing this, go right ahead and plant them contrary to her best interests, there is then introduced a moral issue. Another illustration. God does not care whether you paint your house purple or orange, but He does care if you and your companion come to blows or scold each other over the issue.

When Jesus comes again and raises the dead, we shall all be changed. Our minds will be brought back to the proficiency that God originally intended for mankind. Then our memories will be unfettered from the infirmities of sin. Our minds will have much greater capabilities for thinking and doing (COL332.7; GC677.4). Our capacity for reasoning, deduction, and recall will be profound, greater than we can imagine.

When that is accomplished by the great Restorer, the mind's eye will have free access to all the mental pathways. To prepare us for this, God intends to blot out the record of sin. He wants nothing there that will be a seed for sin, nothing there that would tempt us to sin. The yearly service of the sanctuary on the day of atonement defines what Jesus plans to do for us in the examination of the records and the blotting out of sin. From that also we see the price that our Redeemer and the Father have paid for this restoration of the soul temple to its rightful state (DA161).

1. *Encyclopedia Britannica*, 1952, 1:145.
2. W. Penfield, *Annals of the Royal College of Surgeons of England*, 29:77-84, 1961.
3. Louis Nizer, *My Life in Court*, Doubleday & Co., 1961.
4. *Medical World News*, Sept. 12, 1969.

Chapter 7

A SPECIAL LOOK AT THE RECORD

At the end of the 2300 day time prophecy the Father arose from His throne in the first apartment of the heavenly sanctuary, went into the most holy place, and sat down upon His throne there. Soon thereafter, Jesus arose and followed His Father (EW55.4). It was then that the Son of Man came to the Ancient of days (Dan. 7:13; GC426.3). It was then that the Lord suddenly came to His temple (Mal. 3:1; GC426.3). It was then that Christ went into the marriage (Matt. 25:6; GC426.3). It was then that the work began which will culminate in the cleansing of the sanctuary (Dan. 8:14; GC426.3).

God expects us to follow our High Priest there by faith; (GC430.4, 431.1) and yet, as late as 1890, Ellen White stated, "The people have not entered into the holy place, where Jesus has gone to make an atonement for His children" (RH02-25-90). We are called to arouse from spiritual lethargy, study the plan of salvation in connection with the "day of atonement," and, intelligently, under the Spirit's guidance, participate in the service. Our study in this chapter begins with that phase of the examination of the books of record, the investigative judgment. This phase began in 1844 and extends until probation closes.

Some Adventists seem to believe that the cleansing of the sanctuary with the blotting out of sins for **the living** [please note] has been going on ever since 1844 or even prior to then. Some believe that the sins are blotted out when they are confessed. Two references are quoted to support these beliefs. They are:

"God judges every man, according to his work. Not only does He judge, but He sums up, day by day and hour by hour, our progress in welldoing" (7BC987.6).

"When probation ends, it will come suddenly, unexpectedly—at a time when we are least expecting it. But we can have a clean record in heaven today, and know that God accepts us; and finally, if faithful, we shall be gathered into the kingdom of heaven" (7BC989.7).

God **judges** everyone, nations, families, and individuals, continually but this is not the **investigative** judgment. When the record account for an unrepentant nation or person is full, then probation for that one is over, and that one is devoted to destruction (PP165.8; 7BC987.9). In this manner probation has closed for some of the wicked while they were alive ever since sin began on the earth. This happened to the Sodomites (PP165.1). The **investigative** judgment, however, began in 1844 and is only for those who have their names written in the book of life (GC480.5).

God **judges** how each person is progressing day by day (TM448). He decides (judges), at the time of the thought or action whether it is suitable to be remembered in the **book of remembrance** or considered as a record of sin (4T63.1, 646.4; 4BC1171.9; 5BC1085.7; GC480-1). Of necessity our records are kept up to date (CH416; MM184.3). But it is not until **this** life is over, either by death or at the time for the close of God's work for the living,* that the heavenly court scene takes place, the books are **opened**, **investigated**, and the record of sins blotted out (GC486.2, 483.1, 428.5). We are told that it is **impossible** for the sins to be blotted out until after the investigation of the record of that person (GC485.5). The investigative judgment closes the probation for that person when it occurs suddenly, unexpectedly (7BC989.7; GC490.7). There is no second investigative judgment for a person.

The blotting out of sin for the **living** occurs just a short time before Christ's second coming (GC485.4, 352.7). It happens as part of the "special" or "final" atonement, (EW251, 253) and is part of the "last work" of mediation (GC428.1). It is done for the righteous

---

*   Note: None were examined before 1844 except Enoch, Moses, and Elijah, the forerunners, and the first fruits of the dead who ascended with Christ.

living at the time of "refreshing," the time of the latter rain (GC485.4, 612.1).

Ellen White stated as late as 1900 that the investigative judgment had not started on the books of the **living** (GC490.6; EW280.2; 1SM125.3; 6T130.7). The generation of the living is the last one to come up in the investigative judgment (GC483.2). The investigative judgment of the living **could have taken place shortly after 1844**, but something on the part of God's people was lacking (Ev696; GC458.1; EW71.8; 1SM174.9). What is the cause of the delay? Apparently the Lord has something else to demonstrate to the universe about the nature of sin that requires our cooperation (4T34-35; PP41.4, 42.6; 5T526.2; 6T9-13). Perhaps the remnant church has not yet grasped fully all the truths that they need to know and practice for the end of time. For example, few, if any, of His followers in 1844 were worshipping on the seventh-day Sabbath, nor did they know the health message. God's mercy for sinners and full vindication of His name are at stake.

Two main groups who have professed belief in Christ will be examined in the **investigative** judgment, (a) those who have died before this judgment and (b) those who will be investigated while they are yet alive. Since we know from references above that the investigative judgment did not start until 1844, the question naturally comes up, when did Enoch, Elijah, Moses, and the first fruits of the dead who ascended with Christ have their investigative judgment and when were their sins blotted out? The answer to that question has to be obtained from an understanding of the main group. Exactly **when** this was done for the forerunners, we cannot say; but we know that they had to be examined and their sins blotted out before they were taken to heaven (5T467.3; MB141.9). The times and seasons, however, are in God's hands. He could have let them all remain in the grave and have dealt with them after 1844, but He decided to prepare some and take them to heaven earlier than the main groups to give us hope (PP88.3). Just because He did this should not disturb our understanding of the basic tenets of the plan that God has for the restoration of sinners.

Before we go further, we should consider briefly God's reason for bringing every motive, thought, word, and action into the judgment (5T466.4; 5BC1085.7; 4BC1171.9; PP218.1). **We must not misjudge His motives in this**! The Godhead, in fact the whole unfallen universe, has a deep loving interest in every soul. The record of our own evil deeds and Satan both accuse us before God. God wants us to be clean. He wants the mind's eye to be able to examine all the mental "halls of memory" without being tempted to think evil or to have a propensity to commit evil. For this to occur He must examine us closely to help us to be rid of every spot and wrinkle in our character (GC487.4). If we really want to be freed from **every** record of sin, then we should appreciate this close examination and express thanks to the Father, the Son, and all those who have ministered unto us (4T354.6).

On some occasions when I talk about the record of sin being blotted out of the mental record so that it will not be remembered nor come into mind, there are some who consider this a form of amnesia and are disturbed by such a concept. For some reason, even though they have given up sin, they seem reticent to part company with some of their memory pathways. Personally, I will be glad to give up those evil thoughts even though my natural tendency is not to do so. By the grace of God, I do not want to be tempted to think them again.

Furthermore, if we have, time after time, rejected our sinful thoughts and overcome them, wouldn't it be a blessing to have them erased, so that they could never come to mind? Would it make any difference to us in heaven to have that part of our memory bank missing? My conclusions are that we will not need them. We will realize that we were sinners and that we had quite a mental battle with sin without the actual recorded segment of it still present in the heart.

God knows how to erase the filthy pictures (the record of sin) from the halls of memory and leave the good ones (the book of remembrance), leave the thoughts that will be safe to examine mentally throughout eternity. I shall trust His judgment.

Earlier in this chapter we quoted a statement to the effect that "we can have a clean record in heaven **today**." The question needs to be answered, "How can this be true if the record of sin remains until the investigative judgment of the person and the close of probation?" The answer lies in what God can do for us now. He can create a clean heart in us, **today** (2SM32.1). He can transfer the guilt of every sin from us to the sanctuary and write pardon over every sin, **today** (GC420.2). He can cover every sin that is confessed, by the blood of Jesus, **today** (COL311.7). And by fulfilling every known duty **today**, by overcoming every temptation and trial through the strength that is available to us from God **today**, we can be kept from sinning **today** (GC425; 8T46.8; DA664.7; 1SM409). The promise has been made that there is no excuse for sinning (DA311.7). Every provision for success has been made; but we do not strive to be under the control of the Holy Spirit nor resist unto blood. We do not love righteousness and our Saviour enough nor hate iniquity enough. We are lukewarm to Christ, content with our state, and spiritually passive.

The examination of the records at the investigative judgment is to see if the imparted character recorded in the mind is like Christ's as well as to see the attitude of the person and to see that all sins are confessed, pardoned, and covered. The guilt of all the sins of that person will have been removed to the sanctuary in heaven. Both our **book of remembrance** and our **record of sin** are to be examined (GC481). The parable of Matthew 22 about the King coming to examine the wedding guests emphasizes the examination of the **imparted** character (COL310-14). Also, the oil in the lamps of the virgins represents character (TM234.1; 4BC1179). The character robe that God imputes to us was built in Christ (4BC1179; MB9.2; COL203.5). It covers the record of sin. The imparted robe was built in me and is mine to wear throughout eternity (COL310-12, 204.4; 4T429.5; Revelations 19:8).

Gratitude should flow from us to the Father. He agonized through the position of judge, divested of the attributes of a father, toward the Sin-Bearer at Calvary (TM246.2). He is the presiding judge for the investigative phase of the court duties (GC479.5; Dan. 7:9,10; Acts 17:31). Our Saviour serves as Mediator and Advocate for that phase, but He has a position as judge also (GC482.8; DA210.6; 9T185.6; RH03-12-01). He advocates only for those that He decides are worthy of His ministry by having fulfilled their part of the conditions of salvation (6T363.9). Our Saviour does not take border-line cases upon His lips to plead their cause in hopes of obtaining a new interpretaion of the law in the courts of heaven. What was sin six thousand years ago is still sin today. There is no "new morality," only old immorality disguised in a new dress of rationalization.

By virtue of His death on the cross, Jesus has made a way to the throne of God for all who will respond (GC489.4). With sorrow only partially sensed by humanity, Jesus and the Father turn from those who will not respond to His love and mercy (TM245-6). Hosea describes it, "Ephraim is joined to idols: let him alone" (Hosea 4:17). "How shall I give thee up, Ephraim" (Hosea 11:8)? Those Israelites would not let Him cast down their sacred groves (their evil imaginations) nor bring their sinful thoughts into captivity (Hosea 10:8-13; 2 Kings 15:3, 4; MB142).

After the investigative judgment for all, Jesus gives up His position as mediator and becomes King and Judge (GC485.6; EW280; 7BC989.7; 4T387.8). In this capacity He passes sentence upon the righteous and the wicked (RH11-22-98; GC490.9, 666.3). God has appointed Christ as judge for the final, the executive, phase of the judgment to carry out the decisions of the court of heaven (DA210.4; John 5:27; Jude 14, 15). It will be seen that the wicked have, in effect, destroyed themselves (Hosea 13:9; COL84.9; DA764.1). They have rejected the only Way out of the flames that God sends to remake the earth and to recompense them for their persistent rejections of His offers of forgiveness. Their punishment will be according to their deeds in rebellion (GC666.5).

Chapter 8

GUILT

When we discuss "sin," it is helpful to consider it from several aspects in relation to the sinner. After a known sin is committed, the sinner has three things: a **sense** of that sin, **guilt** of that sin, and a mental **record** of that sin (GC420-1, 480; DA752-3; MH85.4). These are in the person's mind and in the exact copy in heaven. They will stay there unless something is done about them. Guilt of sin poisons the well springs of life (TM518.8). The record of sin may either initiate a temptation from within or serve as a responsive chord (a mental association pathway) to temptations from without via the senses. Both the guilt of sin and the record of sin must be removed, and it is important to realize that they are disposed of differently. If we cling to sin, we will be finally destroyed with the guilt when God cleanses the earth of all sin (COL123.7; DA763.8).

It is difficult in a study of the Scriptures and the writings of Ellen White to determine in many instances when the writer uses the terms "sin," "iniquity," or "transgression of sin" whether he (or she) is referring to **guilt** of sin or to **record** of sin or to **both** together. One must use the context as well as determine what the writer indicates is done with "sin" to distinguish which is under discussion.

Guilt of sin is real. It is as real as the laws of God are real. Some Christians have trouble with this. They seem to believe that guilt is not real. They say that guilt is not something that can be moved from one place to another.

Let us imagine a court scene on this earth. The criminal has been brought to trial for stealing. There are witnesses to substantiate the facts of the crime. Through a coincidence the police have a sound track movie of the deed, and the criminal admits the offense. Is he guilty? Yes. Can you see the guilt? No. Then how can you tell that there is guilt? First, there is a law. Second, there is a remembrance, a record of the deed, with witnesses. Third, there is the effect of the crime on the criminal and on the others involved.

Guilt is a spiritual thing. Law is a spiritual thing. Love is a spiritual thing. Even though we cannot see them, they exist; and we can see the effects of them. Guilt can be "felt" by the mind.

The universe consists of material things and spiritual things. Both material and spiritual things were made at the creation, and they are sustained by the power of a personal Being,–God (MH414.9).

God has made provisions for the removal of guilt from us. When we truly repent of a sin, the guilt of that sin is **not cancelled** but is borne from us by Jesus (GC420.2; PP356.2). Ellen White presents it this way. The guilt of sin is "in reality," is "in fact," **transferred** from the repentant sinner to the heavenly sanctuary (GC420-1). This statement could not be referring to the **record** of sin since the **record** is marked pardoned (GC483.5), and remains (GC421.5), and is finally "blotted out" after the investigative judgement (GC422.1, 483.5).

This **guilt** from the repentant sinners is the entity that pollutes the heavenly sanctuary (PP355-6; GC420-1). The guilt of the wicked stands registered against their records in heaven and does not defile the holy places since it was not transferred by the blood of the Lamb.

When the investigative judgment is completed **for all**, by virtue of His sacrifice Jesus takes upon Himself as High Priest all the **guilt** of all the sins of the righteous (GC422.5; PP356-8). Then, in the presence of all heaven, He places the guilt on Satan because of his responsibility as the originator of sin and the tempter to sin (EW280-1). Every sin must be accounted for (DA761.8; 5BC1087).

It becomes apparent why Jesus is called the "Sin-Bearer" (SR225.8; DA111.7, 685.7, 756.1). He **bore** our guilt when He was in Gethsemane and on the cross. As mediator He bears it from us at confession, and finally places it upon Satan who must suffer the consequences for all the sins that he caused the righteous to commit (GC485.9). Christ paid the penalty for our part in the sin so that He could obtain the privilege to bear our guilt of the sin (RH09-29-96).

The "cleansing of the sanctuary" includes the investigation of the books of record, the blotting out of the record of the sin, and the placing of the guilt of sin on Satan (GC421-2).

Satan knows that this guilt will be rolled back on himself (EW178). Naturally, he will do all he can to prevent this from happening. You can see this from the several false theories prevalent regarding guilt.

Many people go to psychiatrists because they have guilt feelings. In some circumstances they feel guilty unnecessarily. They may feel guilty because they broke one of their own or another person's standards. If the rule was unwise in the first place, they need not have guilt feelings. Other poor souls imagine guilt. Such persons need to be educated as to what constitutes real guilt. The former group should recognize that they are not really guilty if they can legitimately repeal the law.

There is, however, real authentic guilt from disobedience of God's laws. Some psychiatrists try to absolve this guilt in the same way as they do the above mentioned types. Let us say, for example, that a man commits adultery. After a while his feeling of guilt eats away at him until he is a nervous wreck. So he goes to a psychoanalyzer. The psychiatrist says, "Do not let that bother you. Why, down in some south sea islands they do not even get married. In our land getting married is merely a custom. Our marriage regulations are folk mores, nothing more." So the man feels better. However, his improvement is only temporary, so he seeks the advice of a preacher. What does the preacher say? Some mistaken preachers would say, "Do not feel guilty, the law was nailed to the cross." Now, let us suppose that the remorseful individual next goes to a priest. The priest agrees that the person is guilty, and advises a certain amount of good works and acts of penance; and after that he, a sinful priest, will forgive him and take his guilt away.

All such mistaken attitudes toward God's laws and the plan of salvation have resulted in a worse hell then Dante's Inferno. There is no peace for the wicked (Isaiah 48:22).

There are some thinkers who acknowledge that there is real guilt, but they try to diffuse it so extensively that it is hard to locate. When President Kennedy was assassinated, there were many who were trying to blame society for the murder. There is a great deal of agitation in medical and legal circles to find a way to reach a consensus of opinion between the attitudes of lawyers, psychiatrists, and sociologists in regard to criminal justice. It really amounts to this:

the sociologists and psychiatrists would have us believe that a man is a product of heredity and environment, without free moral choice; and that when he is faced with a certain set of circumstances and stimuli, he must react in a given specific predetermined fashion (W. M. McGauhey, *Calif. Med.* 99:318, 1963). This now places the blame for the deed, whether good or bad, upon some poorly demarcated entity called society. So society must accept the guilt and flagellate itself, and let the criminal go free.

By **multiple** choices a person places himself where he is. Just as a person who starts on a journey must continue to choose the right road at every intersection, so we must choose correctly in spiritual things repeatedly. A person may travel along with unregenerate companions, load his mind with the bawdry leavings of filthy authors, and live on a T.V. diet of passion and carnage, until crime is a natural consequence; but when he does something wrong, the guilt is his and remains his until, and unless, by the element of supernatural rebirth by choice, he turns from that way of life.

It is interesting to note that the very first conversation fallen man had with his Creator was regarding guilt. Adam tried to blame Eve for his sin and indirectly implicate God since God created Eve (PP57-8). Eve then tried to shift her guilt upon the hypnotized serpent and back upon God for creating such a subtle creature. About this time the serpent had lost its voice.

My guilt cannot be removed by the dexterous reasoning of psychiatry, or by crucifying the law, or by sociologically smearing it thinly over all mankind, so that it cannot be seen. Neither knowledge of the law nor ignorance of the law can remove guilt (Rom. 3:20; 1 Cor. 13:2; DA744.9). We cannot foist it upon God with Adam's trick. God has only one way for us to be rid of guilt. This includes repentance, confession, and belief in His plan of salvation.

It is a very difficult thing to accept our own guilt, acknowledge that it is ours, and say we are sorry. But it is a wonderful feeling after it is done, and we are freed **legitimately** from guilt. Jesus has made provisions for the removal of all guilt from us. Let us accept His way, the only way that brings peace.

Chapter 9

CHARACTER

"A character formed according to the divine likeness is the only treasure that we can take from this world to the next" (COL332.7; cf 5T466.5). These are startling words. Do you know what a character is? Something as important as that should be on the top of our list for study.

The words "character" and "habit" do not even appear in the King James Version. How can we know what heaven has revealed about this important topic? A dictionary definition is not enough for we are dealing with spiritual things. The concepts of God are not subject to private interpretation (2 Peter 1:20). We must study how the words are used by inspired writers. We will have to look to Ellen White, the author of the above quotation, to see how it is defined. With her insight we see that God uses other words, parables, and symbols in the several translations to teach us about character. In some places the translators have used the words, soul, spirit, or mind in place of the word character. Words like way, wont, custom, manner, and inclination may be used to denote habit.

The parables and stories of Jesus dealt mainly with character building (COL23.4, 269.8). With these our Saviour more accurately expressed how the mind works. The white raiment of Revelation 3 from the heavenly Merchant represents imparted character (4T88.8). The oil of the wise virgins symbolizes not only the ministry of the Holy Spirit but also the fruit of the ministry, an imparted righteous character (COL407.1; CG173.3; TM234.1). The wedding garment of Matthew 22:11 typifies the imparted character which we are to wear while it is being "woven" in our minds by the "loom" of heaven

(COL311-2; 4BC1179; DA762.5). Revelation 14:1-4 indicates the nature of the character that God's people will have in the last days (7BC978).

The four formal statements below about "character" written by Ellen White are of special help.

"...the thoughts and feelings combined make up the moral character" (5T310.3).

"Thus actions repeated form habits, habits form character, and by the character our destiny for time and for eternity is decided" (COL356.6; cf. FCE194.5; MLT269.8).

"The spirit, the character of man, is returned to God, there to be preserved" (6BC1093).

"The mind is the garden; the character is the fruit" (4T606.8).

From the above references it appears quite clear that character is a result of the working of the mind. The character is in the brain and is kept on record in heaven; and it is, indeed, the record of the thoughts, words, actions, motives, and feelings of the individual (CG562; 7BC987; 5BC1085).

What happens to the character at conversion? At conversion the **heart** is changed, but the **character** is not (COL97.3, 163.2; 1SM336.8). New motives take over the heart, and the person works with God to **develop** a **righteous** character, the **new man** in Christ Jesus. Character is "formed," "molded", "transformed", and "developed". (COL100.1, 331; DA407.5). It is through action that character is built (MB149.9).

The development of a **righteous** character has always been a mandate of God (COL391.3; 5BC1085; SC62.2). I find no statement by the pen of Inspiration that says that Adam was created with a character. Adam was to **form** a character (SC62.4). Christ **developed** a perfect character (DA762.5; COL345.3). Christ came as "the character builder" (COL345.4).

As we study the topic of character, we read of **natural** and **cultivated** traits of character (TM416.8; FCE278.1). Since character consists of acts and habits, feelings and thoughts, how can children inherit traits of character from their parents? Is there some kind of mental pattern or record of thought, a sort of instinct, implanted in the brain by the genes?

Answers to those questions are not precisely given to us. The statements of Ellen White that I have found which come nearest to clarify them are quoted below:

"Your children have had transmitted to them your traits of character, and, besides this, they are daily copying your example of blind, unreasonable passion, impatience, and fretfulness" (4T495-6).

"In the human heart there is natural selfishness and corruption, which can only be overcome by most thorough discipline and severe restraint; and even then it will require years of patient effort and earnest resistance" (4T496).

"If before the birth of her child she is self-indulgent, if she is selfish, impatient, and exacting, these traits will be reflected in the disposition of the child. Thus many children have received as a birthright almost unconquerable tendencies to evil" (AH256.3).

The degree of parental temperance or intemperance is reflected in the child as changes in physical strength, mental prowess, and moral power. These are part of the heritage along with what worldly goods he receives (PP561.5).

Perhaps the child begins to sense ever so subtly the attitudes of the mother even before birth on its clean mental "polished plate" (cf. CDF217.5; AH436.5; Romans 9:11). The fetal heart begins to beat by the fifth week. Swedish investigators, Drs. Wedenberg and Westin, (*Medical World News*, 4-10-70, pp. 28) have demonstrated that the unborn baby can hear tones as early as twelve weeks before full-term delivery. Even though the mental capabilities of the fetus are quite limited, it has a degree of response and remembrance.

Apart from those **natural** traits of character that the infant may have inherited, the child obtains his greatest legacy of character traits, good or bad, by the day by day example of the parents. The children of wicked parents "inherit" by imitation the sinful life (3SG291). "The children will develop characters similar to their parents." On the other hand, we are promised that the children may also inherit habits of righteousness from the example of God-fearing parents (3SG291). "Infant children are a mirror for the mother in which she may see reflected her own habits and deportment" (AH267.7).

A few years ago our family spent a year in Michigan. On one clear morning after a winter storm, my four-year-old son and I set out for a hike in the snow. We had not gone far, when a little boy's voice behind me said, "See, Daddy, I'm walking right in your tracks." The impact of the words chilled me for a moment, when I realized their deeper meaning. Momentarily, I dreaded the responsibility of parenthood. I replied, "Fine, I'll take shorter steps; just don't follow me when I go wrong." Back came the answer, "But how will I know when you are wrong?"

Have you noticed how easily a child learns to scold? If I am a fretful, scolding type of person, it is not too long before my child will return the scolding. If the child is rebuffed for such impertinence, the toys or the pets get the scolding. Could it be that the "terrible teens" are a result of the example of "terrible parents" during their early childhood? How important it is that, "Whatever traits of character she [the mother] wishes to see developed in them [the children], she must cultivate in herself" (AH267.7).

Not all traits of character in a child come from the influence of the parents and other associates. The Devil is still active. All too soon children begin to originate and cultivate a few of their own traits. Parents have a right and duty to pray a hedge of angels about their children (CPT110, 118.9). A noble all-round character is not inherited (PP223.4; COL331.3); but by the power from our Saviour and by the ministry of the Holy Spirit and the angels, we each can develop a righteous character (5T579.3; GC469.7).

God has given us the talents, and we are to form the character (4T606.7; COL331.4). Work and prayer are both required in perfecting Christian character (4T459.8). The **imparted character** of Christ is given to us, moment by moment, day by day, as we do God's will, from self-renouncing love, by the power He bestows upon us (AA483.2; DA312.5; 1SM366.8). The strength for character development is imparted to us as we submit our wills to Christ and request this power to work for God (MH514.4; DA667). As fast as the soul resolves to act, in accordance with God's will, God imparts power (TM518.1). As soon as the paralytic responded by willing to obey, God supplied the power, and he walked (John 5). There is no time on this earth when we can say that we have attained to all the character development that we shall have (7BC947).

During our probationary time now, our Saviour would have us "weed" in our own character garden (4T337.8). We are to "wear" Christ's robe of righteousness now (Ed249.5; 5T472.5). Now is the "washing and ironing time" (5BC1131). We are to wash our robes of character in the blood of the Lamb (5T215-6; 4T387.2). God has left it with us to remedy the defects in our character, and to cleanse the soul temple (5T214.7).

> "The work of overcoming is a great work. Shall we take hold of it with energy and perseverence? Unless we do, our 'filthy [character] garments' will not be taken from us. We need never expect that these will be torn from us violently...." (EGW RH10-12-61).

Character will not be transformed at the second coming of our Lord (AH319.5; 4T429.6). The Refiner plans to do all the "transforming" and "reshaping" during probationary time (2T355.3; TM236; GC425.4).

I hear some say that we will not cease sinning until Christ changes this vile body at His coming in glory. Some teach that provisions have been made for forgiveness of sin after probation closes. When I hear that, I am reminded of this statement: "Some of these persons will never attain to perfection of Christian character because they do not see the value and necessity of such a character" (2T519.9).

True, when I look at those about me and examine myself, I agree; I cannot see how I can live without sinning. When I look back in history, I see the example of only one Person, who lived on this earth with the inherited effects of sin on His physical nature yet did no sin. I only know that it can be done, merely because God says that it will be done (CH634.1; 2T355.5; GC623.1).

It is by faith that I grasp the promise of perfect obedience. If the Lord delights in us, we shall succeed (Numbers 14:8).

> "It is not the work of a moment, but that of a lifetime. By growing daily in the divine life, he will not attain to the full stature of a perfect man in Christ until his probation ceases" (4T367.1).

When Jesus was here, He neither inherited nor acquired a mental record of sin (5BC1128-9). No tendency nor inclination to sin "rested" upon Him (5BC1128-9), yet He had to resist the inclination to use His own power when tempted (7BC930) so that He might be tempted and overcome as we are to overcome (5BC1082-3; Hebrews 4:15). Christ did not "possess" "the passions of our human fallen nature"; but, on the other hand, He was not exempt, not immune, from temptation by them, but was tempted as we are (2T202, 509).

Christ's character was perfect, free from sin (DA72, 762.4; 5BC1128-9). By the blotting out of the record of sin, He accomplishes the same state of the character for His followers who will live on the earth during the Great Time of Trouble (GC623.3, 425.4; COL69.2). As a result of their prior experiences with God's keeping power and with the full outpouring of the Holy Spirit, their characters will remain spotless throughout eternity (5T579.2). We are told that God has done His part in making provisions for the restoration of man (5T610.5). The Spirit and the Bride say, "Come" (Rev. 22:17). The atoning blood of Christ is available, knowledge is available, mental-moral power is available, and yet as a church we are indifferent or asleep (5T457.2). "I was shown God's people waiting for some change to take place–a compelling power to take hold of them. But they will be disappointed, for they are wrong. They must act, they must take hold of the work themselves...." (1T261.3). There is another power and light source on the field of controversy, and unless we choose for God, Satan will take over (EW56.2; cf. Ev599.3).

Chapter 10

PICTURES IN THE HALLS OF MEMORY

Let us illustrate the "book of remembrance", "character", and the "record of sin" in another way. The pen of Ellen White uses the phrase "pictures in memory's halls" (5T610, 744). Perhaps if we use this analogy, we can gain additional insight into the workings of the mind. Of course, we realize that we cannot make use of it beyond a certain point; the mind is fearfully and wonderfully made.

The phrase "pictures in memory's halls" conveys the idea that bits of information and mental images are present in the brain as pictures hung along circuit corridors of the mind.

Some of these corridors of the mind have been traversed by the "mind's eye" many times. Other mental corridors are seldom if ever traversed. Pleasant experiences in the past are more easily recalled (mentally revisited) than are unpleasant ones. The mind's eye hesitates to traverse some corridors because of the unpleasantness encountered.

By some means, a frequently used corridor of the mind can be found (recalled) easily by the mind's eye. The eye of the mind can traverse it rapidly with great ease and with less apparent effort. Such is a result of learning or of habit formation. Some of the pictures are silent whereas others have attributes of sound and other sensations accompanying them.

More could be said in this connection, but let us turn specifically to the mind in relation to sin and righteousness.

As a rebel, we have within the mind many pictures of "sin" hung on the walls of our memory. At some time in the past the mind's eye went that way for the first time and hung a sinful mental picture. The sin was desired at the time. At the site there is an aura of guilt and sinful pleasure.

We notice that in many instances some pictures have been embellished, enlarged, and magnificently framed by additional pleasurable imaginations. Each time that the mind's eye went that way, it added an additional touch to the picture.

We notice also that there are pictures in the halls which have no moral significance. They are neither good nor evil as judged by the moral law. As we examine the halls of memory of an unconverted person we find some good pictures. There are some that are cultured and refined, but we find no "righteous" pictures (MB94.7; GC509.5; AA233.8).

What happens to the mental pictures at conversion and repentance? We see some changes. New desires, new interests, new motives hold sway. The aura of guilt is gone. All the sinful pictures in the halls of memory are covered, covered by the blood of Christ. Now, the mind's eye walks with the Holy Spirit and has begun to place a new type of picture in memory's halls. Assisted by our Saviour, new pictures of Bible verses, righteous acts of kindness, prayer, and hymn singing appear on the walls. As the mind's eye walks with the Spirit, it notices that not every picture is a good one. If the picture represents a sin, the Holy Spirit eventually will call it to the attention of the dedicated Christian so that it too can be confessed, forsaken, and left covered. By sanctified reasoning, prayer, and Bible study, through the merits of Jesus, God is cooperating with the Christian to write His law in the heart and put it in the halls of memory. A righteous character is being built, bit by bit.

From our own experience, we see another event with the mind's eye. At times, in traversing a mental pathway, the mind's eye is attracted to one of the pictures that Jesus has covered. By the embellishments and sinful attractiveness, the eye is drawn to reexamine it. The Holy Spirit pleads with the mind's eye, but He must turn away as the mind's eye goes its own way, removes the covering, and entertains the reexamination of the sinful picture. The aura of guilt returns. What is to be done? The Holy Spirit pleads! Once again that sinful picture must be rejected, confessed, and covered through the ministry of our Saviour and the Holy Spirit.

As our mind's eye traverses the halls of memory, God would have it walk with the Spirit (Rom. 8:1; SC63-64). He would have us, instead of sinning, remain dedicated to Him and call for His power (enabling grace) when the mind's eye is tempted to turn aside to reexamine the sinful pictures on the walls of the memory or to entertain some new sinful thought which presses for recognition through the senses or from the imagination. That call for help is recorded in the hall of memory at that point and becomes a reminder of the occasion when next the mind's eye goes that way (GC481.4).

With sufficient time and with repeated rejection of the sinful picture, the attraction of that sinful picture becomes less and less. Yet that covered sin remains (GC487.1, 420-21).

There will come a time, in God's order, that something more will be done for His faithful followers. At the time of the investigative judgment, God will essentially ask, "What is the attitude of that person toward Me and My government? Does he love Me and want to live with the holy ones of heaven? Are all of the sinful pictures in his halls of memory forsaken and covered? (GC483). What is written in the halls of remembrance"? (GC481, 483). If the answers to these questions meet with the approbation of heaven, then the command will be given, "Erase those sinful pictures. Blot them out (GC483.6; 5T475; 4BC1178). My child has overcome them and does not want them." The character that remains is perfectly free from the record of sin. There are no hidden sins to be revealed. They have gone beforehand to judgment (4BC1178). That person had allowed the Holy Spirit free access to the corridors of his mind; and as the evil pictures with their habits had been revealed in their true light, they were faithfully rejected in the strength of the Lord. God's Spirit dwells in fulness in the mind of that follower.

After the blotting out of sin and the full outpouring of the Holy Spirit, the mind's eye continues to hang **righteous** pictures in the mental halls. Character, feelings and thoughts combined, will be developed throughout eternity. From the time of the blotting out of sin, the close of probation, until Jesus comes in the clouds of heaven and changes the physical nature, the mind's eye will still be handicapped by the infirmities and degeneration of the brain; but, by the power of God under the guidance of the Holy Spirit, that person does not sin. No sinful pictures will then be hung in the mind (5T216.5). For after the blotting out of sin and the close of probation, there will be no future time when guilt can be removed, the sinful pictures covered, and then later on blotted out. The mediatorial work by our High Priest that provided for this from Adam's first sin to the close of probation, has ceased forever (GC425.5,614.2).

The saints will **not** say that they are sinless for they still have the sinful physical nature (AA562.1; 2SM33.8). They do not have "holy flesh" (2SM32.7). They will still be tempted as Jesus was tempted until He comes in the clouds. They will realize that they could sin, but they will depend upon that "needed grace," that power to obey from God, just as Jesus did (AA56.1).

During this time of trouble, the mind's eye knows - as it examines the corridors of the mind—the corridors had suffered from the effects of sin. There is plenty of evidence of a struggle. There are scars left (TM447.5; OHC227; 8T66.5). The picture frame, as it were, remains; but the part in the heart that pictures the love for sin, cannot be recalled because it has been blotted out (GC620.4).

The mind's eye is well aware by those things which remain in the halls of memory just how unworthy a person he is (GC620.4). But there are signs of overcoming recorded there (GC481.5). The calls to the Lord are written everywhere. Those mental corridors which had the troublesome enticing pictures have many evidences of repentance (GC481.5). The mind's eye clearly sees that without God's help all would have been lost (DA98.7; GC641.8). It can see nothing about which to boast (GC619.1).

During the time of trouble, with the help of God, the person exercises faith, hope, and patience to an extent much greater than ever before (GC631.2). The person will continue to learn lessons, lessons of faith and obedience. Just as Jesus learned obedience by the things that He suffered (Heb. 5:8), so also will God's people be allowed the cup of affliction (GC641.8). He has promised to keep them in the "hour of temptation." The promise is, "My grace is sufficient for you" (GC486-7; PP218.1; MLT291.4). This is the enabling grace for obedience, the grace for which Jesus prayed (AA56).

One final point should be made. As stated in Chapter 6, all the mental feeling and thought pictures are recorded in the brain of the person on this earth and in the record in heaven. Whatever occurs in the original record here is copied exactly in the book in heaven (GC482-3, 427-8; MM184.2). It is this "book" in "the hall of records" in the holy place that represents us there in heaven (GC428). It is by this record that the saints are considered to be "in heaven" before they are taken physically there (see EW55, 92; GC427.6). Conversely, whatever is done through the ministry of Christ to this record in heaven, such as the answers to prayers and the blotting out of sin from the heart, causes the same thing to happen to the mental record of the living people here.

Chapter 11

THE SUBTLE CHANGE OF THE MIND

After Adam and Eve ate from that tree, why did not God accept their repentance and say, "I will forgive you this time. You may stay in Eden. Don't you ever do that again."

Since they had confessed their sin (PP61) and promised for the future implicit obedience (SR41.2), what was the problem? Was God an ogre setting out to teach them a lesson? The answer revolves around the difficulty with "appetites," "desires," "propensities," and "tendencies."

We have learned that an act repeated becomes a habit, and that habits make up the person's character (COL356.6). Moral acts repeated become moral habits, and the moral habits compose the moral character.

We have also learned that feelings and thoughts combined make up the character (5T310.3). Feelings repeated become appetites and desires. These feelings and thoughts, registered in the mind, sway the decisions, serve as impulses, inclinations, lusts, passions, proclivities, biases, prejudices, and propensities in our daily life. An invalid may develop a strong habit of feeling morose by brooding upon and sighing about his ailments and problems.

We are told that after that one sin of our first parents, their "nature" had become depraved (PP61.8). Since the physical nature certainly had not changed that quickly, this statement must refer to changes in the spiritual and/or the mental natures. Spiritually, they were in rebellion, but true repentance should have brought them back into harmony with God, at least for a while. The problem was with the little seed of sin that had been planted within the garden of the mind. With the mental record of sin within their mind, the drawing power of sin was too strong for them to overcome. They had sown one seed; imperceptibly it would grow into a tangle of feelings and thoughts with the resultant bends and biases toward evil which would yield even more seeds. The ingredients for a desire for sin had been planted in the heart. Their minds would "cultivate" these plants because of the deceptiveness of sin.

Many times it is difficult to tell a weed from a desirable plant. Young sprouts are especially challenging to identify. Mature plants may try to hide their true reputation under fragrant blossoms or artistic leaves. The locoweed may be decked out in blue or purple flowers and the poison oak in leaves of yellow and crimson, but the poison lies waiting under the disguise. Just so, certain feelings and thoughts may at first appear harmless. Time and a degree of development may be needed to portray the true nature of an act or concept.

Just how the mind of man functions is, in many respects, a mystery (6BC1105; SD105). The mind of man was designed to have appetites, desires, inclinations, and propensities for the good things in God's universe (CDF167; 2T408; 4T498; 3T491). The entrance of evil perverted this functional design to the harm of man. Now we must contend with sinful tendencies and propensities.

These changes in the mental nature which cause evil tendencies or propensities may be, as far as their origin is concerned, classified as follows: (a) natural, from our ancestors, (b) inherited, from our parents or guardians, (c) cultivated, from our own seed planting through the senses and from our imaginations.

From our ancestors we receive physical derangements, intellectual or moral weaknesses of varying degree, and animal (natural) instinctive (?) pathways within the mind which give us tendencies to respond in favor of sin (5BC1128). Even the smallest infant responds with anger when all of its wants are not met according to its instinctive desires.

During infancy and childhood we "inherit" mental traits of character from our parents and close associates by living with them. Unconsciously we receive the impress of their accents, mannerisms, and habits for good or for evil. We see examples of this all about us. The anatomical organs of speech are the same for the Southerner in America as for the native of England, but somehow the articulation of the words makes them sound so much different.

Impure thoughts can seize the imagination. These may be dwelt upon, "cultivated" or "entertained." We may devour a novel of lust and bloodshed or sit entranced with the intrigues and lawlessness of television. All these plant seeds of the cultivated variety.

Again we ask the question, why did not God allow Adam and Eve to start out all over again in the garden as though nothing had happened?

Satan had made three major criticisms of the law of God. He stated that is was imperfect; it needed to be changed; and it could not be kept (DA761-3; PP38, 69). These accusations had to be met. Initially, it appeared that Satan was right. God's plan was to prove with the very ones who had failed and with their descendents the falsity of the accusations.

Adam and Eve were given a second period to help vindicate God's design for the order in the universe. Besides provisions for forgiveness and removal of guilt of their sin, God anticipated the need for removal of the sinful seeds, roots, stems, branches, and flowers of evil in the heart. The mental entities that would induce sinful passions, desires, and propensities were to be removed from the garden of the mind by the blotting out of sin, but first these drawings, these magnetic attractions, to sin had to be rejected and overcome.

God did not leave them, nor has He left us, to be the tools of our prejudices, propensities, pronenesses, or proclivities (MB142.1; MH176.5; CH440; 7BC943). At conversion He wants to give us new desires, new motives, and good tendencies (COL98; 5T82; 6BC1101). We are to overcome the natural, hereditary, and cultivated tendencies by allowing Christ with His power to come into the soul temple and cast out all that pollutes its environs (DA161.5). We are not to be deceived into thinking that **we** can cast out some of the cherished idols in our own strength (DA161.8). Neither can **we** fill the cleansed dwelling with holy thought without His help (DA323-4). The development of righteous propensities, righteous tendencies, and righteous desires comes from united effort, God working with man.

By faith Jesus works in us to build righteous habits. We get the benefit, the righteous character; we give Him the glory. The Father calls it, "the righteousness of the saints"; We call it "the righteousness of Christ" (Revelation 19:8; Romans 3:22).

Under the impress of the Holy Spirit and the angels, we are to plant good seeds of memory verses, psalms, hymns, and meditations in the mental garden. The soil is moistened by the grace of Christ, the Living Water (PP412). The Sun of Righteousness is to energize the plants (DA468.7, 677.2; 6T67.7). The pure air of prayer is to gently sway the plants heavenward. Thus we are to encourage, entertain, and cultivate the tender plants to maturity in the heart.

Regardless of which avenue that evil desires, etc. enter the mind, they must be recognized for what they are, rejected, and overcome. The Holy Spirit, aided by the holy angels, leads us to the Scriptures. These words are to "remain", to be cherished, in the mind (John 15:7; 4T355.3; MH215.6). Christ, working by the Holy Spirit through the Scriptures produces in the mind a good conscience. The conscience is to be in control of the appetites and passions (MH319.7, 399.1; 8T63.8; Tel45.8, 216; 2T408.2; 5T314.5). An enlightened **reason** is to control the workings of the mind (AA311.5, 423.9; 2T473.9; 5T177.4; COL114.8). Our **will** strengthened by the power of God is to dominate the propensities and inclinations (3T183.2; 4T215; 5T514). God is willing to send every angel out of heaven to our aid in the battle (EW88, 262; GC560.6; 7T17). But one angel is sufficient if we are "willing to be made willing" (ML302-5; EW170; 2SG278; MB142.8).

Perhaps the battle within the mind and the overcoming can be illustrated by the following diagram.

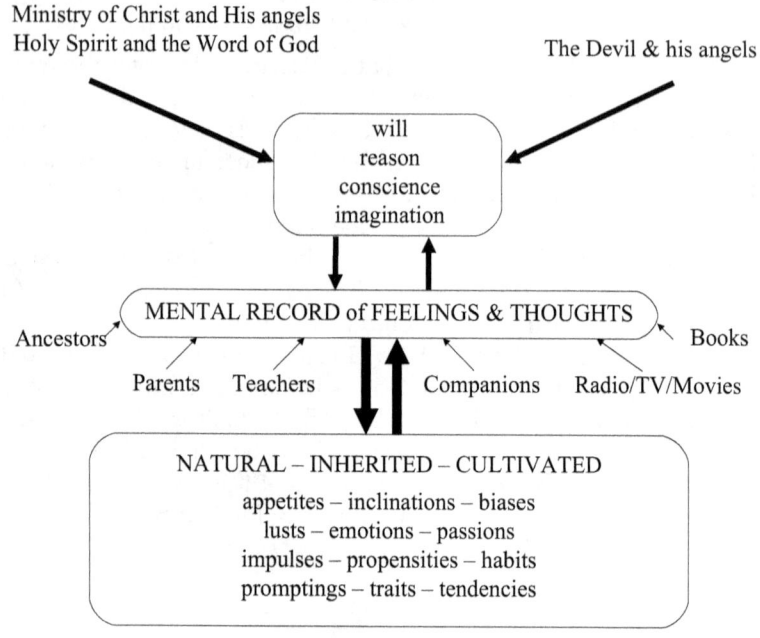

Now, must we battle those evil passions and promptings forever? Shall we be plagued by sinful propensities of the heart throughout eternity? No! No! The promise is that at the proper time and in the proper season, God will remove, blot out, erase whatever is necessary in the mental record so that whatever remains will not originate a temptation from within the mind nor be a responsive chord to a temptation from without the mind. He has not promised to remove the record of sin immediately after our repentance any more than He promised to remove those of Adam and Eve right after their repentance. He will cover the sin after repentance and help us overcome that old man of sin and assist us in building up right tendencies **now**, but we must wait for the time when the soul sanctuary is to be cleansed for the blotting out.

Will we miss those old sinful tendencies after they are removed? How can we? During our lifetime of repentance and obedience we have rejected them and called upon the power of God to keep from thinking them. We do not care to have them come into mind. In heaven we will thank God that they are gone.

If we have in reality followed the leadings of God and "cast down" every sinful "idol" trait, then God will feel free to blot out every sin. However, will the loving, considerate God of the universe remove from us a desire or propensity that we cannot give up? Will He tear from us an idolized appetite or tendency? No! He will have to turn from us in sorrow and say, "Ephraim is joined to idols; let him alone" (Hosea 4:17). But the agony of the Father and the Son is heard elsewhere saying, "Say unto them, As I live, saith the Lord God, I have no pleasure in the death of the wicked; but that the wicked turn from his way and live: turn ye, turn ye from your evil ways; for why will ye die, O house of Israel"? (Eze. 33:11).

If we look at the working of a personal computer, we find some very interesting things that help us to understand the blotting out. In the "word-processor" program with which I am familiar, there is an interesting sequence. When I ask the computer to erase a certain segment of information in its memory, the computer responds by asking, "What do you want erased"? I must mark the beginning and the end of the part to be blotted out. When I specify what is to be blotted out, it asks, "Are you sure that you want that erased"? I have to say, "yes" or "no."

Just so, God will test us repeatedly, after we have repented of our sins, "Do you really, when the time comes, want that sin that is covered to be blotted out"? If our answer is a consistent yes for all the sins, Jesus will blot them out after the investigative judgment is finished with our record.

There is a further point that we can make from the computer. The computer has a certain memory capability. While I am working on a manuscript, the computer is working away storing the bits of information in the computer memory. In order to keep the information, before I shut off the computer, I must store it on a floppy disc or its equivalent. What would happen if the power should go off while I am working on the material? Everything in the computer memory will be lost, erased.

God is keeping a continuous record of whatever goes on in my mind of my feelings and thoughts. This record is being recorded simultaneously with what is occurring in my mind. If the power should go off in my mind (by death), within ten minutes whatever that was in my mind has been lost. However, God can create a new body and use His record to imprint my thoughts in the new mind, and I will be the same person.

God has made provisions for little children and infants to be there (2SM260.4; CG566). The relationship of one or both parents toward God "sanctifies" the child (1 Cor. 7:14). The Lord knows those that are His (John 10:27).

Chapter 12

TEMPTATION WITHOUT—ANSWERING CHORD WITHIN

A study of the topic of temptation reveals that human beings are tempted by "allurements of the world," "clamors of the carnal nature," and by "direct temptations of Satan" (5T102; cf. TM445). We read elsewhere that, "Through sin the whole human organism is deranged, the mind is perverted, the imagination corrupted. Sin has degraded the faculties of the soul. Temptations from without find an answering cord within the heart, and the feet turn imperceptibly toward evil" (MH451).

How does the world tempt us? Temptations of the world come to us from the goings-on in the world about us, the pressures, the enticements, the intrigues, all such "allurements." Moses, no doubt, had much of this in the courts of Egypt. In our day we face books, magazines, billboards, televisions, etc. We are influenced by the ways of our friends and our enemies. These temptations come to us through the sensory nerves of sight, touch, hearing, and the others.

How does carnal flesh tempt us? This cannot mean the somatic (physical) body although the physical equipment is needed for transmission of the sensation and for performance of the response. This "carnal nature" is the *sarx*, the "old man of sin" within us. The *sarx* represents the aggregate total of that person's mental record of past sins in the heart, the ones that he acquired directly from his own imagination as well as those that he inherited from his parents (2T74).

Those sinful thoughts or acts, forgiven or not, become evil habits which in turn make up the moral character. They can not only initiate a temptation as they would initiate a memory of anything else from the past; but because of the association pathway capabilities of the mind, they may also serve as an additional enticement or drawing from within the mind to unite in strength from an analogous stimulus from without by the senses. This conglomerate of mental records of sin can thus serve as source material for the mind's eye or an imagination worked upon by Satan to initiate a "temptation from within."

The devil plays a role in the preparation of the two above ways of tempting a person, but he has one other way by which he can tempt us. This is the one called a "direct temptation." We are told that Satan used his power of hypnotism on Adam and Eve and that he tried to use it on Christ (5BC1081). We read repeatedly in the Scriptures of devil possession. No doubt, this represents the extreme of devil control upon humanity. Ellen White tells us, "We must inevitably be under the control of one or the other of the two great powers that are contending for the supremacy of the world" (DA324.4).

Even though we realize the extent that the devil is capable of controlling the minds of men, under ordinary circumstances a "direct temptation" does not represent the control of the mind to the same degree as in hypnotism or in devil possession. God holds back his influence in the former (GC506-17; 1 Cor. 10:13). Our guardian angels strive to keep back the cloud of evil influence from Satan and his angels (MB119).

Are we alone in this battle against temptation? No! "For we have not an high priest which cannot be touched with the feeling of our infirmities; but was in all points tempted like as we are, yet without sin" (Heb. 4:15). Our Example was born with the same instinctive reflexes that regulate bodily function and response to external stimuli that we have. His physical equipment, the body, the genes for His brain and physical organs, had been subjected to the deterioration of four thousand years of hereditary damage (DA117). Before we go further, we must realize that we should study the nature of the humanity of our Saviour in the same frame of mind as was Moses at the burning bush (5BC1128-9; YI10-13-98). The statements must be carefully phrased and even then may be misinterpreted.

Christ had no natural, inherited, nor cultivated record of sin (5BC1131). He maintained His character without a taint of sin

(DA311; E.G.W. in Questions on Doctrines, p. 657). He had no evil propensities nor evil passions (5BC1128; 2T509). No inclination or tendency to corruption "rested" upon Him (5BC1128). When Satan came to Him, he found that "not a single thought or feeling [of Jesus] responded to temptation" (RH11-08-87; 5T422).

And yet, we are told that He "was in all points tempted like as we are," and He "suffered being tempted" (5T422; 5BC1082; 7BC927). When he was tempted, He knew that He could do His own will (DA117). He was "inclined" to use His own strength in the battle (7BC930). How it was arranged so that He would be tempted in all points **like** we are, and how He was inclined to sin without having a propensity to sin and without a tendency or inclination to corruption resting upon Him, is a mystery (5BC1128).

However, it has been revealed that He overcame as we are to overcome. The law of God was in His mind and written upon His heart (7BC926). He was controlled by the full indwelling of the Holy Spirit (DA123; 5BC1124). He overcame by the power of God and by the Word of God (DA24; 5BC1082-3; 7BC929). He prayed for that **enabling** GRACE from the Father, and did not depend on His own human or divine strength (AA56; 2T202, 508; 5BC1080, 1082, 1127; 7BC930).

Christ felt the full strength of temptation **from the world** as we do 5T422; 5BC1117). He was not blind to the beauty of a woman, but He resisted by power from His Father the temptation to lust (5T422; 5BC1080-2, 1117; DA71-2; 7BC929). He had the necessary physical organs and reflexes to retaliate to the verbal and bodily abuse heaped upon Him so many times (5BC1127, 1130), but He overcame the temptation to respond in kind by saying, "Not My will, but Thine be done" (DA687-9, 208; 5BC1108; 7BC929).

Christ suffered from **direct temptations from the devil** just as we do. Here again, He did not meet the enemy with His own words or power, but depended upon that same power that we have free access to (5BC1082, 1108).

He did not need to have within Him a mental record of sin to be tempted as strongly as we are. The temptations that He had from the world and the direct temptations from the devil were stronger upon Him than any that we will ever have to face from the world, from carnal flesh, and/or from the devil (DA116, 4T45; 1SM289).

To be tempted is not a sin (Te192; 4T358). Having a tendency or inclination to respond wrongfully to a temptation is not sinning (7BC930). But "entering into"; or "entertaining" a temptation constitutes the sin (Te192; TM453-4). If we dally with temptation, we allow Satan to amplify our inner desires, or start a chain of rationalization, and gain the leverage that he needs (4T258; DA121.1). The following points have been helpful to me in overcoming temptation. They have given me hope of victory.

1. Have a settled committment to God in heaven (DA324; MB92; 2T517). At your morning and evening worship ask the Lord to cover you with His robe of imputed righteousness so that you will be "in Christ Jesus" all day (1SM344; 6BC1078). **Ask Jesus To Write His Law In Your Heart So That You Will Just Love Doing His Will** (Heb. 8:10 Living Bible).

2. Do not place yourself needlessly or presumptuously where you might be tempted (DA126; 3T47, 482; 2T222). Remember Eve's first mistake was that she wandered from her companion; and, then, thought that in her own wisdom and strength she could meet the enemy (PP54.1).

3. Expect to be tempted or tried or have opportunity to be of particular service to God at any moment (James 1:2; PP457).

4. Expect to be inclined to go along with the temptation to sin (FCE423.2).

5. Expect the people in our generation to be morally weaker and in need of more power now than in past ages (3T488).

6. Expect temptations to be stronger as we near the end of time on this earth (3T571).

7. Close to sin every avenue of the soul that you can and still do your God-given work (PP459-60). In other words, avoid the books, magazines and TV programs that might contain material which would tempt you to enter into one of the sins "that would most easily beset you."

8. Do not dally with the temptation lest you rationalize away the reasons for obedience (3T482-3; 4T258, 493).

9. Do not expect to overcome even the weakest temptation in your own wisdom or strength (4T355; MB142; 1SM101, 333; DA382, 676).

10. **ASK FOR HIS HELP** (DA300, 311)**!!** Believe that you can overcome every temptation **perfectly** by the enabling power of God (MH514; 6T306; 1SM409). Be "willing to be made willing" and God will work in you both to "will and to do of His good pleasure" (MB142; Phil. 2:13; 2 Cor. 8:12).

11. When you are tempted or sense the danger of imminent temptation, immediately pray to Jesus for power to obey (COL172; 4T542.9). Take an active stance in the battle. "Say to your soul, 'How can I dishonor my Redeemer? I have given myself to Christ; I cannot do the works of Satan'" (SL90). Remember that Jesus has explained that "the secret of their [the disciples] success would be in **asking** for strength and grace in **His** name" (DA667.5).
12. Study the Scriptures as well as pray since power comes from God's Word as well as from His Spirit (Ed126; DA324, 466; GC600). Study especially the life of Christ, our Example.
13. If a particular temptation repeatedly annoys your mind, stop what you are doing, agonize with God in prayer (COL175; MB141-2; 1SM409; 2T93). Let it be known to yourself, to the Lord, and to the devil that you have forsaken that sin. The Lord then has free rein to control your will. When the Lord was most severely beset, He ate nothing, committed Himself to God, earnestly prayed in perfect submission to the Father, and came off victorious.
14. Avoid intemperate health practices and drugs that interfere with reason (MH130; Te17-8, 174).
15. If you stumble and make a mistake, do not become discouraged (COL332; SC64.4; 1SM337). God has not deserted you (MB93.1). Remember that so long as His ministry continues in the sanctuary in heaven, if we confess our sin, "He is faithful and just to forgive us our sin and cleanse us...." (1 John 1:9).
16. Remember to thank the Lord for the victory (Ed258). Be thankful that He has made you "willing to be made willing" and enabled you to do what He wants (MB142; SC47).
17. As your confidence in the power of God increases, and your trust in self fades, God will reveal more and more of your faults and give you opportunities to extoll His name (DA208-9, 310, 313; MH513.9). You become a living witness of His redeeming power to glorify His name. Make the most of the opportunities with God's help (TM510; MH100, 513.9; AA600).

Consider the sufferings of Jesus in temptation when He went forty days without food or water (SOC10). He was near death (1SM272, 288-9). In this state of near complete physical exhaustion He was extremely vulnerable, and Satan tried to make the most of the situation. But, by power from the Father, Jesus overcame. This gives hope to even the most severely debilitated person. In our lowest point of physical degradation, mental weakness or distress, in the time of our gray hairs, we can trust in victory (Isaiah 46:4).

We have the promise that God will not allow us to be tempted "above that we are able," but will make a way of escape from the temptation (1 Cor. 10:13). The way that He has in mind is not through temptation – transgression – repentance – forgiveness – temptation – transgression – repentance – forgiveness, and on and on, although that is available for a time. He wants to bring us off more than conquerors through the power that He has made available at our **request** and our **demand** (MH514.4; Rom. 8:38; DA672). "To obey is better than sacrifice" (1 Sam. 15:22). Be ye transformed by the renewing of the mind is the promise given (Romans 12:2).

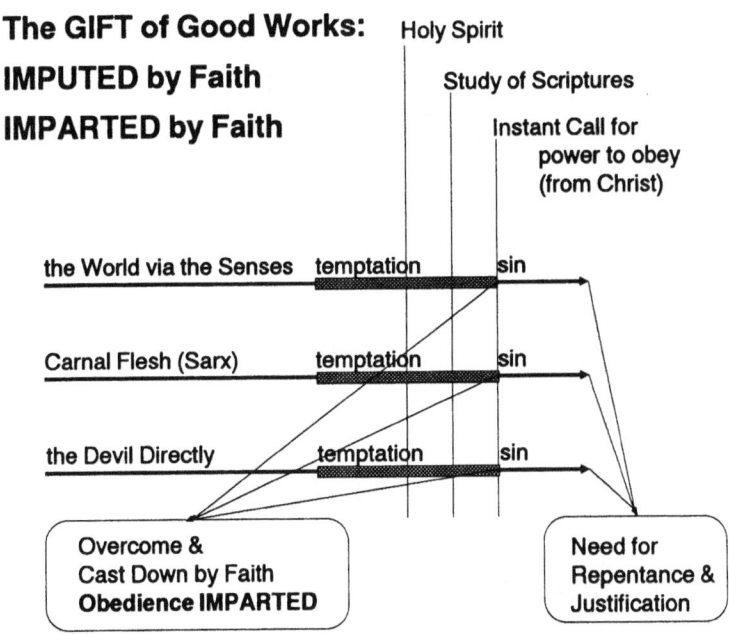
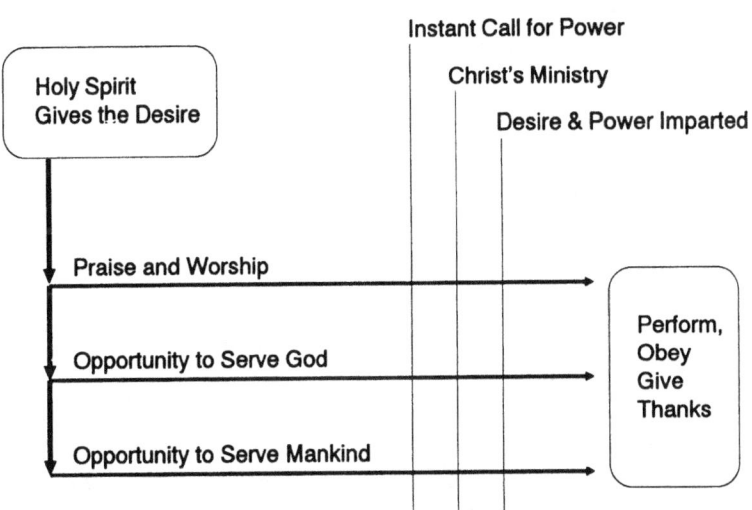

Chapter 13

RIGHTEOUSNESS

This is a much discussed topic. What does it mean in the simplest terms?

One simple basic definition states that "righteousness is right doing" (COL312). The phrase "Christ's righteousness" or the "righteousness of Christ" has two main applications in common usage.

Christ's righteousness refers to His sinless "robe" of character which God developed in [imparted to] Jesus while He was on this earth, which He can impute to us for past sins (1SM392-3). It is Christ's righteousness because He wrought it out and it belonged to Him.

The term Christ's righteousness in a broader sense amounts to this:–

(a) doing the right action in the right way, - whatever God says (DA310.2; FCE238).

(b) from the motive of love (*agape*), - love to our God and to our fellow men (MB18.3).

(c) by the power of God available to us through faith in Jesus (TM92.3; DA466; MH514.3).

Whenever these components are associated in the work of Jesus in His followers, this, too, is called Christ's righteousness. We are the instruments in God's hands just as Jesus was. It is what Jesus would do under those circumstances. God worked in Christ to produce right doing, and He wants to work in us for the same purpose (GC343.5).

"Man's righteousness" consists of the "good deeds" that a man may do based upon what he thinks is right or what he may do in his own strength. Culture and refinement are not necessarily a sign of the working of the Spirit of God (GC509.5; MB94.6). Some may choose to exhibit these talents to serve self or the devil.

The Scriptures abound in principles or laws to guide us. These laws may be divided into three great categories. God has given laws to govern actions, pointing out what should be done and how it should be done. In this category we would place laws such as the ten commandments and those governing the sanctuary service. Next, God had laws governing the motives. The key law here is that "new commandment" of which Jesus spoke. God has also laws which determine how we may accomplish, or perform the first two categories of laws. This is the "law of the Spirit of life in Christ Jesus" (DA209-10; Romans 8:2).

There are some Christians who profess to keep the commandments of God who are, you find after questioning them more fully, referring almost entirely to the "new commandment" of Jesus which has to do with the motive. They see little light in keeping the Sabbath of the Lord for, according to their thinking, the ten commandments were nailed to the cross. They essentially say, "If you love, you need no rules; for if you love someone, you will **naturally do** what that person wants you to do." There are two serious dangers with this tenet. First, we cannot know how to please God nor anyone else unless we ask them what pleases them. We must read His Word and listen to His Spirit if we are to learn His will. Unless we do, we may not be doing what He prefers. Second, since sin entered this race, we **naturally** choose wrong and are unable to obey (GC505).

Same take the above idea a step further with the catch phrase, "Love God and do as you please!" If your desire is to please the Lord, then this might work. But there is a hazardous existential overtone to such a statement. Satan himself originated that concept before ever he was cast out of heaven. He taught that, "¤angels, being more exalted needed no restraint, for their own wisdom was a sufficient guide. They were not beings that could dishonor God; all their thoughts were holy; it was no more possible for them than for God to err" (PP37.7; GC499.8). He has not changed this maxim yet. Spiritualism still teaches that, "each mind will judge itself and not another" (GC554.8). We must reject this concept. God alone has the right to decide what is right (James 4:12). We have the right to agree or disagree with Him, but the results of separation from God have not been the utopia that Satan promised.

There are other professed Christians who claim to be "baptized by the Spirit." They talk a lot of "love." They may have some fruits which superficially resemble the good (Gen. 3:6) but they, too, do away with a key component of righteousness, obedience to God's law that governs the actions. In truth they are worked by an evil spirit to produce a counterfeit. Neither speaking in tongues nor miracles are a sign of the working of the Holy Spirit since these can be imitated (2SM54.5; 5T698; Ev599.3).

Seventh-day Adventists are accused of keeping only the laws which govern the actions. It is possible to be morally good without being a true follower of Jesus. We should not be tricked into being a "mere human moralist" (COL315.8). On the other hand, we dare not be deceived into disobeying any of the laws in the three categories merely because some do not see the whole law, and falsely make their accusations against us. We are to show this accusation to be what it is, a lie, by combining love and the working of His Spirit in our lives, as we go about letting God work in us in every respect.

Let us consider these three categories further.

Actions: There was nothing wrong in the act of paying tithe that was done by the Pharisee (MB79.2; DA617.2). It was his motive that was wrong. He did it to be seen of men or for a reward from God. He thought that since he paid his tithe, God then owed him justification. However, true righteous works are done to fulfill, from faith, an expressed command of God, not for the recompence nor for earned salvation, but simply because it is expected of us (Luke 17:7-10). The tares in the church have what appears to be good works, but they are motivated merely by fear of punishment or hope of a reward (COL71.8).

Motives: Humanly speaking, Uzzah had a good motive when he reached out to steady the ark, but his act was wrong. He was held accountable for knowledge he may not have remembered or may not have known (GC597-8; PP705-6). The lesson for us is this; we cannot do things just like the Philistines about us, ignoring the light available to us, even though we have a right motive. With light available to us, we are required to look up God's will and not presume upon His mercy (GC598).

Strength: Eve made the mistake of thinking that in her own wisdom, and in her own strength, that she could discern evil and withstand it (PP54.1). Abraham took Hager and set out with his own strength to fulfill God's promise of a son through whom the Messiah would come.

Reason and wisdom are important, but these must be kept in perspective. "God is the source of all wisdom.... Before men can be truly wise, they must realize their dependence upon God, and be filled with His wisdom" (CPT66). Reason must acknowledge the Authority above itself (MH438.9). Our faith and trust are based upon what God has revealed; and, to a lesser extent, upon what we have experienced in the past.

Abraham was chosen to be the example for those who **trust** God (PP147.4). He was asked to slay his own son, the son who was to be the ancestor of the Saviour of himself and of all mankind. At that time there was no history of a resurrection to bolster his faith. In addition, God had a standing law that said, "Thou shalt not kill." God expects implicit obedience from faith in Him whether we think His requirements are reasonable of not. But it is reasonable to be sure what the will of God is and be sure that it is He that is speaking and not another.

In some matters our faith is to be based solely upon His Word (5T701.1). For example, what is reasonable about keeping holy a period of time from sundown Friday night to sundown Saturday night? Could you find that law by deduction? God is authoritative, but contrary to the accusation He is not arbitrary (1BC1084; MH114). We are called to exercise faith, reason, and the other faculties of the mind; but if obedience is not necessary until **after** we can determine a reason for the command, at what point does faith and trust come into use (SC105-6; GC527.4).

Man has been endowed with powers of the mind, intellectual and spiritual powers. Yet even with all his endowments he cannot keep himself from sin for one moment or overcome a single temptation (DA676.3). But there is mental-moral power available to us to overcome temptation and to serve God (MH514.4; 1SM101.7, 381; DA604). Everything we do by ourselves unassisted by God is defiled by sin (COL311.8; 1SM364.4). But we **can** do **all** things right if we recognize our need and call for Christ's help (Phil. 4:13). Christ exercised no power in His own behalf that man may not have through faith in Him (DA24.5, 664.8). All truly righteous works are dependent upon a power outside ourselves (8T316.4). We are told that **the secret of success will be in asking for this power in His name** (DA667.5; PP509.2). Jesus waits for us to decide

(DA300.2). He does not force His power on anyone. (MH114.5; MB142.5). Shall we ask His help or shall we try it alone?

We must strive to be under His control (1SM409.4). Not only should we confess our sins and consecrate our whole life—body, mind, and soul—to Jesus at our morning and evening devotions; but we must be instantly ready when we are challenged by trials or temptations to call for help **then** (DA382, 667.7; 5T177.5). It should become a strong habit for us to ask for this strength at the moment of trial (8T314.4). We obtain imparted righteousness by calling for the imparted power to do right (DA310-2, 668.8). "Sanctification means habitual communion with God" (7BC908). This is how Enoch "walked with God" (1BC1087).

As we obtain the imparted gifts, we are in turn to impart to others (TM510.5). The circuit of loving deeds is to continue unbroken (DA21.7). "One of the divine plans for growth is impartation. The Christian is to gain strength by strengthening others" (7BC947). This is what Jesus wants to see in His church (DA827; 9T22).

Now, some may say that this sounds like righteousness by works. Brothers and sisters, God requires works (1SM381.3; TM240.6), but not **merely** from hope of reward or fear of punishment (PP523.6). He says, "Come and work in my vineyard." It is true that works cannot save us; but it is also true that we cannot be saved without works (4T89.2; 1SM377.9). Even so, think again, how can I ascribe credit to myself for what I have done or can do, when **every** righteous thing that I do is by the imparted power of Christ (SC63.4; TM377)? I am to have habits of thought to overcome evil which serve me in my battle with sin and the devil, but these I have obtained from the repeated right acts of Christ working in me (8T314.5; 6T162.8; PP460.8). These good habits must be maintained by further right acts (4BC1182). True grace is only obtained through faith and humble, prayerful obedience (4T89.3).

Our understanding and presentation of righteousness by faith should be balanced by statements such as the following three:

> "Man can accomplish nothing without God, and God has arranged His plans so as to accomplish nothing in the restoration of the human soul without the cooperation of the human with the divine. The part man is required to sustain is immeasurably small, yet in the plan of God it is just that force that is needed to make the work a success" (MS113, 09-08-98).

"The proud heart strives to earn salvation; but both our title to heaven and our fitness for it are found in the righteousness of Christ. The Lord can do nothing toward the recovery of man until, convinced of his own weakness, and stripped of all self-sufficiency, he yields himself to the control of God" (DA300.2).

"But man is no passive being, to be saved in indolence. He is called upon to strain every muscle and exercise every faculty in the struggle for immortality; yet it is God that supplies the efficiency" (CPT366.4).

For both the natural and the spiritual life we are to take advantage of the facilities that God has made available to us (AA284; PP279.2). God will not force-feed us either material or spiritual food. We must seek for these. God longs for us tenderly and touches us by His Spirit because we are so weak that all that we can do is "**be willing to be made willing**" (MB142.8).

What is meant by "righteousness by works?" When a person does "good deeds" with the aim in mind to earn salvation, **that** constitutes righteousness by works.

The apostle Paul wrote **against** certain works (Romans 3:20-31). The apostle James wrote **in favor of** certain works (James 2:14-26). How can we correlate what Paul wrote with what James wrote, both men under inspiration?

Paul was **against** the works that would be done to fulfill a promise of God to man or to bring God into debt to the worker (Romans 4:4). Paul used the example of Abraham, Hagar, and Sarah to discuss this subject. Rebecca's scheme to help Jacob get the promised birthright is another example. They were trying to help God out of an apparent predicament.

As we do what God tells us to do, we are not in any way to consider that we have **earned** justification, sanctification, or any other reward (Gal. 2:16; DA300.2). In the parable found in Luke 17:7-10, Jesus tells us that we are to do God's bidding; and after having done all, not to expect even thanks, but to consider ourselves unprofitable servants. We have only done what was expected of us.

Some, however, have carried this thought too far to another extreme and recline back in their mental couches with the thought, "Since conditions are so diffucult, and since what we do is not worth much, we might as well let the Lord do it all." Perhaps they add the thought, "After all, it is the Lord's work."

From our zeal to let our critics in other churches know that we do not believe in justification by works, we have left unsaid the value that God places on our good works. God compares true righteous acts with pure gold (4T88-89; 1SM381.3). The works that God accepts, the works that James advocates, are works from belief and trust in God to fulfill a command of God (James 2:20-24).

Nothing would be more chilling to the ardor of a servant than to tell him to go do a certain job, and then say as a parting shot, "Before you go, let me tell you this; what you do will not amount to much." Would you expect to find very much missionary work being done by the church members that believed such a concept?

The only good deeds that have "merit" in the plan of salvation are the works of Christ. Furthermore, even though I am to feel in all sincerity that I am an unprofitable servant, the Lord considers my good works as of real value. "In His divine arrangement, through His unmerited favor, the Lord has ordained that good works shall be rewarded" (5BC1122). But that is not the reason for doing them!

The good works that Jesus builds up in us, God calls, "the righteousness of the saints" (Rev. 19:8). However, the saints do not take credit for those; they refer to those good deeds as "the righteousness of Christ" (Phil. 1:9-11). All runs smoothly so long as we maintain that attitude of mind. We give the glory to Jesus, He glorifies the Father, and the Father glorifies Jesus and the saints (John 17:1-11; cf. Matt. 25:31-40).

I propose that we carry out the admonition of our Lord to buy of Him "faith which **works** by love and purifies the soul…" Rev. 3:18; 4T88-89). Let us also follow the advice of Paul to "…esteem them [the brethren which labor among you] very highly in love for their work's sake" (1 Thess. 5:13).

Chapter 14

THE MINISTRY OF THE SPIRIT

Up to this point we have not emphasized the agency by which God gives us power to do right. The Holy Spirit is the agent of communication of God to man (PP405.5; 1SM134.2). Without the workings of the Spirit we would have no desire to repent (8T64.9). He is our "counselor, sanctifier, guide, and witness" (AA49.4). Notice, though, the spiritual graces poured out by the Holy Spirit in the early and in the latter rain come sequentially, in the **times** and **seasons** determined by God, and are poured out, not in the course of events, but as a consequence of our supplication for them (AA54-5; TM506-8).

"So the life-giving power of the Holy Spirit, proceeding from the Saviour, pervades the soul, renews the motives and affections, and brings even the thoughts into obedience to the will of God, enabling the receiver to bear the precious fruit of holy deeds" (AA284.5).

The Holy Spirit speaks to the mind throught the Scriptures (1SM134.2; DA671.3). We receive power from the Holy Spirit and from the Scriptures (TM518.1; MB150.3). The work of the Holy Spirit on the heart is to be tested by the Word of God (1SM43.6).

What are the various relationships of the Holy Spirit to mankind?
- Some are merely restrained by the Spirit (GC36.2, 614.2).
- The Spirit creates a craving for something men and women have not (SC28.1).
- Some are just "touched by the Spirit" (MB150.1).
- Some "now and then yield to Its power" (MB150.1).

- Some are **led** by the Spirit of God; **these** are the sons of God (MB150.1)!

A friend of mine once stated that he was afraid to allow the Spirit to freely control him lest he be led to do something foolish or fanatical. In reality, just the opposite is true. God gives the Spirit of a sound mind (2 Tim. 1:7). The gospel may seem foolishness, and the gospel worker may appear to be fanatical in the eyes of the unconsecrated, but not so in the eyes of unfallen beings.

In order to be led, we must be willing to follow. We are not to use the Spirit; the Spirit is to use us (DA672.5). Those who follow the Lamb "whithersoever He goeth" in heaven will need to have followed Him on this earth "whithersoever He goeth" (AA591.5). God desires that all be **led** by the Spirit. The fault lies with the individual. "If all were willing, all would be filled with the Spirit" (AA50.4). It is our privilege to place ourselves in right relation to God, then precious conquests will be obtained (1SM101.8; TM240.5).

If my friend, referred to earlier, does not wish to be controlled fully by God, then who is controlling him? Is he under the control of his own will? Does God have a sphere in the universe that He controls; the Devil have a sphere that he controls; and each man or woman have individual control over themselves?

One of the main points that Satan made in his plan of rebellion was that each angel (GC495.7; PP37.6) and each human being (Gen. 3:4,5) should follow the rules of his own making, and each be under independent control (GC499.8). Each one was to be his own judge (GC554.8, 555.8). But, has it turned out that way? Why did he ask Jesus to worship him, and then say that he would give Him the world (1SM286.2)? Jesus has revealed to us the true situation.

> "Every soul that refuses to give himself to God is under the control of another power. He is not his own. He may talk of freedom, but he is in the most abject slavery. He is not allowed to see the beauty of truth, for his mind is under the control of Satan. While he flatters himself that he is following the dictates of his own judgment, he obeys the will of the prince of darkness" (DA466.3).

> "But unless we do yield ourselves to the control of Christ, we shall be dominated by the wicked one. We must inevitably be under the control of the one or the other of the two great powers that are contending for the supremacy of

the world. It is not necessary for us deliberately to choose the service of the kingdom of darkness in order to come under its dominion. We have only to neglect to ally ourselves with the kingdom of light. If we do not cooperate with the heavenly agencies, Satan will take possession of the heart, and will make it his abiding place¤. We may leave off many bad habits, for the time we may part company with Satan; but without a vital connection with God, through the surrender of ourselves to Him moment by moment, we shall be overcome" (DA324).

The control exerted by our Saviour is very delicate so that, "Under the influence of the Spirit of God, man is left free to choose whom he will serve" (DA466.5).

"God does not control our minds without our consent; but if we desire to know and to do His will, His promises are ours" (Ev626.3). What promises are ours? Promises of deliverance from the control of error and sin.

In order to be controlled by the Holy Spirit, we must strive and earnestly seek for it (TM459.8; HP263; AA56.5). By way of contrast, the devil takes control of any who are not decidedly under God's control whether they want his control or not (TM79; DA324, 587). As it serves his own purpose, Satan exerts control ever so subtly so that we think that we are really in command of our own ship. Sooner or later, though, we will recognize the pilot and the port of call.

Being "for Christ" consists of more than just not being "against Him" (Matt. 12:30). When the final day of decision came for Lucifer and the angels in heaven, they each had to make a choice (3SG37-8). Their "investigative judgment" was at hand.

At that time in essence God said, All who want to live under Christ's command, gather around Him. All who wish to be under Lucifer's control, gather around him. In response to that, one-third of the angels followed Lucifer (SR18.5). In portraying this history Ellen White makes a transition at that point from the name Lucifer to Satan (PP41). The challenge was then given to the holy angels, if you are indeed on Christ's team, show it by casting Satan and his followers out of heaven (MB119.3; Ev704.8; 7BC973). Angels had to enter into combat with former friends. No one could stand by watching and simply say, "I'm not against you, Lord!"

As a result of this battle, the holy angels were more firmly settled on the side of God that ever before. Then, at Calvary, the enmity exhibited by Satan and his host quenched the last flicker of sympathy that they had for their former companions (7BC974). When the holy angels look at the cross, they are secure from Satan's deceptions (ST12-30-89).

God could have spoken and cast out the devil and his sympathizers, but He chose a way that would involve His helpers in heaven.

The battle lines are now drawn here on this earth. Are we decidedly **for** Christ or are we wavering in our decisions? If you are **for** Christ, God wants you to be spiritually awake, earnestly seeking for the outpouring of His Spirit moment by moment, and thus be able to participate with fervor in the great controversy between Christ and Satan. The limitation is with our will, not in the availability of the Spirit.

> "Were it possible to force upon you with a hundredfold greater intensity the influence of the Spirit of God, it would not make you a Christian, a fit subject for heaven. The stronghold of Satan would not be broken. The will must be placed on the side of God's will. You are not able, of yourself, to bring your purposes and desires and inclinations into submission to the will of God; but **if you are 'willing to be made willing'**, God will accomplish the work for you, even casting down **imaginations**, and every high thing that exalteth itself against the knowledge of God, and bringing into captivity **every thought** to the obedience of Christ' " (MB142.5 emphasis supplied).

We are to yield our will to God, but does that mean that He takes away from us the freedom of choice? God could have withheld Adam from eating the forbidden item (1BC1084), but he had been given the will to exercise (MH176.5). "Our will is to be yielded to Him, that we may **receive it again**, purified and refined, and so **linked in sympathy** with the Divine that He can pour through us the **tides** of His love and power" (MB62.5 emphasis supplied).

As God works in us to will and to do His wishes, we are to work out our own salvation (8T312.7; 7BC978). The world will then know about God. "In working **out** what divine grace works **in**, the believer becomes spiritually great" (RH11-01-92).

> "The third angel's message is to lighten the earth with its glory; but only those who have withstood temptation in the strength of the Mighty One will be permitted to act a part in

proclaiming it when it shall have swelled into the loud cry" (RH11-19-08 emphasis supplied).

We as a people, definitely need a personal, experimental relationship with the Holy Spirit and with this power that is available to us through the cross of Christ that is more then able to keep us from sinning. **This** is the experience that we need now and steadily to the end (5T213.5, 219-221).

"The wind blows where it wills,
and you hear the sound of it,
but you do not know
whence it comes
or whither it goes;
so it is with every one
who is born of the Spirit."

— *Jesus Christ*

(in John 3:8, R.S.V.)

Chapter 15

PERFECTION VERSUS MATURATION AND THE NATURE OF HUMANITY

The subject of perfection is very important in the context of the nature of humanity. What should we know about perfection? In what respects can we be perfect?

There are some who teach "absolute perfection" and others who teach "relative perfection." When Jesus said, "Be ye perfect," did He mean, "Be ye almost perfect"?

Relative perfection teaches that no one ever ceases to sin, they just cease to commit known sins. They live up to all the **power** that they inherently have. The theory works on the logarithmic scale so that there is an infinity beyond of unrecognized sins to be stopped. This would mean that provisions must be made for forgiveness of sin after probation closes. According to some Adventists the 144,000 would continue to sin and need forgiveness during the great time of trouble. This concept of relativism confuses sinlessness and cessation from sinning with growth, maturation, and development.

The Saviour's command, "Be ye perfect," is also a promise (DA311.4). God has committed Himself (covenanted) to prepare us so that after Christ's mediatorial service ceases, we will **not sin again**, **ever**, either a known or an unknown sin. He has **not** agreed to forgive sins and cleanse us from sin after the High Priest throws down His censor and becomes only Judge and King. If one sins even a single sin after that moment, he is in the same situation as Adam after that first sin. He has within him the "knowledge" of evil with the guilt and record of sin.

God wants to lead His people to believe that they can live after probation without sinning, but the trouble is that all too many of us do not see how **We** can do it. Is there an Adventist who does not believe that God can keep His people from sinning perfectly in heaven throughout eternity? If they can believe that, why can they not grasp by faith the promise that He can and will do that same thing for His people after probation closes while they are on the earth?

In general, we know the law. We realize that it must be kept. Our problem seems to be that we have not concentrated our studying and teaching on the **HOW** to perform that which we know. When a person is convicted of what he should do and yet knows by experience that he cannot obey the law in his own strength, he may well become discouraged, repine, and even give up. Some professed Christians try to get around this by doing away with the law. Some say, "Do all that **YOU** can, and God will do the rest" (see 1SM381.5). Then others come up with the erroneous theory of relative perfection.

Threefold Nature of Man: The Bible and the Testimonies reveal that the nature of man is threefold, - physical, mental, and spiritual (FCE57.2). There is a possibility of confusion on the subject of perfection because, as we shall see, not all three natures of a person can be perfect until the proper time or season for each to be perfect is at hand. The times and seasons are in God's order (1SM189.4).

For example, holy flesh (perfection of the flesh) is not given until Christ's appearing in the clouds of heaven (2SM33.7). We cannot say, "I am sinless," until that act of redemption is done (AA562.1; SL10.3; GC620.4). Furthermore, the record of sin will not be blotted out until after the investigative judgment for that particular person (GC485.4). All the effects of sin on the character, thus, will not be completely eradicated until that is done.

Two lines of reasoning help us establish that **the character** will not be perfect before probation closes, but it will be perfect before Christ comes in glory. Until the blotting out of sin, the follower of Christ has a righteous character as part of **the character** within him.

> "As he advances toward perfection, he experiences a conversion to God every day; and this conversion is not

completed until he attains to perfection of Christian character, a full preparation for the finishing touch of immortality" (2T505.8).

"When He comes, He is not to cleanse us of our sins, to remove from us the defects in our characters, or to cure us of the infirmities of our tempers and dispositions. If wrought for us at all, this work will all be accomplished before that time. When the Lord comes, those who are holy will be holy still.... No work will then be done for them to remove their defects and give them holy characters. The Refiner does not then sit to pursue his refining process and remove their sins and their corruption. This is all to be done in these hours of probation. It is **now** that this work is to be accomplished for us" (2T355.3).

Some Adventists object to consideration of the three natures of man separately. True, the spiritual nature and mental nature are not something encased in the physical body to be liberated at death. When a person dies, all three natures are no longer living even though the ingredients still exist. A person may be mentally and physically alive while he is spiritually dead. Nicodemus was in this state without realizing it (John 3:3; Eph. 2:1). With our modern medical equipment, we are able to keep a person physically alive long after they are mentally dead. Organs can be transplanted from one person to another.

Satan has tried to confuse this doctrine of the threefold nature of man by various false doctrines. He has used the dualism of the Greek philosophers, the reincarnation of Hinduism, the apparitions of spiritualism, and the three forms of pantheism to overshadow clear thinking on this important topic.

Pantheism is of special interest in connection with the consideration of the threefold nature of man. Pantheism would do more than make a non-entity of God. It would endeavor by the mental gymnastics of redefinition of words to consider the universe as a single nature, a **unity**.

One form of pantheism would consider the mental and the spiritual natures to be physical nature and thus make the whole universe into **material**. The matter, the flower or the tree, becomes God. The second form would convert the mental and the physical into spiritual nature and make the whole universe **supernatural**. In that form, God becomes just an all-pervading power such as law or love or faith. The third form attempts to convert the spiritual and the physical into mental nature and make the whole universe **mind**. The first form is represented by atheistic communism of Marx. The second form is the most widely accepted theory of the nature of the universe in the western hemisphere and was held by such philosophers as Hegel, Plotinus, or Spinoza (See "Actuality" in *Encyclopedia Britannica*, 1952 Ed., Vol.1, p 145). The third form is represented by the Christian Scientist theories of Mary Baker Eddy.

The forms of pantheism would tear down the distinction between material things and spiritual things, between the natural and the supernatural, between the common and the sacred, and between humanity and Divinity.

When God made man, He took whatever He needed from material and spiritual things and made man with it and started him breathing (MH414.9). This did not include a "spark of divinity." He made man so that he was a **unit (not a unity)** with a physical, a mental, and a spiritual nature (Ed55.2; FCE57.2). Man was placed under the laws for the physical, the mental, and the spiritual realms (DA827.6; 6T306.6). When man dies, the integral components, whatever they are, God knows, return to the state they were before use; but man's spiritual, mental, and physical natures cease to exist in relation to that person. All that remains is God's record of the thoughts and feelings that the person had had while he was alive (COL332.7; 5T466.4; 6BC1093).

Perfection vs Maturation: There is another problem which retards our ability to understand perfection. A certain degree of confusion stems from the failure to distinguish between "perfection" and "maturation."

We may, by the help of God, have all of the **fruit** of the Spirit and may stop sinning every **known** sin completely, but whether or not we receive one of the **gifts** of the Spirit is another thing. We should not equate perfect cessation from sinning with the ability to perform miracles or do any other great deed. As far as our ability to perform deeds for God is concerned, these depend on our talents and how we develop them, as well as on the workings of the Holy Spirit. We are to be perfect in our sphere in the same manner, but not with the same capabilities as God (MB77.8). A child is not able to do what is expected of an adult (AH196.4; CG122.5). But a child can perform perfectly as a child to the extent a child can perform, in the strength of the Lord. The infancy and early life of Christ teaches us this (DA71-4). A **perfect** rosebud may develop into a **perfect** rose in Eden yet the bud differs from the full bloom. This change from one stage to another in development is what we call maturation, but maturation does not indicate whether the change is perfect or imperfect, good or bad.

The perfect love of the Father for the Son was even greater for Him after He gave His life for us (SC14.3).

The perfection for which the plan of salvation was instituted was to give us complete, absolute, freedom from the effects of past sins and freedom from sinning now. As I study the word of God, I find that this recovery from the effects of transgressions is accomplished in stages. Christ's spiritual kingdom has been established (Luke 17:21), but His temporal kingdom has not yet been set up (John 18:36; GC347.8).

Through the merits of Christ we can have **perfect** justification now (2SM32.9) and receive power and guidance for the **development** of a **perfect character** during "this life" (CH634.1; 5BC1147; Sp.T 2:32.5). God has made available to us all needed facilities to cease all known sins **now**, and to examine ourselves **now** for sins of ignorance; but there are some further things in store in the plan of salvation. "This life" ends at the close of probation for all the living or at death. All the saints from Abel till now have had access to the ministry of the "daily sacrifice" in their lives. Something more is to be done for the last generation, the saints who go through the investigative judgment, while they are alive. Yet, they do not have this exclusively. The same thing must be done for all other generations; but it is done for those who will be translated from among the living **while they are alive** on the earth, and for those who are asleep in the Lord while they rest in the grave (EW254.8, 280.3; GC486-91; 5T692.2).

In addition to the development of the righteous character in the early rain experience, the full effect of sin on the character is to be cared for. During the "little time of trouble" the character will be tried and tested further (EW33, 85.5; GC490, 528.9; PK589.5; 5T214.7, 474, 570.3). After the investigative judgment the record of sin will be blotted out and the mental record will be freed from the effects of sin. The sealing and the blotting out of sins complete the ministry whereby the character will be made perfect (5T216.5; GC425.4; 4T367.1).

Those who go through the great time of trouble will have a perfect heart toward God and a mental record free from sin; but they will still have their same degenerate weak body. Then, when Jesus comes, the infirmities of the flesh will be taken care of (GC645.2). After the millennium the effects of sin upon this part of the universe will be removed (GC674.1).

Chapter 16

THE HUMANITY OF CHRIST AND THE PERFECTING OF HUMANITY

In the preceding chapter we summarized the sequence whereby the threefold nature of man is made perfect. Now let us consider these points in more detail.

Perfecting of The Spiritual Nature:—At conversion God creates within us a perfect heart (COL97.4; 4BC1165). We are to turn from all **known** sins perfectly and hold nothing back from God. We dedicate ourselves and all that we have completely to Jesus and resolve to do **with His help** all that He asks or will ever ask of us. After we set ourselves aside for holy use ("sanctify" ourselves), Jesus takes all our guilt from us to the heavenly sanctuary and sets us aside for holy use (sanctifies us). The **Spiritual nature** is then perfect. Under these conditions we have the right to claim sanctification, recognizing that sanctification is a process whereby sin is taken away **and** the vacuum is filled with the graces of the Holy Spirit (2SM32.9; AA566; COL420.1). With this perfect heart we receive our title to heaven (MYP35.9). It is like being "in the city of refuge" (PP516.9). We are "in Christ Jesus," and this relationship must be maintained by our **striving** for a pure heart continually PK591.1; 2T505-6). It is in this sense that Noah and Job were perfect (Gen. 6:9; Job 1:1).

A perfect heart comes with deep earnest soul searching, with fervent prayer and study. It is not something that we can keep once obtained, but it must be continually desired and sought after. Conversion has to be renewed if and when we commit a known sin, but we must hasten to add humbly that God says that there is no excuse for committing a known sin with the facilities that He has made available (DA311.6).

Perfecting the Mental Nature:—With this perfect heart we are to set out in cooperation with our Redeemer to **develop** a perfect character (PP460; 1T158.5; 2BC997). This is also called "perfecting a character" (4T459.7; CPT365.8). This is the first phase of the perfecting of the mental nature. It is called "walking not after the flesh, but after the Spirit" (Rom. 8:1-11). Even with conversion and consecration we still have evil habits, hereditary and cultivated propensities to do wrong, and false concepts of the things of God. God does not tell us at once all that He expects of us, lest we become confused. "He tells them [His children] just as much as they can remember and perform" (DA313.9; cf. 568.6). As God reveals our weaknesses and faults to us, **our** "work" is to **strive** to be under the control of the Spirit for power to cut loose from wrong. In other words, the righteous are not to give themselves up to the control of evil (5T474.4).

Since God tells us that there is no excuse for sinning, and since He has said, "Be ye perfect," we should avail ourselves of these promises **when** the times and seasons are at hand. Right now He is testing our hearts and characters (4T85.1). He wants it to be known to us and to the universe just what our attitude will be toward Him under all circumstances. Right now He is trying us with little and big opportunities, with little and big temptations, and with little and big trials. The question is, will we try to overcome in our own strength, or will we turn to Jesus in prayer for **His** help? Where is our faith? Is it in **ourselves**, or is it in our Saviour who wants to be invited to work in us and with us to keep us from sinning? When we seriously want to be through with sin, then He can do something with us; then our lives will be a series of victories, with victory over every besetment that He permits to come to us (EW71.8; AA531.5).

All of God's saints from Abel until the present time have had the perfection described in the preceeding four paragraphs while they were living.

More, however, is to be done for those who will go through the time of trouble, stand without a mediator, and be translated. The character must be brought to the state of Christ's character. Our characters must be such that Satan can find nothing within them that will respond to his temptations (GC623.3). The heart is to be so that it will not cherish any sinful desire (GC623.3).

God knows how much development of character we need for the little time of trouble. The great time of trouble requires additional preparation (GC622). God has revealed that growth is necessary. This growth has been compared with plant growth, "first the blade, then the ear, and the corn in the ear." Some will have to learn in a few months what others have been years learning (EW67.8). Yet it must be done. It cannot be sidestepped.

Now is the time for us to let the Spirit dig deep into our minds, examine all the halls of memory, find all of our propensities to evil, help us recognize them, and strengthen us to overcome them. A most solemn preparation must be made to receive the seal of God and the "latter rain" (EW71). By the fires of affliction and temptation, kindled by Satan, the Lord will prepare His people for the investigative judgment and the blotting out of sins. Thanks be to God that He watches the furnace of affliction closely! (PK589.9; 1T706.8; 2T269.2). Do not be surprised at all the things in your past life that Jesus will bring into your mind during this process. Admit it, repent of it, and make it right when needed.

Even though the Christian has a perfect heart toward God with all guilt of sin removed, even though he has been walking with God in the development of a perfect character and has been overcoming all revealed sinful tendencies and propensities, there still remains something more to be done for him in order for him to have a perfect character. The old man of sin, the *sarx*, the sum and total of former habits recognized and unrecognized, even though they may have been "overcome," remains yet in the memory of the heart and must be blotted out (cf. GC421; PP202.6, 356-7). Furthermore, all of God's law for mankind must be put into the mind as well as in the heart so that the person will know what God expects on each and every occasion as well as love doing it. God plans that we commit neither a known sin nor a sin of ignorance after probation closes (cf. 2T691-2; EW254, 281.5; 1BC1104).

At conversion God writes His law of love in the heart by the Holy Spirit (DA176). The Christian now loves God's law. God then proceeds to put His law into that person's mind. Adam and Eve at creation had within them the knowledge of and love for God's law (1BC1104; PP363; 3SG295.5). Years of sin have partially obliterated it from the minds of mankind (cf. PK376, PP363-4). Through a study of the Scriptures and of nature under the guidance of His Spirit, God reveals to His followers," ¤as much as they can remember and perform" (DA313.9). But, if mankind is to be kept from going against God's will ignorantly, God must put His requirements into the mind as He did for Adam at his creation. *The Living Bible* phrases the everlasting covenant this way, "But this is the new agreement I will make with the people of Israel, says the Lord: I will write my laws in their minds so that they will know what I want them to do without my even telling them, and these laws will be in their hearts so that they will want to obey them, and I will be their God and they shall be my people" (Heb. 8:10, 11). The blotting out of the record of sin from the heart and the completion of the writing of the law in the mind occurs in connection with the final atonement and the investigative judgment and not before then (GC422, 485; 1BC1104).

After the character development during the early rain, **after** the trials of the little time of trouble, **after** the sealing and the outpouring of spiritual power in the latter rain, **after** the blotting out of the record of sin and the putting of the law in its entirety into the heart and mind, **then and not until that time will the character of the person be perfect** (4T367.1, 429.6; 2T355.3; 5T216.5). This does not imply that the character will not develop (mature) further from that time onward. It will develop further, but the mental nature will be free perfectly from the effects of sin even though the mental-moral power is yet weak from the effects of sin on the physical brain (cf. 1SM271.9; DA117.3; 2SM33.7). Character will be developed further **but completely without sinning** through the great time of trouble and on into heaven (COL332.8). The weak mental-moral power is made strong by the imparted power of God.

At this stage of events, the close of probation for the living, God's people will be like the **humanity** of Christ in certain vital ways (5T235-7; COL69.2; GC623.2). [Note: Christ was divinity clothed in humanity, but mankind can never be this (DA671, 675; 5BC1127-8)].

	The Living Saints	Humanity of Christ
They will love righteousness and hate evil	3T266.8	Heb. 1:9
They will be sealed	5T212.6	John 6:27
The Holy Ghost will fill them without measure	MB21 GC477	5BC1124 GC477
They will have no guilt of sin	GC620.3	DA685 5BC1114

	The Living Saints	Humanity of Christ
They will have no record of sin in their hearts nor in the copy in heaven	5T214.6 GC623 GC421-2	5BC1131 GC623
With the record of sin erased, they will have no passions nor propensity to sin	GC623 EW271	5BC1128 5T422
They will have sinless human spiritual nature and sinless human mental nature, but they will still have the sinful physical nature. "He [Jesus] took upon nature. "He [Jesus] took upon His sinless nature our sinful [physical] nature...." (MM181.7)	GC425, 623 5T216, 235 4T366.7 2T355	GC623.1 5T422 MM181.7 MH422.3
	The Living Saints	Humanity of Christ
Until Jesus comes they will yet have the infirmities of the flesh,– decreased physical strength, decreased mental power, and the decreased moral worth that has accrued.	GC491.2 cf.GC645 2SM33	DA49, 117.3 5BC1081 5BC1127-31 RH09-04-00
They will be tempted by the devil and by the things of the world through the senses, but will no longer be tempted by that old carnal man of sin.	EW271, 277 GC619 GC623, 625 cf.GC489	7BC927, 929 1SM255 DA116.9
They will still need the ministry of the spirit, ministry of angels, and the enabling power from God.	EW271, 279 GC618, 620 GC631 5BC1080	DA114, 126 4T109
They will go directly to the Father without an intercessor for needed wisdom and enabling grace (power) just as Jesus did (AA56.1).	EW48.2 EW280, 283 GC614, 620 5BC1123 7BC926	PK691.5 AA56.1 5BC1080-2 7BC929-30 1T339-40
They could sin, but they will not. There is no forgiveness after probation closes.	EW281 5T212-3	DA117.5 5BC1082 5BC1128
They may have a "sense" of sin, but to have that is neither sinning nor sinful.	GC618-9	DA753.6

They, unlike Jesus, will have "a sense of their unworthiness." They remember the "pit from which they were dug" and realize that their state of sinless perfection of character is a gift of the Lord.	EW272 PP202 GC619-20 GC650.1
They will not say, "I am sinless," because they still have the sinful flesh.	2SM32-33 AA562.1

> ONLY THOSE WHO ARE TO BE TRANSLATED WITHOUT SEEING DEATH WILL HAVE BOTH THE PERFECTION OF THE HEART AND PERFECTION OF THE CHARACTER, DESCRIBED IN THIS CHAPTER AND THE ACCOMPANYING TABLE, WHILE STILL LIVING ON THE EARTH AFTER THE CLOSE OF PROBATION AND PRIOR TO CHRIST'S SECOND COMING.

The first fruits of this group is presented in the Scriptures as the 144,000 (Rev. 14:1-5; 7BC978; GC649). We can say that Paul and the other righteous dead did have a perfect heart and were developing a righteous character by the grace of God during their lifetime, but their character was not perfect while they were yet alive because the blotting out of the record of sin is a necessary part for this to be, and the blotting out of the record of sin could not occur until after the investigative judgment (PK591; GC483-7). The investigative judgment did not start until 1844 (GC480-3).

There are two parts to the perfection of the character. Man does his part by the help of the Lord while he is alive. By this means he is prepared for our High Priest to complete the work He alone can do; namely, blot out the record of sin and complete the writing of the law in the heart and mind.

We can say that the forerunners, Enoch, Elijah, Moses, and those who went with Jesus at His ascension, had their investigative judgment and their records blotted out earlier than those who remain until His second coming, for this must be done to live in God's presence (EW71; 1T705-6; GC485, 646.9; SL26.5; 5T467.3). We cannot prove **when** this happened to Enoch and Elijah prior to their translation for this has not been revealed to us.

God's part of the perfection of our character which includes the blotting of sin out of the heart is done for the righteous dead **while they are dead**. This is called the "final" or "special" atonement, an atonement by our Mediator for the righteous dead while they are asleep and then for the righteous who are to be translated without dying, **while they are alive** (EW251.3, 253.9). An interval of time elapses after the "final" atonement of the living during which time the 144,000 live on the earth without sinning (EW271; GC485).

Surely, if God can keep His saints from sinning in heaven for a thousand years or more, He should be able to keep them from sinning for a short while after probation closes on this earth.

Perfecting of the Physical Nature:—When Jesus comes in glory, the dead will be raised. He creates a new body for them with a much finer arrangement of material and imprints the thoughts of their character into the new brain (6BC1093). Their thoughts will begin where they ceased at death (GC550.5). Physical features will be preserved enough that friend will recognize friend (6BC1092-3; DA804; LS66).

The living saints will be changed in a moment. The new body will be perfect. The deformity, the enzyme defects, the diseased cells, the results of senescence will all be corrected. The finishing touch of immortality is given to each (6BC1093). We shall grow up with these immortal bodies.

Christ, in heaven before His incarnation, was taller than the tallest angel (4SG115.5). While He was here during His days of ministry, He was "but little taller than the common size of men" at that time (4SG115.5). When He arose from the tomb, He was of the same size as before His death (4SG119.4). He came forth glorified yet the soldiers and later His disciples recognized Him (DA780.8, 804). When He ascended to heaven, He attained to the same stature as He was before He came to live among men (4SG119.6). We too shall grow to mature height in heaven (GC644-5; 4SG119.6). The infant will not remain so forever there.

Further Comments:—It now becomes apparent why it is important to understand some things about the human nature of Christ. In His humanity Jesus had sinless spiritual nature and the sinless mental nature like Adam before the fall, but He had the sinful physical nature of Mary after Eden. Unless we understand His nature in that light, we will have difficulty in explaining many statements in the Bible and in the writings of Ellen White such as the following:

"He took upon His sinless nature our sinful nature..." (MM181).

"...His *spiritual nature was free from every taint* of sin." (EGW in *Questions on Doctrine*, pp. 650-660).

"He was the son of Mary; He was of the seed of David according to human descent" (ibid).

"For four thousand years the race had been decreasing in physical strength, in mental power, and in moral worth;

and Christ took upon Him the infirmities of degenerate humanity" (DA117).

"...notwithstanding the humiliation of taking upon Himself our fallen nature..." (DA112).

"He also himself likewise took part of the same..." (Heb.2:14).

"He vanquished Satan in the same nature over which in Eden Satan obtained the victory" (EGW in Questions on Doctrine, pp. 650-660).

"In taking upon Himself man's nature in its fallen condition, Christ did not in the least participate in its sin. He was subject to the infirmities and weaknesses by which man is encompassed..." (ibid).

"Do not set Him before the people as a man with the propensities of sin. He is the second Adam." (ibid).

"When Adam was assailed by the tempter in Eden he was without the taint of sin.... Christ, in the wilderness of temptation, stood in Adam's place to bear the test he failed to endure" (ibid).

"Never, in any way, leave the slightest impression upon human minds that a taint of, or inclination to, corruption rested upon Christ, or that He in any way yielded to corruption¤. let every human being be warned from the ground of making Christ altogether human, such a one as ourselves; for it cannot be" (ibid).

"He was born without a taint of sin, but came into the world in like manner as the human family" (ibid).

"Though He had no taint upon His character, yet He condescended to connect our fallen human nature with His divinity. By this taking humanity, He honored humanity. Having taken our fallen nature, He showed what it might become, by becoming partakers of the divine nature" (ibid).

"He is brother in our infirmities, but not in possessing like passions" (2T202).

"He was to suffer the inconveniences, and ills, and afflictions of the human family. He was not to perform miracles on His own account" (1SM277).

"As a member of the human family He was mortal, but as a God He was the fountain of life to the world. He could, in His divine person, ever have withstood the advances of death, and refused to come under its dominion; but He voluntarily laid down His life..." (RH07-05-87).

If we take the statement in MM181 at face value, Christ must have taken upon Himself something that was sinful. Yet the only sinful nature that we have that Christ could have taken upon Himself without being a sinner was our sinful physical nature.

If in His humanity He had taken our sinful spiritual nature on Himself, He would have been out of harmony with God and thus a sinner. If He had taken our sinful mental nature upon Himself, He would have had a mental record of sin with all its passions and its propensities to evil.

If I take the statements available at face value into my theological reasoning without distorting their meaning, without trimming them to fit a location in the picture of the nature of Christ, I conclude that He took upon **His sinless *spiritual* nature and His sinless *mental* nature our sinful *physical* nature**.

This is one of the profound topics. "The study of the incarnation of Christ, His atoning sacrifice and mediatorial work, will employ the mind of the diligent students as long as time shall last" (GW251).

This much insight into the nature of the humanity of Christ helps us understand and believe how the last generation of the earth can live, **by the power of God, without sinning** for a space of time even though they suffer the effects of six thousand years of decreasing physical strength, mental power, and moral worth.

The 144,000 during the great time of trouble will be like the humanity of Christ while on this earth in their spiritual, mental, and physical natures. This comes not because of some special virtue on their part, but simply because they are the last generation, the one which shall be translated (GC649.3).

The history of the Israelites on the way to Canaan teaches us many lessons. Salvation is a cooperative venture. We may not be able to stop the Jordan River, but we can walk by faith up to the edge and step into it. We may not be able to cause the walls of Jericho to fall, but we can march by faith around according to God's instructions, keep our mouths shut when asked to, and shout for His help when the time is right. He surely will work with us.

God purposes that no one who is saved will be able to say that he made it to heaven in his own strength (4SG64.3). In the judgment parable, what do those on the right hand say to the King? They are heard saying, "When did we do this kind deed or that humane work for you?" Were they zombies? No! They realize that God was working in them all the way after they set out to serve Him because they always asked Him to do so. They refer the merit to Christ. They know by experience that it was the Saviour who make all this possible. The Father acknowledges the part of His saints. Even though their part was little, it was the deciding factor; they did the deciding.

What would happen if the saints were to answer the King, "Yes, I remember that time when I helped those people. It turned out very well, didn't it"? No. God cannot compliment His people nor give them a reward if they take a particle of credit to themselves. The kingdom of heaven does not work that way. Jesus does not seek His own glory (John 8:50). He glorifies the Father and the Holy Spirit (John 17:4). The Father glorifies the Son (John 17:5). The Spirit glorifies the Saviour (John 16:14). We are to glorify God (1 Cor. 6:20). The Father extols His church. We give honor to our colaborers and above all to Christ (1 Thess. 5:12, 13; Rev. 5:13). God calls what we do, "the righteousness of the saints" (Rev. 19:8). We call it, "the righteousness of God and our Saviour" (2 Peter 1:1). The circle of love thus abounds and continues (DA21.7). Only sinners enter and take credit to themselves.

Elijah on Mount Carmel did not receive the answer to his prayer for rain until he had thoroughly searched his heart about giving honor to God; and until he thoroughly realized that, "he was nothing, and that God was everything¤" (2BC1035).

At times, when I hear some Adventists talk about perfection, I get the impression from their expressions that no created being, not even an angel, can perfectly obey God's laws. They seem to set the standard super high, so high that only God can keep it perfectly (cf. DA668.5; GC489.8).

For those who say that it is impossible to obey the law perfectly, let us remember that it is not God who says this. Here is but one of His promises. "Exact obedience is required and those that say it is not possible to live a perfect life throw upon God the imputation of injustice and untruth" (MS 148, 1899).

It is the Evil One who states that God's laws are faulty and cannot be kept (PP69.2; DA761.8). Here is a statement to that effect. "Therefore he [Satan] is constantly seeking to deceive the followers of Christ with his fatal sophistry [lie] that it is impossible for them to overcome" (GC489).

True, when I look at my strength to do a righteous act or at my fellow church members, I agree with the devil. I do not see how it can be done. **But I believe that it can be done simply because Jesus says that we can** (Mark 9:23, 24; DA664, 668.4; AA531-3). Jesus has shown us that it can be done, and He promises us the same victory (DA24.7, 667.5; 1SM409.1). "Jesus, considered as a man, was perfect, yet He grew in grace" (1T339).

The standard that God has set for His people is high (TM121). "Higher than the highest human thought can reach is God's ideal for His children. Godliness–Godlikeness–is the goal to be reached" (Ed18). We are promised that His grace is sufficient (2 Cor. 12:9). "The Lord does not ask for anything unreasonable. He does not expect the smaller vessels to hold the contents of the larger ones" (MYP96).

Whatever I do is as "filthy rags," but **everything that God does is perfect**. Whenever someone asks whether or not we are perfect, we can say that we are not. If someone asks if we have ever done anything perfectly, we can say, "No"; but we can hasten to add that God has worked in me to do a perfect act from a perfect motive because I have asked Him to do just that. **Jesus receives all the glory**.

God is working in His people. He will be satisfied with nothing less than perfection. For this we should be thankful. When the Master Artisan is through with you and me, He wants to be able to say, "Here are they that keep the commandments of God" (Rev. 14:12; MM184; COL361). They will be without spot or wrinkle (Eph. 5:27).

It would be helpful when we study, discuss, and write about "perfection" that we understand what aspect of a person is under consideration in the context. We cannot use texts and references which are discussing perfection of the character and apply them, for example, to perfection of the heart or to perfection of the flesh without causing confusion in our thinking and in the thinking of others.

To help clarify these concepts, I have tabulated the various types of relationships between man and his God on separate pages to follow.

DEFINITIONS FOR THE FOLLOWING TABLE

"Heart" — used in the sense of the seat of the emotions or determiner of the motives of the person

"Character" — essentially the sum and total of the mental records, habits, memory of the feelings and thoughts, pictures in memory's halls. The "spirit" of man.

"Body" — the "soma", the physical brains, nerves, bones, muscles, glands, and other organs.

"Sinless" — the state of being free from the effects of sin.

"Perfect" — absolutely correct and free from defects or the effects of sin.

"Mature" — relates to growth. The blade matures into the ear, etc. A perfect rosebud can develop into a perfect rose. It can be perfect in each stage of growth, but the change is called maturation. Similarly, a perfect rosebud may develop into an imperfect rose if sin enters.

"Sinful" — the state of having the effects of sin on that nature. The effects of sin on the spiritual nature is rebellion against God and the presence of guilt. The effect of sin on the mental nature is the memory record of the feelings (attitudes) and thoughts that occurred at the time that each sinful act or thought occurred. The effect of sin on the physical body consists of the genetic changes from the sins of our forebearers, plus the changes which result from our own disobedience of God's laws. Jesus suffered the genetic changes; but since He was obedient to the laws of health, further damage was limited to that extent.

	Adam & Eve Before their Sin	Unconverted Person
SPIRITUAL NATURE "Heart" or "will" Attitude toward God	*sinless* loved God perfectly*¹	*sinful* loves evil indifferent to God
Relationship with God	child of God	"property" of God
Relationship with the Holy Spirit "touched by"	full	"restrained by" in dwelling "occasionally responds to Him"
MENTAL NATURE	*sinless*	*sinful*
Righteous character or "new" man in Christ	was being developed	has none
Feelings recorded in Heart evil habits or record of sin or "old man of sin" = "sarx"	none	present & alive being developed
Thoughts recorded in Mind	none	present
PHYSICAL NATURE	*sinless*	*sinful*
Body including brain flesh and blood (Gr. "soma")	no defects from heredity or disease	infirmities subject to ailments

1   Perfectly dedicated to God steadily
2   Intermittent, more or less. Must be renewed = reconverted

---

*   **Perfectly dediated to God steadily**

Converted Person	Humanity of Christ	144,000 After probation closes before translation
sinless "striving for perfection" toward God**[2] *	sinless perfect toward God[1]	sinless perfect toward God[1]
spiritually a child of God	Son of God	spiritually a child of God
led by the Spirit has the "earnest" of the Spirit	full indwelling	full indwelling
sinful being developed	sinless was developed on earth	sinless being developed
present but covered being "crucified" or "overcome"	none	none,-erased or blotted out
present	none	"scars" present
sinful infirmities subject to ailments	sinful infirmities subject to ailments	sinful infirmities subject to ailments

---

*   Perfectly dediated to God steadily
** Intermittent, more or less. Must be renewed = reconverted

Chapter 17

GOLD AND SILVER AND PRECIOUS STONES

In this chapter let us consider character building from the standpoint of 1 Corinthians 3:9-17. We find that Ellen White applied these verses in two main ways. First, these verses direct our thoughts to the church of God on the earth as a whole; and, second, they are applied to individual character development (5T466-7; 8T173).

The Church as a Temple:—In the first instance, the one most commonly referred to in the Spirit of prophecy, we realize that there are both righteous and wicked in the church. The works of the ministers have something to do with this situation.

To sanctify His church, God gives opportunities to the church and allows affliction and trials to come to cleanse the church. Further than this, we are informed that there will be a mighty shaking, sifting, of the church (5T80; 1T181). When the "mighty shaking" occurs, the results of the work of the ministers and laymen for God's church will be manifest (5T81, 474; PK589).

The Character Temple:—The other main application of these verses has to do with the character of each human soul temple (5T466-7; 8T173.1). Each of us must build character upon the foundation, which is Jesus Christ and His Word (DA314, 599; MB150.5). Upon His sinless imputed character (**our title to heaven**) we are to build our character (**our fitness for heaven**). Both are gifts. The first is imputed to us; the latter is imparted to us by the Holy Spirit (MYP35). We build brick by brick, deed by deed. Each righteous thought and action, purified by His merits, is gold, silver, or precious stone in the character (5T129; 4T89). Morally wrong thoughts or actions, all selfishness, all false religion are likened to hay, wood, and stubble.

By helping us get enduring material into our character and through afflictions burn out the dross, God works with us for the cleansing of our soul temple. This is the removing of the "earthliness" which is especially applicable to those who will be sealed, have their sins blotted out, and live through the time of trouble (GC621.3). This refining-testing process will begin soon and build to a climax during the little time of trouble (9T11; EW85.8) which precedes the close of probation (PK589-90; 2T355.5, 430.9; 5T214.9).

Christ carefully watches every human soul (8T123-4; 5T754.9; MB121.8). He gives opportunities (PP223.4; 3T511.6). He allows trials and temptations to come our way (4T85; DA301.2; MB10-11), but no more than we are able to bear through faith in Him (4T89; 1 Cor. 10:13; 5T474-5). The true Christian will overcome every besetment. He will put that "old man of sin" to death. He will not give himself up to the control of evil (5T474.4). He may make mistakes; but, when he recognizes them, he turns from them with true repentance (COL173.2, 332.6). "We shall often have to bow down and weep at the feet of Jesus because of our shortcomings and mistakes, but we are not to be discouraged" (SC64.3).

By the **exclusion** of every sinful thought, work, or deed and by the **incorporation** or the good, the dross is kept out and solid structures are brought into the character. It is for this reason that we should take care in the use of our time and be selective in what we think, see, and hear. In this sense the soul temple is being cleansed even today, i.e., by exclusion of the bad (FCE428.9; 5T72.9, 214.7; DA161).

In addition to the cleansing of the soul temple by the process of sanctification, discussed above, there is yet another lesson to be learned from the text in first Corinthians. If we compare GC426.3, 5T570.3, Malachi 3:1-4, and Isaiah 4:3,4 with 1 Cor. 3:9-19, we find that "**the day**" that declares every man's works will be the day of investigative judgment for that person. After the investigative judgment of the person, the command will be given, "take away the filthy garments from him" (Zech. 3:4; 5T475; RH11-19-08). In other phrases, burn up the hay, wood, and stubble; **or** bury forever that "old man of sin"; **or** blot out his record of sin. The righteous person will then be left with the "gold, silver, and precious stones" in his character; left with the "book of remembrance"; left with the imparted character; and he will be saved (GC481.3; 6BC1088). God will not remember his sins (Isa. 43:23; GC483.6), and the righteous person will not remember them either (GC620.4; PP202.7).

Notice then the significance of verses 16 and 17 in their context in 1 Corinthians 3. Paul here applies these to the soul temple when he says, "Know ye not that ye are the temple of God¤" (cf. 6BC1085-87).

There are some Bible students who say that after the blotting out of sins, only God would not be able to remember our sins (Isaiah 43:25). The reference (GC620.5) plainly states that the righteous will not be able to remember them as well. If the blotting out of the thought record were only performed on the books in heaven, then God could still know of my sin because He can read my thoughts. Once He read my thoughts again, He would remember them then. Furthermore, the only record that God has of the righteous dead is in heaven. If He blots the sin record out of their record while they sleep in the dust, and uses that corrected record to imprint in their resurrected body, they will not remember their sins, since, while their soul temple here did not exist, the final atonement was made in heaven (EW253, 254, 280). The blotting or erasing of the record of sin must be done for the original record (the earthly mental record) as well as for the copy of that record in heaven at some definite time for those who will not taste death if they are to have the same advantage as those who die in the Lord. And this is the promise, "Those who are living upon the earth when the intercession of Christ shall cease in the sanctuary above, are to stand in the sight of a Holy God without a mediator. Their robes must be spotless, their characters must be purified from sin by the blood of sprinkling" (GC425.5; see also 5T467; 4BC1181).

Perhaps part of the confusion about the timing of the blotting out of sin lies with the location of the following statement in the context of the time of Jacob's trouble. "The assaults of Satan are fierce and determined, his delusions are terrible; but the Lord's eye is upon His people, and His ear listens to their cries. Their affliction is great, the flames of the furnace seem about to consume them; but the Refiner will bring them forth as gold tried in the fire. God's love for His children during the period of their severest trial is as strong and tender as in the days of their sunniest prosperity; but it is needful for them to be placed in the furnace of fire; their earthliness must be consumed, that the image of Christ may be perfectly reflected" (GC621.4).

We know from that statement by Ellen White that the "fires of affliction" will continue and be most dreadful during the great time of trouble. After the close of probation, Satan will be allowed to foment trouble such as never was throughout the world (GC614.5). In addition the seven last plagues will be poured out by angels from the throne in heaven (GC627-29). This affliction with the watch care of God is presented as follows: "And even after the saints are sealed with the seal of the living God, His elect will have trials individually. Personal afflictions will come; but the furnace is closely watched by an eye that will not suffer the gold to be consumed. The indelible mark of God is upon them..." (TM446.4).

The question is this, even though the "furnace of affliction" is allowed to continue after probation ends, will the righteous still undergo cleansing from dross? Or is this period of affliction merely the time when, "The people of God must drink of the cup, and be baptized with the baptism" (GC630-31)?

We know that after the close of probation, the saints will have to "wait trustingly for the Lord to work." They will be led to "exercise faith, hope, and patience" more fully during this time shortly before Christ's advent (GC631.2). But is this when the earthliness will be removed?

I believe that the above questions may be answered best from a comparison of references.

In the discussion about "Joshua and the Angel," we read essentially the identical words as those written in Great Controversy on page 621 about the removal of the "earthliness" (PK589.9). In that context the removal of the earthliness and the taking away of the "filthy garments" occurs in connection with the final sealing and the decision to retain the names of those who receive this in the "Lamb's book of life" (PK591).

There will be a time of "refining," "shaking," and "sifting" for the living that will prepare them for the Latter Rain and the blotting out of sins (EW50.8, 270-1; 5T80.5; 7BC911; 1T251). The "refining" that will remove sin and corruption will be done only during the hours of probation. "The Refiner does not then [at the time of coming in glory] sit to pursue His refining process and remove their sins and their corruption. This is all to be done in these hours of probation. It is *now* that this work is to be accomplished for us" (2T355.5).

After the "mighty shaking" and the "sealing," God's company will have "obtained the victory" and the evil angels can have no power over them (EW271). Can we grasp that? About this time for the saints, we are told, "The despised remnant are clothed in glorious apparel, nevermore to be defiled by the corruptions of the world. Their names are retained in the Lamb's book of life,¤ Now they are eternally secure from the tempter's devices" (PK591). This "glorious apparel" is the spotless robe of Christ's righteousness (PK591). Yet it is called "the righteousness of the saints" (Rev. 19:8). They have received it as a gift, woven in them as they have chosen it moment by moment, day by day. This imparted character shines forth from their faces by their outward reactions to the trials (PK591; COL310-12; DA173.1). "Their features, marked with severe internal anguish, now shone with the light and glory of heaven (EW271). This is not the robe of light given to the living saints after the resurrection of the righteous (GC665.6; COL310-11; PP57.5).

Let us thank God for all His goodness to us. None of us will ascribe salvation to ourselves. We can, however, cooperate with God and let Him work in us. We can call earnestly for His strength to be manifest in us by obedience. God will reward us for even that. Praise His name. God intends to prepare His people so that the temptations and trials by Satan directly and from the world via the senses will find no answering chord within their minds after probation closes.

Chapter 18

HE WAS REJECTED

When we think of sin and its effect, we often forget the impact of evil on the three Persons of the Godhead. For a few moments let us consider what our Saviour has endured. It can be summed up in the words of Isaiah.

"We despised Him and rejected Him - a man of sorrows, acquainted with bitterest grief" (Isaiah 53:3 Living Bible).

The emotional trauma from rejection is one of the most difficult feelings to endure. A child unwanted, unloved bears the scars, suffers the warp in mental attitudes throughtout life.

Have you experienced rejection as a child? Have you suffered the heartbreak of young love when your betrothed, for no reason, desires your company no longer? Perhaps you have trained up a child in the way that he should go and then sorrowed as you saw him seek another path. Has your life's companion wrung the depths of your emotions until tears of agony came no more? There is One who knows your grief by experience.

Six milleniums ago, through the visions of the prophets, we see the eye of jealousy turn against Christ. Lucifer, His closest helper, restrained not the stirrings of envy (SR15-6; PP35-7; GC494-5). This mighty commanding angel aspired to the position of Christ, to be equal with God (PP35.5, 41.5; GC495). And what about Christ? *He was rejected!*

Satan with his subtle questions, insinuated doubts, and deceptions (PP37-8, 41; GC497) was able to persuade nearly half of the angels of heaven to give him their allegiance (SR18.5). Instead of joyous service to the Meek One, they turned their backs as He went by. They chose to "follow their own will, which would [supposedly] ever guide them right" (GC499.8; cf. GC495.7; PP37.7). Oh, the anguish in heaven, **He was rejected**. Now the loving merciful One must endure as His loyal followers expelled these, their former bosom friends, from heaven (SR17.5; Rev. 12:9).

When the loving Creator came to the garden on that fateful day, what reception did He get? "Adam, Eve, where art thou?" Eve had chosen to "be like gods"; Adam had chosen Eve. **He was rejected**. The Majesty of heaven must find a way to define His own "offering" for reconciliation, select the symbol, and, for the first time, see death, death of a lovely lamb (SR42.8).

And then nine generations of giants came upon the earth. What did they do with the One who is pure in heart? Billions chose their evil imaginations (SR62.6; Gen.6:5). **He was rejected**. One family accepted Him and sought safety in His promises.

He spoke to Abraham and Sarah, called them out of Ur, led them into a new country. Their descendents multiplied in Egypt and were made slaves. By many miracles and with a cloud for shade by day and for light at night, He led them from bondage. At Sinai the unfaithful ones chose the meat, garlic, and the sacred bull of Egypt. **He was rejected**. At Kadesh-Barnea they chose to trust in their own strength to enter Canaan. **He was rejected**.

He established them a mighty nation, even gave them a king. Yet they chose to have their children pass through the fire (3SG303-4; PK57.8). They chose the lustful sensuality of fertility gods; they chose the fiery arms of Moloch to cradle their babies (PP454-5; PK57-8; CG277; 2BC1039). **He was rejected**.

He sent them as slaves to Assyria, Babylon, and Medo-Persia. Yet He preserved them, and they prospered in the land of their captivity. He called them once, yes a second time, out of Babylon. Some returned, but many chose their ease and real estate in the land of their sojourn rather than the sacrifice of rebuilding waste places in Jerusalem in preparation for the coming Messiah. Because of Tammuz and Ishtar they turned their backs on the temple and worshipped the sun (Eze. 8:14-16). **He was rejected**.

"He also Himself likewise" (Heb. 2:14) became one of us in the flesh. Yet no one hung a wreath at His manger. No one decorated a fir with tinsel. His only gifts came from three foreigners. No reporters, only a monstrous king, checked the rumor of His birth (Matt. 2:1-8).

When He entered His ministry and had a major confrontation with the devil in the desert wasteland, no one fasted and prayed for His safety. No one sent a rescue party for Him. None applauded when He returned. Only one person went looking for him (5BC1132).

His mother did not comprehend His mission (DA56.6, 82.1, 90). His brothers were ashamed of Him (DA87, 88, 321, 325). The Gadarenes chose pigs instead of Him (DA339-40).

No colosseum filled in His honor. The religious leaders were preoccupied with other matters. The Pharisees retained their pride and self-sufficiency (DA279; COL278). The Scribes continued to pore over the Torah (DA610, 612). The Sadducees sought material advantages since their god had gone into a far country and left them to make out the best that they could (DA603-5). When the resurrection of Lazarus threatened these leaders and struck down their doctrines of death, they showed that their traditions and tenets were more important then the Life-giver (DA537-41, 387.3, SR209). **He was rejected**.

His own disciples looked for a king to conquer Rome's legions (GC594; DA378-80). The threat of persecution in Gethsemane caused His closest followers to flee. One of them betrayed Him for silver. **He was rejected**.

Caiaphas preferred the proceeds from the money-changers. Herod went back to his Salomes. Pilate selected his politics. After the nails and the formality of cross raising, Roman hands returned to their gambling. **He was rejected**.

Jerusalem, **Rome**, was it not enough just to turn from Him? Was it really necessary to crucify Him? Hear His agony, "**Their contempt has broken my heart**" (Psalm 69:20 (Living Bible); DA746.5, 772.6).

He was despised and rejected of men, and yet there is more. One more experience of woe is yet to come. In the garden He moaned, "Let **this** cup pass from Me." On the cross He cried, "My God, My God, why hast **Thou** forsaken Me"? For our transgressions, **He was rejected!** (SR225; DA753-4). Divesting Himself of the attributes of a loving Father, our God withdrew His beams of love and light and glory from His Son (TM246; SR225; DA693, 753-5). The tender Father agonized through His office as judge (5BC1114; TM246). The Lamb could not see past the tomb (DA753). The cup of rejection for my guilt must be tasted to the last bitter drop. When the Father had to reject His Son, it was like a knife thrust in His heart (Zechariah 13:6,7; DA686).

Why did Heaven undergo these experiences? How could our Master withstand this without sinking down into discouragement? He loved me and you, yet He hated sin! (DA462; TM519; Heb. 1:9).

Rather than sink down into a careless stupid state (EW111, 113, 119), rather than curse the day of His birth (Job 3:1; Jere. 20:14), rather than revile His persecutors (DA744), rather than lose His temper at the injustices of His trial, He "endured the cross" and despised the shame (Heb. 12:2). Christ chose eternal separation from His Father rather than a course contrary to His Father (GC348; Luke 22:42; DA693). Sustained by His knowledge of the Father and by the cry of humanity, "Lord, remember me when Thou comest into Thy kingdom" (Luke 23:42; 8T43-4), He could say as did Job, "Though He slay me, yet will I trust Him" (Job 13:15).

What can we say to this love? Can we reject such love just to be first over our fellows? Will pride, self-sufficiency, or evil imaginations separate us from Him? Is anger, strife, and evil temper, or harsh behaviour worthy of such nobleness? Are the "new morality" Asherahs of sensuality, evil desires, adultery, or homosexuality all that enticing? Are houses or land or currency worth the price of one more rejection of Him? What will cause us to turn from Him? The answer must come from each person. The decision is at every juncture in the path of life (SC62, 70, 72).

Lord, we choose you! You are our help. Strengthen us, too, so that we would rather die than reject you even one more time. Let us say, "I am persuaded that, neither death, nor life, ... nor any other creature, shall be able to separate us from the love of God" (Rom. 8:38, 39).

Yes, He **was** rejected, but hear **now** the mandates of the Father.

"Thus says the Lord...to one deeply despised, abhorred by the nations, the servant of rulers: 'Kings shall see and arise; princes, and they shall prostrate themselves; because of the Lord, who is faithful, the Holy One of Israel, who has chosen you'" (Isa. 49:7 RSV).

"...He raised Christ from the dead and seated Him in heavenly spheres at His right hand, high above all government and authority, power and lordship, and every name that is named, not only in this but also in the future world" (Eph. 1:20, 21 MLV).

When we preceive what our heavenly Father and Jesus have suffered as a result of the rebellion, can we ever doubt the tender love and care that they have for each sin-tossed soul? Let us add our voice to this, "Thou art worthy, O Lord, to receive glory and honour and power" (Rev. 4:11).

Chapter 19

VITAL LESSONS FROM THE 1888 EXPERIENCE

As we review the experiences of Israel from Egyptian slavery to the partition of Canaan, we see portrayals of how God leads His people. Their experiences revealed wherein their love for God and trust in Him were lacking. From them we can also see some of the sidetracks of Satan not only for the individual but also for the church.

In a similar manner God is leading the remnant church. "God has shown me that He gave His people [in 1844] a bitter cup to drink, to purify and cleanse them. It is a bitter draught, and they can make it still more bitter by murmuring, complaining, and repining. But those who receive it thus must have another draught,¤ and another, until it does have its designed effect, or they will be left filthy, impure in heart" (EW47.1).

In a series of studies entitled *The Exodus and Advent Movements in Type and Antitype* by Taylor G. Bunch, he likened the 1844 experience to the Israel's crossing of the Red Sea, (GC457-8) and the 1888 episode to the Kadesh-Barnea sequence of events. God intended to lead His people into Canaan in such a way that no one could take credit unto himself (TM214.3). He has the same intent for His people who would enter the heavenly Canaan (DA122; TM456.5).

An examination of letters by Ellen White and the discussions of A.T. Jones, E. J. Waggoner, A. G. Daniells, and others about the events in the time period around 1888 reveals that more can be learned about the closing events of this earth's history than just an understanding of imputed and imparted righteousness. Other questions can be answered such as:– What other major issues were at stake? And, what sidetracks did the devil set up to counteract the truth?

Five major points loom prominently, points that God needs to get across to His church in preparation for closing events on this earth. In summary, they are:

(1) **What God is like**: We are to have a clear, correct conception of the **character** of God, not what His **essense** is like. One cannot reflect fully nor distinctly the attributes of Jesus without knowing Him well. Two important aspects of His character, both love and justice, must be kept in balance. These are plainly stated in Exodus 34:6, 7.

(2) **What we are like**: This is the message of how the True Witness sees Laodicea, God's church in the last days. A message to a church which has been described variously as asleep, indifferent, unconcerned, lukewarm, fence-sitting, and/or trusting in their own inherent capabilities.

(3) **A clear balanced, practical, experiential understanding of How we are to reflect Jesus**: This is a clear perception of the twin gifts, (a) forgiveness by faith (justification) and (b) obedience by faith (the character development of sanctification). In other words, imputed and imparted Righteousness by Faith.

(4) **A clear understanding of the gospel of salvation**: This would include a straight, truthful understanding of what God must do to separate us from sin and to remove the consequences of sinning on the **threefold nature of man**:

A correct understanding of spiritual topics particularly the sanctuary service and the prophecies of Daniel and John.

A balanced understanding of what Jesus plans to do to renew the mind so that the effects on the mental nature are dealt with and the character of Christ is developed in us.

An accurate presentation of the health message in such a way that His people will apply the true remedies in their lives for healthful living (MH127).

(5) **The need to witness for God**: An appreciation of the privilege and duty to witness for Jesus in such a way as to save souls and to vindicate God's character before the universe.

THE CHURCH IN 1888

God's Plans and the Devil's Sidetracks:

The emphasis on righteousness by faith by Ellen White had been building up for many years prior to the confrontation at the 1888 Minneapolis Conference (5T84; MS-5-89 cf. RH08-13-89). Her early emphasis on that topic was later assisted by the teachings of Elder A. T. Jones and Dr. E. J. Waggoner (TM91). Also, for over twenty years Ellen White had been given light for the reformation of the health habits of the people (4SG120-151). Dr. J. H. Kellogg and his staff, to a large measure, carried the burden for education of the church in the health message (MS-13-01).

In the church, however, there had been a growing feeling of doubt and disbelief in the testimonies (5T217). The message to the Laodicean church pictured it as in need of gold, – love which works by faith and purifies the soul, eyesalve, – spiritual insight, and white raiment, – the imparted character of God (4T88; COL158). This call of the True Witness was met with cold formalism, legalism, and lukewarm indifference (RH07-23-89; Letter O-19-92; RH12-23-90). The message of righteousness by faith was ignored or rejected by many, and the messengers were criticized and ridiculed (RH05-27-90; TM79-80; Letter O-19-92). Preconceived ideas, peer pressure, and pride on the part of others prevented widespread acceptance of the message (RH05-27-90; TM79-80; 1SM234).

Many ministers turned against the principles of health reform (MS-13-01; Letter B-38-99). As a result God could not proceed with His plans for the "Loud Cry" and the closing up of the work (RH11-22-92). The situation seems comparable to the time when Israel preferred to believe the ten spies rather than the two faithful ones and Moses (Numbers 14:5, 6).

Two quotations from the Lord's messenger shortly after 1888 portray the situation.

"Had the church of Christ done her appointed work as the Lord ordained, the whole world would before this have been warned, and the Lord Jesus would have come to our earth in power and great glory" (DA634.1).

"We may have to remain here in this world because of insubordination many more years, as did the children of Israel, but for Christ's sake; His people should not add sin to sin by charging God with the consequences of their own wrong course of action" (Ev696).

The development of the "Alpha" and Other Heresies:

In addition to the cold formalism and lukewarm indifference, the devil had other sidetracks. Since many ministers of the time had not accepted the messages of health reform, they did not appreciate the work of Dr. Kellogg in health education (MS-13-01; Letter B-38-99). This caused the docter to lose confidence in the ministry. Such a relationship resulted in an interchange of criticism and faultfinding between the ministry and the medical workers (ibid). To make things worse, Dr. Kellogg began to foster the concept that the medical missionary work should be the **body** of the message; he was not content for it to be just "the right arm" (Letter K-55-99; K-204-09). Perhaps this concept fostered the ideas of pantheism or was an outgrowth of them from the same source.

This state of affairs prepared the way for his pantheistic speculations about the **essence** or **nature** of God which resulted in the "alpha of deadly heresies" (1SM200). Instead of concentrating their thinking about the character of God, those involved were deceived into theorizing that the things of nature, such as the sunflower or the tree, were the very essence of God (Letter B-242-03; GCB 1901, 2nd. quarter). In an address in 1901 Dr. J. H. Kellogg asserted his pantheistic ideas such as, "It is God in the sunflower that makes it do this [follow the sun]" (D.D. Robinson, *The Story of our Health Message*, 1943, p. 268). Dr. Kellogg seemed to be saying that the whole universe was material, and that each tree or flower was a part of God. Instead of considering the soul temple as the physical place where the Holy Spirit works to develop character, it became to him a part of the very essence of God. His teachings were so subtly pantheistic that he could not distinguish these ideas from those presented in the Spirit of Prophecy (SPT #B7:60). The pantheistic views were referred to by Ellen White as "spiritualistic views" (SPT #B7:4).

After repeated pleadings by letter to Dr. J. H. Kellogg, Ellen White was finally led to reveal that his teachings, as portrayed in his book *The Living Temple*, were fully pantheistic (Letter B-242-03) and that it was not safe for people to go to Battle Creek for their training (SPT #B7:15, 33, 34).

Offshoot movements of other types also developed. As a rule their adherents pretended belief in the writings of Ellen White but later repudiated them (2SM12-100). Attention was diverted away from the study of the character of God and how to be like Him as embodied in the messages of Righteousness by Faith. Ellen White characterized the church as "steadily retreating toward Egypt" (5T217).

THE CHURCH IN THE LAST DAYS

God's Plans and the Devil's Sidetracks:

The church in the last days will be brought around again to an understanding of these five major points that the church needs to know. Satan obstructs wherever he can in this.

The Last Church and the Character of God:

God calls upon His people to have a true understanding of His character so that they may tell the world "the truth about God" (MM91-4). "The last rays of merciful light, the last message of mercy to be given to the world, is a revelation of His character of love" (COL415).

When Moses asked to see God, he was shown very little of His form (Ex. 33:22, 23). Instead, God revealed the attributes of His character (Ex. 34:6,7; Ed35). Seven phrases describe His love; two phases describe His justice (ibid). When Philip wanted to see the form of God, Jesus pointed him to the character of God as revealed by His own ministry to the people of Palestine. (5BC1141-2; 5T739; John 14:8-12).

The Old Testament portrayal of His character shows His justice with mercy; the New Testament, His love with justice.

Satan has tried to portray God to be arbitrary, cruel, and vengeful (GC534; 5T738). Remember the antediluvians, he would say. If people do not serve God, He will drown them (PP99-100). He would have others believe that God's justice demands that after a brief time on this earth, the sinner must spend eternity in the fires of hell (GC535-6). But since that approach is so unreasonable and distasteful to many, Satan promoted the doctrine that all will ultimately be saved. The atheist and even those who opposed God most vehemently nevertheless will enjoy lives of bliss in heaven (GC537, 557).

Specifically, here is one statement of the teachings of Satan, "Love is dwelt upon as the chief attribute of God, but it is degraded to a weak sentimentalism, making little distinction between good and evil. God's justice, His denunciation of sin, the requirements of His holy law, are all kept out of sight." (GC558).

Satan propounds theories that are pleasing to the carnal heart. He leads some to believe that God's law is done away with. There is nothing then to condemn the sinner. God will not judge. "Each mind will judge itself," we are told (GC554).

On the other hand, the record of Scripture is too plain to be mistaken. The love of God, as manifested to the nation of Israel and as defined by the life of Christ, is too clear. Through it all we can see the mercy that has tempered His justice. The Lord God caused the flood, and in this sense caused the death of the antediluvians. Only eight believed God and went into the ark. The others doubted that God would do what He said He would do. What would have happened if He had allowed another 100 years or a 1000 years to elapse? Would there have been a Mary, a Joseph, or twelve apostles? What choice did God have?

God opened the earth under Korah, Dathan, and Abiram (PP400-2). The Lord and His angels went to destroy Sodom (Gen. 18:1 to 19:25; PP159-165). He directed Israel in their overthrow of the Canaanites (PP423, 434, 491). Did these events enlighten them? Many in Israel still followed Ashteroth, Chemosh, and Baal.

God had to preserve a people for the coming Messiah. Saul was judged harshly for not eliminating Agag and the Amalekites. (1 Sam. 15:1-16). Why did God order the destruction of those people? They had defied God. They had made an oath to destroy every Israelite (PP300). Years later Saul's relatives, Mordecai and Esther, had to meet the family of Agag in Haman (Esther 2:5; 3:1; 3BC469, 472).

We are presented with another aspect of God's dealings with man in the following quotation. "God destroys no man. Everyone who is destroyed will have destroyed himself" (COL84, See 5T120). How do the above examples of God's destroying force harmonize with quotations like the one just above?

God stated to Adam that the wages of sin would be death, (Gen. 2:17; Rom. 6:23); and, yet, the antediluvians lived 900 years before they died. Was that death their punishment?

Many recognize that a life without the sustaining power of God results in degeneration of the mind and body with death as the endpoint (PP68.2). But there appears to be a second element in disobedience. It is rebellion against the Sovereign of the universe (PK185; Ev365; PP78; 1SM222). And what is the penalty for rebellion? Is it also merely a gradual loss of vitality until death sweeps in on its victim? If the only penalty for sin was the suffering of the results of sinning: - namely, disease, degeneration of cells, and damage to genes, then what would be the need of the resurrection of the wicked? They have paid their penalty for sin already, haven't they? Why not let them be?

No, there is more to be accounted for. They have been deceived and misled by Satan and his agents. They have been in open rebellion. They must see that there is a controversy between good and evil. For God to be fully vindicated, they must have their day in court. They must grasp the love of God and must have a glimpse of the grandeurs of heaven and know this as Satan and his angels know it. Man has not seen this (DA761).

There must be no doubt in anyone's mind as to what the controversy was about and why they are where they are. After viewing the city, after the law of God is displayed in the heavens, after the panoramic presentation before every eye of the details of creation, the origin of evil, and history of God's dealing with the saints and sinners in all ages, the trial and crucifixion of Christ, and after the revelation of God's character of love, they realize fully what they might have had. Yet they still reject it. They are still in rebellion. They still hate God, but have no love for the devil either (GC666-672).

Will they then be allowed to die of old age? Will they be given a second time to suffer the natural consequences of sinning? No, God does not wait for them to die one by one of the ravages of disease. They begin to attack each other, but God says, "Vengeance is mine." He is the only one who can stop the ordeal. They are enveloped and perish in the flames that come from God to recreate the earth (GC672). Before they perish they will suffer knowing that their existence will cease forever, but can this sensation equal that of the Son of God in Gethsemane and at Calvary? (GC668).

The one who loves another person cannot bear the thought of separation. The thought of temporary separation from a loved one is unpleasant, but the thought of permanent separation is too dreadful a thought to endure.

But what is the feeling of one who hates another? Will he dread the thought of eternal separation? Perhaps, but certainly not like the Son and the Father with their great love (DA754; 2T207-9). There was physical suffering heaped upon the Son of God, but others have been tortured as much. The thought of eternal separation from His loved ones, far outweighed the physical suffering that Christ endured (ibid).

A question that is difficult to answer is: why will some remain alive in the flames and suffer longer than others? Why does not God give them all an anesthetic? These are difficult questions. I can say, however, on the word of God that some will suffer longer than others (GC673). Note, however, the decision as to how much punishment, will have been determined by the courts of heaven during the millennium by the living saints working with Christ (GC661). What group in all the universe would be more fair, more sympathetic, and more lenient with the lost souls than Christ and His followers who have lived on the earth? The degree of punishment is not an **arbitrary** exercise in sadism, but it is merciful justice in proportion to their guilt (3SM415). It is called "retributive justice," the "strange act," of God (1SM190; GC541, 627-8; Hebrews 2:1, 2, margin; Isaiah 28:21).

After the wicked have viewed the portrayal of the scenes of the great controversy between Christ and Satan and acknowledged the justice of God in closing their existence, the **glory** of God, described as fire, descends and remakes the earth (GC37, 672).

Some say that it is the revelation of God's love that destroys the wicked. The reference states, "the manifestation of His glory is to them a consuming fire," to those who obeyed not the gospel (GC37).

There are two aspects to the glory of God. To Moses, God revealed His **spiritual** glory of love and justice (Ex. 33:18 to 34:7). On Mt. Sinai God also revealed His **physical** glory as a representation of the glory that will be a consuming fire to the wicked (PP339-40). The description of that event and of the destruction of the wicked at the beginning and end of the millenium leaves little doubt that there will be a revelation of God's character of love, His spiritual glory; but there will also be a revelation of His physical glory which has been veiled and shielded from man for his own safety until the time of the executive judgment (GC657).

If God does not destroy the wicked with His physical glory, then we are presented with a problem. Who does destroy them? Do they commit suicide when they see that every chance of salvation is gone? No, where in the Bible or the Spirit of Prophecy do we find such a concept presented? Instead we read that the sentence of death is passed upon the wicked, and then that sentence is executed (GC661, 668-72). In love to His true followers and in justice to the wicked, He removes evil from the universe forever (PP101, 325; GC543).

Satan would picture God as having nothing to do with this destruction (PP96, 283; GC557). We read in Psalm 10, "He [the ungodly] thinks, in his insolence. 'God never punishes'; his thoughts amount to this, 'There is no God at all'; the dealings of thy justice high are far beyond his sight" (Ps. 10:4 Moffatt).

Since the wicked did not avail themselves of salvation, they are identified with sin (DA107; COL123). Since God intends to destroy all vestiges of sin, they will be caught up in the flames that God uses to cleanse the earth of sin (EW52, 295; GC674). God causes the fire of the last days (GC672). It is not a natural consequence of sin. The wicked destroy themselves by choosing to be outside the city that God protects from the holocaust (7BC986; Heb. 2:2, 3; DA466, 764; GC543, 654.6, 668). The wicked do not run and leap into the flames. For these rejectors of mercy there is no way of escape. No, it is not a time of rejoicing. The tears of those who remain will be wiped away by God Himself (Rev 21:4).

The Last Church and Attitude Toward the Bible and the Spirit of Prophecy:

What will be our reception of the Spirit of the Prophecy now?

"Spiritual darkness has covered the earth and gross darkness the people. There are in many churches skepticism and infidelity in the interpretation of the Scriptures. Many, very many, are questioning the verity and truth of the Scriptures. Human reasoning and the imaginings of the human heart are undermining the inspiration of the Word of God, and that which should be received as granted, is surrounded with a cloud of mysticism. Nothing stands out in clear and distinct lines, upon rock bottom. This is one of the marked signs of the last days" (1SM15).

"The very last deception of Satan will be to make of none effect the testimony of the Spirit of God¤. Satan will work ingeniously, in different ways and through different agencies, to unsettle the confidence of God's remnant people in the true testimony" (1SM48).

It is with **words** that we communicate with each other and with our God. It is Satan's plan to destroy confidence in the Word of God by challenging the Scriptures or the writings of the Spirit of Prophecy. Where he fails in this, he endeavors through the diabolic plot of the human reasoning of philosophy and vain deceit to undermine confidence in **words** themselves as a means of communication.

With some philosophers the very definition of words needs to be clarified, for in their discussions they may shift the meaning of a word to suit their own purposes. Since words may have several meanings, some dialecticians may tacitly undermine confidence in **words** as a means of communication of definite truths. Such philosophy and vain deceit on word meanings may lead theologians to devitalize trust in the Scriptures. Discrepancies and apparent contradictions in the Bible (or the writings of Ellen White) are sought out and their significance exaggerated. It is of interest that in crucial issues God has circumvented these challenges by the use of symbols (such as the sanctuary services), parables, and the living example of Christ.

The Message to Laodicea:

The message to the last church from the True Witness to Laodicea still applies. We may think that because of a good church organizational structure, a large number of baptismal candidates, or the wealth of the church that we are no longer in Laodicea but in Philadelphia or some other church. Individually, while we may profess otherwise, we can still inwardly be lukewarm, poor, blind, and naked spiritually.

It is true that some believers have accepted the message to Laodicea and have brought their lives into harmony with the Lord (2T217). Although we are not to use that message to tear down the church (TM23), we should recognize that the straight testimony called forth by the counsel of the True Witness will result in a "shaking" just before the "Loud Cry" (EW270.6). When it is heeded to its fullest extent, many will leave the church. (EW271; 1SM179). Others will accept the call and take their places. (EW271).

Each of us is to pray and study earnestly for spiritual insight. We are to work by true love and purify the soul of every defilement of sin. We are to wear the white raiment, the imparted character of Christ, by responding to the promptings of the Holy Spirit to do God's will from love, depending upon the power of God for strength. The door into the holy places has been opened by our Saviour (EW42-5; GC435, 490). He, as Executor, of His estate will take our request to the Father and return the answers to us (Heb. 8:1; 9:15-24). Let every request be according to the will of God (Matt. 6:10).

The Last Church and Righteousness by Faith:

Many and varied have been the sidetracks that Satan has placed to misrepresent forgiveness by faith and obedience by faith. Some think that they must wait until they are "good enough" in themselves before coming to Christ. Some hope to perform some "good deed," and then they can be forgiven.

Others come to Christ just as they are. They are "born again," but stop at that point. Imputed righteousness constitutes their whole gospel. They believe that Christ did all their good deeds long ago. They need no works by faith in response to the power of the Holy Spirit. These are "empty house" Christians (Matt. 12:44, 45; DA324), "foolish virgin" Christians (COL412.2), who have no character imparted to them by the power of God. No righteous deeds are found recorded in their halls of memory. They "come to Christ" but fail to **ask** what God would have them do; they do not **seek** to know His will; they fail to press their petitions to the throne for power to live the life of Christ in their sphere of influence (COL145-8, 77.9).

There are others who come to Christ for the free gift of forgiveness. They see the law of God; but because of lack of spiritual insight, they set out to do the will of God in their own strength. Essentially, they are saying, a person is perfect if he trusts in forgiveness by faith and **lives up to all the power that he inherently has**. The strong willed succeed in having a form of godliness. The weak willed become discouraged and fall by the way unless they see that, not in their own strength but, by the power of God they are enabled to obey (SC47, 63-4; COL160.1).

Some Christians talk much of love but omit the teachings of the law. Others claim to be "baptized by the Spirit"; but when you talk of loving obedience, they say that the ten commandments were done away with. Another class honors the law of God, but do not obey it (DA584).

Truly many and varied are the deceptive sidetracks of Satan.

The Last Church and The Foundation Doctrines:

The distinctive doctrines of the Seventh-day Adventist church that have been studied out and that have made the remnant church what it is, will be under special attack (2SM386-95; GC9-11). These include the Sabbath, the state of the dead, the three angels' messages, the investigative judgment, the sanctuary service, our distinctive interpretation of the prophecies of Daniel and the Revelation, and the health message. We should expect the attack from within the church to be, at first, not overt or blatant, but subtle and indirect. We should expect error to be mixed with the true doctrines in such a way as to attack only a portion of the truth (5BC1094-5). For example, the devil might have his agents present the doctrines of the sanctuary in a pure, clear manner, but one key portion would be omitted or distorted in a manner similar to his second temptation of Jesus (DA125). His agents might leave out the blood for the atonement in the holy place or most holy place (Hebrews 9:10-22; 10:19).

Since the purpose of the sanctuary service was to delineate the plan of salvation in such a way as to obviate changes that may occur in the definition of words, we should expect that Satan would attack doctrines based upon the sanctuary especially. Since the veils of the sanctuary represent the flesh of Christ (Hebrews 10:20), he will have some teach a false Christ, one who was exempt from the passions that corrupt humanity (study M.L. Andreasen, *Letters to the Churches*, Leaves of Autumn, 1980). Guilt will not be transferred from the sinner by the "Lamb of God" to the sanctuary in heaven, and then rolled back on Satan in the final atonement, but will be dealt with differently from that portrayed by the sanctuary. Or perhaps the entire ministry of our High Priest at the altar of incense for obedience by faith, would be be glossed over or omitted from the theology. Our fundamental understanding of Daniel 8:14 and the day of atonement service will be challenged. Satan will have his agents bring in a new understanding of the 2300 days, the 1844 message, the investigative judgment, and final atonement.

The Sabbath of the Lord will be under special attack because the keeping of it is an acknowledgement of the authority of God (2SM105). *The world in general will be tested on whether or not there is a sabbath to keep, the Christian world will be tested upon which is the right day to keep, while Seventh-day Adventists will be tested upon **how** the Sabbath is to be kept holy.*

Near the turn of the century, John Bell, of Australia, appears to have written a book with a new interpretation of Bible prophecies. What evidence that we can find indicates that he was taking, "Events in the train of prophecy that had their fulfillment away in the past" and was making them to be fulfilled again in the future (2SM102-3; see A.L. White, *Ellen White*, Vol. 4, pages 274-5). We see a similar thing happening in our time with the prophecies of Daniel and the Revelation. There are those who acknowledge that the time prophecies in those books were fulfilled in the past based upon the day-for-a-year method of prophetic reckoning, but they also believe and teach that "history will be repeated," and these time prophecies will be fulfilled again with the time in a literal day-for-a-day time frame. This they believe in spite of the warning that, "There will never again be a message for the people of God that will be based on time" (1SM188, see also EW75).

Our message for this time is first and foremost to be the three angel's messages as if there had been no time lapse since 1844 (1SM104-7). Since 1844, God has taken time to further train His people on this earth for the final movements. When He has done all that He deems necessary in this training, so that He will be fully vindicated when He calls for the "mighty shaking," then the closing events will proceed as though there was no great time hiatus between 1844 and the final movements (1SM111-2).

Through psychology, philosophy, and other sciences that deal with the mind, a whole false plan for character development will come into the churches (2SM351). Satanic teachings which foster existentialism and anarchy have been promoted in the public schools of our country through the concepts and role playing techniques of "values clarification" or the six or seven stage theory of "moral development" propounded by Harvard's Lawrence Kholberg, etc. By these and similar "scholarly" methods, the doctrines of the "Humanist Manifesto" promote the spiritualistic teachings, "'that man is the creature of progression; that it is his destiny from his birth to progress, even to eternity, toward the Godhead.' And again: 'Each mind will judge itself and not another.' 'The judgment will be right, because it is the judgment of self¤'" (GC554; EV601).

Kholberg has been quoted in the *National Enquirer* as saying, "A person in the sixth stage can and should violate laws he feels are unjust. This is a principle of moral justice we consider preferable to the common morality as expressed in the law of the land or the Ten Commandments." (See D. Schwartz: "Public Schools are Teaching Children That It's OK to Break the Law." *National Enquirer*, 11-2-76, p.44.) According to Kholberg's tenets, a person who is properly developed morally to above his stage four no longer believes in retributive justice (cf. Hebrews 2:2, RSV; GC540-1).

How extensively have these false concepts been placed in the Bible text material of Seventh-day Adventist schools, academies, and colleges? This deserves careful examination. I have a recording of a meeting on March, 1983, of educators who were members of a committee that was established by the General Conference to rewrite the Bible-course-textbook material of our church schools, colleges, and universities. At this meeting the merits of Kholberg's theories were extolled.* According to the tape recording of that meeting, these educators are on their third revision of those textbooks as of 1983. *Parents are you listening to what is being taught to your children?*

"At the same time anarchy is seeking to sweep away all law, not only divine, but human.... the world-wide dissemination of the same teachings that led to the French Revolution,–all are tending to involve the whole world in a struggle similar to that which convulsed France" (Ed228).

The whole trend of modern medicine and the health care institutions of the church are predominently oriented toward "acute

---

* See J.K. Testerman: *Kholberg's Stages of Moral Development: Implications for Theology*, unpublished manuscript and presentation at the March, 1983, meeting care" medicine. In that medical care system, the patient lives a certain way; he gets sick; he consults with a physician; he receives a prescription; but little or nothing is done to help him correct his faulty life style. The result is that he continues on in his uninformed, health-destroying, life style until the body degenerates to death.

Our merciful Saviour's plan is preventive medicine. The instructions that the Lord gave to Israel in the wilderness were based upon washing cleanliness, isolation of infectious diseases, and a vegetarian diet.

"Christ began this work of redemption by reforming the physical habits of man" (3T486).

"God has permitted the light of health reform to shine upon us in these last days, that by walking in the light we may escape many of the dangers to which we shall be exposed" (CDF22).

"I was again shown that the health reform is one branch of the work which is to fit a people for the coming of the Lord. It is as closely connected with the third angel's message as the hand is with the body¤. Men and women cannot violate natural law by indulging depraved appetites and lustful passions, and not violate the law of God. Therefore He has permitted the light of health reform to shine upon us, that we may see our sin in violating the laws which He has established in our being" (3T161).

"The health reform is closely connected with the third message, yet it is not the message" (1T559; Romans 14:17).

Acute health care has its place. We would not close that down. What we must do is build up the preventive aspects of our health ministry to balance the acute care work. This will take sacrificial work, perseverance, and patience since remuneration for health care from insurance carriers and government agencies are directed toward paying for acute care. Essentially none of it is available for preventive health programs.

The evidence that we have been given is that God does not intend to work in our time as Christ worked when He was on earth. During our time, God intends to demonstrate before the world that His laws are perfect, and just, and good, and that obedience to them results in a rich reward. God could easily perform miracles and cure everyone, but what would that prove? Why should He do that for them, and they continue on in violation of His laws of health? In the realm of health laws we can see the results of disobedience and of the benefits of obedience because they can be visibly contrasted. The advances of science can demonstrate objectively the advantages of living in harmony with God's laws. Satan will attempt to cloud the contrast by the working of miracles; and where God limits these, he will perform imitation miracles, deceptions (2SM52-55). However, only the most obstinate will deny the evidence.

God intends to test humanity in regard to their attitude toward His laws. Will it be loving obedience to His ways or shall we do what we think is right? We need not fear for God will work with his medical missionaries, "Natural means used in accordance with God's will, bring about supernatural results. We ask for a miracle, and the Lord directs the mind to some simple remedy" (2SM346).

> "Let no one obtain the idea that the Institute is the place for them to come to be raised up by the prayer of faith. That is the place to find relief from disease by treatment and right habits of living, and to learn how to avoid sickness" (1T561).

> "And God has pledged Himself to keep this human machinery in healthful condition if the human agent will obey His laws and cooperate with God" (MM221).

> "If our will and way are in accordance with God's will and way; if we do the pleasure of our Creator, He will keep the human organism in good condition, and restore the moral, mental, and physical powers, in order that He may work through us to His glory. Constantly His restoring power is manifested in our bodies" (1BC1118).

The above quotation is loaded with meaning. God has made out a will for His children. Those that are adopted into His family can have access to all power and all wisdom (MH514). God promises to give them **both the desire to change their life style and the mental-moral power to do it, if they are but "willing to be made willing"** (MH514; MB142). God has arranged the plan of salvation so that all glory goes to Him. He does not intend to give His glory to another (Isaiah 48:8). His servants in the health institutes do not take credit to themselves. They are to consider that after they have done all, they are but unprofitable servants (Luke 17:10). God, not man, is to be vindicated before the universe.

In the last days, God intends to establish sanitarium type institutions in many places where "genuine medical missionary work" can be carried out. His servants are to "carry forward a work of physical healing, combined with the teaching of the Word" (2SM54).

This healing is to be done primarily with God's "true remedies" (MH127). When we put into practice proper nutrition from whole foods, as grown, without animal products or refined foods of any kinds, judicious conditioning exercise, water, sunshine, temperance, fresh pure air, proper rest, cleanliness, and the trusting in Divine power for the desire and the power to do this, we see dramatic results in many of our patients with chronic degenerative diseases that are epidemic in our time. We see this taking place before our eyes as many self-sacrificing workers are pooling their talents in several such institutions.

What are the results? In the one with which I am connected, we regularly watch as patients with arteries plugged up to the extent that they need or have had coronary artery bypass heart surgery, obtain regression of their arteriosclerosis. We see that 65 percent of patients who enter with with a diagnosis of hypertension and on drugs can have their blood pressure controlled below 140/90 without medication. We see the sharp shooting, burning pains of diabetic neuropathy disappear in 80 percent of the patients with that, previously untreatable, problem within 15 days, and the pains remain away for at least the forty months that we have followed them on God's original diet of unrefined total vegetarian diet. Arthritis, obesity, and other chronic degenerative diseases respond to the simple application of God's natural remedies along with his divine power.

The advantages of better health that have accrued to the members of the Seventh-day Adventist church have been published in the well known health studies from Loma Linda University School of Health. Adventist's who live on a lacto-ovo-vegetarian diet have a five to ten year longer life span than do those who eat meat regularly. The sad part of the story is that only about half of the church membership have given up the use of flesh foods. Another finding is that, although the lacto-ovo-vegetarian Adventist's may live those five to ten years longer, they end up with heart attacks, cancerous lesions (except for smoker's lung cancer), hypertension, and strokes at about the same percentage rates as do their non-adventist friends.

God is leading His people back step by step to His original diet of fruit, vegetables, whole grains, and nuts (CDF380). Let us resolve to follow "the cloud" of protection that He has placed over us in the health reform message for our time. (For more information, please see Chapters 20-24 of this book.)

The Last Church and Witnessing, The Vindicative Atonement:

It is at sunset that the rays of the sun reflect down to the earth. Then it is that the brilliant orange, yellow, and crimson hues may be seen with a background of blue. We are living in the sunset time of this world's history (John 9:4; EW48.1). We are each called to be part of this "cloud of witnesses" that will reflect the character of God to the world (Heb. 12:1; 9T22; COL415.9). Just as clouds at sunset must be in position to reflect the sun, so also are God's witnesses to stand in their appointed places for Him (COL326-7; PP638.7). Satan knows this and redoubles his efforts to interfere with this testimony in each of their lives (5T462; COL79). He will also put up his own "cloud" of false Christians and miracles to screen the truth.

There will be false conversions (Hosea 5:6, 7; RH04-14-53). The devil will have his "born again" counterfeits (GC464). His servants will "speak in tongues" to imitate Pentecost. His agents will perform real miracles; and where their power is restricted, they will perform imitation miracles (MM110; 5T698) designed to "sweep the whole world into the ranks of spiritualism" (GC562; Ev602.9).

The church will be divided into ministers and spectators. The doctrines of pantheism that would lull the church members into the feeling that it is not necessary to be a missionary will be brought forth by the devil. Through his efforts the true revival and reformation will be labelled an off-shoot movement or fanaticism (GW170; GC464).

We should expect Satan to work in subtle and ingenious ways to cloud our understanding of the sanctuary service, confuse our understanding of the prophecies of Daniel and Revelation, and undermine our faith in the Bible and the Spirit of prophecy. Person after person will come to undermine the pillars of the faith that God has carefully built up in our past and has preserved and illuminated, especially for the "time of the end" (2SM388-9; 1SM208)

God intends that the message of heathful living shall be part of the third angel's message (CDF74-7). Genuine medical missionary work is the teaching of a better way of life for health of body and strength of mind to assist in salvation of men and women from Satanic power (MM21, 23). It encompasses much more than what is usually done in our hospitals (MM27-8). Since Satan intends to put himself up as the great medical missionary (MM87-8), should we not expect the devil to use every tactic to thwart the development of true medical missionary work as he did in the crisis years around 1888? A strong well balanced health reform program would put the lie to Satan's claim that God's laws of health, as well as His other laws, are faulty.

Some will disdain the counsel of healthful living (5T196; 2SM54). They would rather turn to those who can heal with drugs. They may turn to workers of supposed miracles rather than give up unhealthful habits of eating and living (5T197; 5BC1099), and thus they may be led to put their trust in "spiritualistic physicians" (CH454).

Some may **overspiritualize** the health message. They are in danger of making it the body of their message (cf. 6T288-93; Letter K-55-99). They fail to see that even though the health message is to be part of the third angel's messages; it is **neither** the gospel nor the third angel's message (CDF74-7).

Chapter 20

THE PURPOSE OF THE HEALTH MESSAGE

No loving father leaves his children without knowledge of what they can do to enjoy physical well-being, strong mental health, and spiritual vigor. Our heavenly Father is foremost in caring for us. Jesus "went about doing good, and healing all that were oppressed by the devil" (Acts 10:38). God wants us to "prosper and be in health" physically as well as spiritually (3 John 2). This was His plan for Israel when He delivered them from Egypt (Exodus 15:26). It is even more important for the church in the last days when Satan seeks to deceive even the very elect (Matt. 24:24).

The Lord had a unique message of health which He began to present to the last church in the mid-1850's With the health message he wanted to demonstrate that Obedience to His laws resulted in good. Obedience to His laws of the physical nature resulted in improved health, something that could be seen, felt, and measured. This knowledge would open the way for confidence in His laws for the mental renewal and spiritual health.

Every one is elected (predestined) to be saved, but *they* must choose salvation. They must "run" for the offices of "king and priest" that is set aside for them (Rev. 1:6). What is happening to prevent the inhabitants of this earth from *choosing to be saved*? Satan uses deceptions and *chemical warfare* against our minds. His prime weapon is alcoholic beverages. In the last remnant of time he will use every conceivable techinque and chemical agent to impair the reasoning capacity of man. Notice what he is doing with tobacco, alcohol, tea and other caffeine beverages, narcotics, and other mind-altering chemicals. To these agents he adds faulty diet and sedentary living. With these tools, Satan hopes to sweep the whole world into his camp with his deceptions.

God's approach is to teach us of the tactics of our enemy and then give us the _desire_ and _power_ to overcome every natural, inherited or cultivated tendency that goes against His laws of health. In the great controversy between good and evil, turning from disobedience of the laws of health to obedience of them will result in such dramatic changes in physical well-being that it will be considered a miracle. This appears to be God's approach in the last remnant of time.

"The way in which Christ worked was to preach the Word, and to relieve suffering by miraculous works of healing, But I am instructed that we cannot now work in this way, for Satan will exercise his power by working miracles. God's servants today could not work by means of miracles, because spurious works of healing, claiming to be divine, would be wrought.

"For this reason the Lord has marked out a way in which His people are to carry forward a work of physical healing, combined with the teaching of the Word. Sanitariums are to be established, and with these institutions are to be connected workers who will carry forward genuine medical missionary work. Thus a guarding influence is thrown around those who come to the institutions for treatment" (2SM54).

Preventive medicine has been the Lord's main thrust for healing from the beginning of sin. This is quite evident from the laws of health that God gave to Israel through Moses in the wilderness (see Leviticus and Numbers). He has given much more specific information to the church in our time.

In 1853 Ellen White began to write against the evils of tobacco. Later on she was given insights into other unhealthy practices and instructions on diet. In 1865 Ellen White published six health pamphlets on "Disease and Its Causes." Since that date, she has given us much additional advice. The following are a few important concepts which were put into practice in the Battle Creek Sanitarium with great success.

"I was again shown that the health reform is one branch of the great work which is to fit a people for the coming of the Lord. It is as closely connected with the third angel's message as the hand is with the body....

Therefore He has permitted the light of health reform to shine upon us, that we may see our sin in violating the laws which He has established in our being" (3T161, 1871).

"Again and again I have been shown that God is trying to lead us back, step by step, to His original design—that man should subsist upon the natural products of the earth" (Christian Temperance p. 119, 1890).

"*If we plan wisely*, that which is most conducive to health can be secured in almost every land. The various preparations of rice, wheat, corn, and oats are sent abroad everywhere, also beans, peas, and lentils. These, with native or imported fruits, and the variety of vegetables that grow in each locality, give an opportunity to select a dietary that is complete without the use of flesh meats" (MH299, 1905).

"You should keep grease out of your food. It defiles any preparation of food you may make" (2T63, 1868).

"The grease cooked in the food renders it difficult to digestion" (CH114, 1890).

"When properly prepared, olives, like nuts, supply the place of butter and flesh meats. The oil, as eaten in the olive, is far preferable to animal oil or fat" (MH298, 1905).

There are some who wish to make an issue over whether these statements about "grease" apply to "oil" as well. Webster's dictionary fails to distinguish between oil and grease. Grease = "rendered animal fat" or "oily matter." Oil = "Any of various kinds of greasy combustible substances obtained from animal, vegetable, and mineral matter." *Grease* is *oily,* and *oil* is *greasy*. Oil is some kind of grease, and we are admonished not to use "grease of any kind."

Chemically speaking, the distinction between a "grease" and an "oil" may be of academic importance but not of dietary importance since the oily grease can be turned into a greasy oil by warming. Whether a fatty acid compound is more of a gel or a liquid depends upon the length of the fatty acid chains and the number of unsaturated double bonds. Long chain saturated fats (18 carbons or so) which would be unctuous at room temperature are dissolved in the mixture of polyunsaturated and short chain saturated fats. It might take, gram for gram, less emulsifiers to prepare a long chain polyunsaturated liquid oil for digestion than it would a long chain saturated "hard fat"; but, to my knowledge, this has not been demonstrated.

Basically, the intestinal tract works in a water phase and not in an oil medium. All the oily characteristics of free fats, whether liquid or unctuous, need to be dealt with before the digestion of proteins, carbohydrates, or even fat can proceed properly.

Even so, we need not guess about what Ellen White meant in regard to the use of sugar and "grease of any kind." Dr. J.H. Kellogg was a close contemporary of James and Ellen White. In fact, they had encouraged him to become a physician and had helped him financially to do so. Dr. J.H. Kellogg was against the use of refined sugar and oil in the Battle Creek Sanitarium. When, about 1904, his brother, Will, added sugar to the cornflake cereal recipe, J.H. Kellogg strongly disapproved of that move. Also, he must have understood the above statements by Ellen White about "grease" to mean any type of free fat. In 1877, He wrote:

> "The objection is not against fat, per se, but against taking it in a free state. When taken in the form in which nature presents them, enclosed in cells in such vegetable foods as maize, oatmeal, nuts, and some fruits, fats are wholesome and nutritious elements of food. It is only when separated from the other elements and taken in a free state that they become unwholesome. When taken into the stomach in the form in which nature furnishes them, they offer no obstacle to digestion. It is only when taken as free fats that they become a means of producing disturbance of digestive functions. When taken in their natural state, vegetable fats are likely to be taken only in such quantity as can be digested.... It makes little or no difference, so far as the interference with digestion is concerned, whether the fat is animal or vegetable.... The persistent efforts of individuals to discover some cheap vegetable substitute for butter and lard are painfully ludicrous.... We do not recommend the use of any free fat" (J.H. Kellogg, *Health Reformer*, May, 1877).

Free fats were excluded from the food at Battle Creek at least four years before 1875 when J.H. Kellogg graduated from medical school and was connected with Battle Creek. We note the menu for a dinner at the rededication of the Battle Creek Sanitarium as reported by a friendly editor of the local Battle Creek Journal on July 21, 1871. He commented, "It is to be noticed that butter, *grease of all kinds*, tea, coffee, spice, pepper, ginger, and nutmeg, were wholly discarded in the cookery, and were not in use upon the tables...."(D.E. Robinson, The Story of Our Health Message, Southern Pub. Assoc. 1943, p.161).

Ellen White said, "Fruits, grains, and vegetables, prepared in a simple way, free from spice and grease of all kinds, make, with milk or cream, the most healthful diet (CDF92).

She also said, "Let the diet reform be progressive. Let the people be taught how to prepare food without the use of milk or butter. Tell them that the time will soon come when there will be no safety in using eggs, milk, cream, or butter, because disease in animals is increasing in proportion to the increase of wickedness among men....

"God will give His people ability and tact to prepare wholesome food without these things. Let our people discard all unwholesome recipes" (CDF349).

Some respond to the oil question by saying, "oil was used in Bible times for food. In fact, in the time of Elijah and Elisha God helped two widows by miraculously supplying them with oil." Yes, that is true, but we must remember that the Bible records what was done. That, however, cannot be construed to be dietary advice.

In spite of the fact that God had told them not to eat the fat or blood of animals (Lev. 7:22-27), Israel ate it anyway. At their insistence, God gave them flesh foods (Ps. 78:17-31). We can read the menu, a food frequency list, which they selected. It included produce, honey, "oil out of the flinty rock," butter, milk, and the "fat of lambs and rams" (Deut. 32:13,14). Even though all of that came from God, they suffered the consequences of the diet they selected. Their own bodies suffered from the free fat, and their own souls suffered from the lack of faith and trust. They "waxed fat, and kicked: thou art grown thick, thou art covered with fatness." They then forsook God (Deut. 32:15). Whether by heart attacks or strokes we do not know, but Psalm 78:31 tells us that God "slew the fattest of them."

In Proverbs we are given two bits of wisdom. "He that loveth wine and oil shall not be rich"; and "It is not good to eat much honey" (Proverbs 21:17; 25:27).

Archeological studies of the Pharoah's tell us that their eating habits were quite similar to civilized people in our time, even to the use of refined flour. Examination of thousands of Egyptian mummies tells us that they had obesity, atherosclerosis, diabetes, and degenerative arthritis just as we have now.

Chapter 21

THE ROLE OF CHOLESTEROL AND "FREE FAT" IN DISEASE?

Physiology books tell us of five interesting, very important points in the study of cholesterol. First, the body can make cholesterol and does so in many different cells. Second, the body cannot break the phenanthrene cholesterol ring structure once it is made. Third, the more oily-greasy food that we eat, the more cholesterol the body makes in the liver and in the small intestines. The liver makes cholesterol and converts over half of it to bile salts. This is the "soap" of the intestines, to emulsify the oily-greasy food that we eat. The small intestines absorb some of the cholesterol from animal products (flesh foods, milk products, or eggs), some from the bile, but **it also makes some more cholesterol** to be a constituent part of low density lipoproteins (LDL). These LDL particles are really little balls of fat, protein, and cholesterol made up for cell food. Fourth, the main way that cholesterol gets out of the body is in the bile and by riding out of the intestines on fiber and plant sterols (phytosterols). Another ball of fat, called high density lipoprotein (HDL), draws the extra cholesterol from the cells, hauls it back to the liver where it is eliminated in the bile as cholesterol along with bile salts. Fifth, some people have a hereditary enzyme defect, or they acquire an enzyme defect, which causes them to make too much cholesterol.[1]

The result is that a steady diet of foods that are low in fiber and high in free fat causes a few more milligrams of cholesterol to be formed than is removed from the body by HDL, fiber, and phytosterols. Day by day, cholesterol from this natural, cholesterol-containing LDL, cell food gradually accumulates in the body. This is of special importance to the hardworking muscle and elastic cells in the artery walls. The normal pulsatile pressure in the arteries bends the cholesterol crystals in the cells and by a piezoelectric effect damages the cells in the walls of the arteries. Some cells die and plug the inside of the artery. Some cells grow and induce fibrosis thickening (hardening) of the artery. The extra cholesterol in the bile precipitates out in the gallbladder to form stones.[2]

If our usual diet also includes meat, fish, fowl, milk, and eggs, foods which contain plenty of free fat and extra cholesterol without fiber, the atherosclerosis proceeds at an accelerated rate. Vegetarians who eat milk and eggs, but no flesh foods, have a five to ten year longer life expectancy[3-5] than the meat-eating civilized people have. The other side of the coin is that, with a few exceptions, the vegetarians die of the same diseases and with the same degree of arteriosclerosis as do the omnivores. Only aboriginal societies are noticeably free of degenerative vascular diseases. Generally, those natives subsist on a vegetarian diet free of refined foods with perhaps only about ten percent of their calories coming from animal products.[6]

When experimental animals, such as rabbits or monkeys, were fed their regular chow of fruit and cereal plus extra cholesterol, equivalent in the human to two to three egg yolks per day, along with added fat, they develop atherosclerosis. Fat in the free state (outside the plant cell wall) caused their arteries to develop fibrosis and thickening in the artery wall and/or plugging of the inside of the artery from this cholesterol-fatty material and cellular debris. Coconut type oil plus cholesterol caused the typical atheroma (plugging) lesion; peanut oil with cholesterol stimulated an overgrowth of fibrous cells in the artery wall with thickening and extra collagen scar tissue; milk fat with cholesterol produced an accumulation of fatty material in the artery wall.[7] The good news is that these changes from free fat and cholesterol gradually reversed when the cholesterol and oil was stopped.[8] Also, the coronary artery lesions in the human can be reversed on a low fat, low cholesterol, high fiber diet alone,[9-10] or by a modified fat restricted diet plus cholesterol lowering medication.[11-12]

1. W.F. Ganong: *Review of Medical Physiology*, 8th ed. Lange Medical Pub., Los Altos, CA, 1977, pp. 228-30, 356-58, 378-9.
2. G.S. Boyd: In, A.J. Vergroesen, *The Role of Fat in Human Nutrition*, Academic Press, London, 1975, pp. 353-380.

3. F.R. Lemon and R.T. Walden: *JAMA* 198:117, 1966.
4. R.L. Phillips, F.R. Lemon, W.L. Beeson, J.W. Kuzma: *Am J Clin Nutr* 31:S191, 1978.
5. J.W. Kuzma: Why Adventists Live Longer, *Ministry*, Sept., 1989.
6. A. Keys, N. Kimura, A. Kusukawa, etal.: *Ann Intern Med* 48:83, 1958.
7. R.W. Wissler: In, E. Braunwald, et al: *Heart Diseases*, Vol. 2, W.B. Saunders Co, 1980, pp. 1221-1245.
8. M.C. Armstrong, E.D. Warner, and W.E. Conner: *J Atherosclerosis Res* 8:237, 1968.
9. D. Ornish, S.E. Brown, L.W. Scherwitz, J.H. Billings, W.T. Armstrong, T.A. Ports, S.M. McLanahan, R.L. Kirkeeide, R.J. Brand, and K.L. Gould: *Lancet* 336:129, 1990.
10. M.G. Crane and G. Shavlik: *Preliminary report,* Oct.1, 1989.
11. C.R. Ost: Scandinav *J Clin & Lab Investig,* Sup 93:241-45, 1967.
12. D.H. Blankenhorn, S.A. Nessium, and R.L. Johnson: *JAMA* 257: 3233-40, 1987.

Chapter 22

OTHER WAYS "FREE FAT" CAUSE DISEASE

Oil that we usually get in the diet comes in different carbon chain lengths. They may be 12, 14, 16, 18, or 20 carbon atoms in the chain hooked together with a single or a double bond between them. Two oxygen atoms are linked on one end. Wherever there is a single bond between the carbons, there are also two hydrogens hooked to each carbon atom directly opposite from each other. Wherever there is a double bond, only one hydrogen is hooked to the carbon, and that double bond is called, "unsaturated." This is very important because when there is a double bond with only one hydrogen, the chain takes a 60 degree turn at each of the carbons. If the hydrogen atoms project in the same directions from the carbons at the double bond, this is called a "cis" arrangement. This cis arrangement gives a 120 degree "U"-shaped turn in the chain. The fat in plants occurs only as the cis isomer. If the hydrogen atoms project in opposite directions, they make a jagged "Z"-shaped trans fat. Trans fatty acids are formed when fats are heated in the process of refinement or when they go through the stomach of a ruminant animal.[1-2]

The number of carbon atoms in the chain, the number and location of the double bonds, and the direction of the hydrogen atoms are very important because these determine the size and shape of the fat molecules. We will come back to this later.

The body can make saturated and monounsaturated fats, but they cannot make fatty acids with two or more double bonds, called polyunsaturated fats. There are two main oils we must get in the food because we cannot make them. These "essential" oils are eighteen carbons long with two or three double bonds precisely located. Our bodies have a daily need of about three grams of omega-6 linoleic acid or gamma-linolenic acid and one gram of omega-3 alpha-linolenic acid.[3-4] These are used to make very important chemicals called prostaglandins, thromboxanes, leukotrienes, and 18-hydroxy fats.

Most fruit, vegetables, grains, tubers, and green leafy vegetables are relatively low in fat content, usually below 20 percent of calories. On the other hand, the nuts, olives, avocados, and high fat seeds such as soybeans or sunflower seeds are high in fat. In plant produce, the essential fatty acids generally make up over half of the fatty acids. This is not true for the fats in flesh foods, milk, and eggs. Half or more of the calories from beef, pork, milk, and eggs come from fat, and less than 12 percent of beef, pork, and butter fatty acids are of the essential type.[5] The animals have used up the essential fats and stored other types such as monounsaturated or fully saturated fats in their tissues.

The process of refining soybeans to soy margarine further complicates the problem of getting good fat and other fat soluble nutrients. Over half of the essential oils in the soybean have been changed to saturated or monounsaturated oil, and over 25 percent of those fats with two or three double bonds have been bent out of shape from the cis to the trans isomer.[5-6] Also many double bonds become oxidized.

By nine major ways an excess of refined fats and animal fats can upset our health. These are discussed below.

Obesity: The first problem is "empty calories." Fats furnish nine calories per gram which is over twice what protein or carbohydrate furnishes. To be marketed in the free state, they need to be "refined" to remove certain chemicals that discolor the oil, cause spattering in the skillet, or cause the oil to turn rancid easily. During processing nearly all of the protein, carbohydrate, minerals, vitamins, fiber, and plant sterols are removed. Other foods must then provide for this imbalance. The average American adds about an ounce of this high calorie, oily-greasy material daily to his food. One would have to eat fifteen medium sized ears of corn or four ounces of soybeans to get that much oil. One of the serious ailments afflicting civilized nations is obesity. We can understand how easy it is for a person to become overweight on high calorie fatty foods.

Interference with Digestion: When they are in the free state, outside the plant cells, oily grease interferes with digestion. Fats have the highest caloric density of all foods. They prolong the emptying time of the stomach,[7-8] coat the foods, and interfere with the proper action of digestive enzymes on protein in the stomach. Studies need to be made to determine the effect of the free fats on the absorption of large complexes of amino acids, macromolecules, which may be absorbed as they are and upset the immune system. Studies should also be made to determine which way the small intestines will absorb fat. Shall it be absorbed into the lymph channels as cholesterol-containing chylomicrons and VLDL or absorbed into the portal vein as lecithin–like phospholipids? To put it another way, if the fat is presented more slowly to the gut such as by a gradual release of fat from within the plant fiber, does it go directly to the liver through the portal veins rather than go to the lungs and body first through the lymph system as it does when free fat is eaten?[9] This would make a difference in the way the body metabolizes the fat.

Cholesterol Build-up in Body Tissues: The combination of increased formation of cholesterol to emulsify and utilize the added free fats, along with the lowered fiber intake, results in a gradual accumulation of cholesterol in the body cells. In the arteries the repeated change in pressure with each heart beat distorts the fibrous tissue and the cholesterol crystals. It appears that in the artery wall, this repetitious irritation by the cholesterol crystal through its piezoelectric effect induces thickening of the fibrous tissue and causes the death of the cholesterol-loaded phagocytes. The result is hardening of the arteries and/or plugging of the inside of the artery.[10]

Fatty Acids Make Cell Membranes: Fatty acids are used for more than a source of energy. Every cell has a double lining of lecithins which are fatty acids chemically hooked up with a phosphorus complex. Some cells change their cell walls ever five minutes. Inside this doubly-lined cell wall there are a number of "cell workshops" which also have a double lining of lecithins. The body does not use lecithins directly from the food, but breaks them down and makes its own lecithins, designed especially for our bodies from the fat, protein, and glucose that we eat.

The important thing is this. If we eat too much saturated fats or trans fats and get them into the cell walls, the cell walls will be too stiff to work properly. An excessive build-up of cholesterol will also cause the cell walls to be stiff. Polyunsaturated fats in the wall help it to be flexible. Stiff cell walls are subject to easy attack by viruses and germs. They are more likely to succumb to cancer and other problems.[11] From studies that Aloia and I made on trans fats in fat stores and cell membranes, these trans fats gradually leave the body fat stores and cell membranes so that within a year they have been exchanged for fresh new ones from the diet.[12]

Proper Cell Fats Produce Proper Cell Chemicals:[13-14] The cells use fatty acids from their cell walls and from elsewhere as raw material for the formation of four kinds of key chemicals in body function. These are prostaglandins, thromboxanes, leukotrienes, and 18-hydroxyfats. Omega-6 fats are channeled through the arachidonic acid pathway, and the omega-3 fats are channeled through the eicosapentanoic acid pathway. If the major chemical pathway is through arachidonic acid, the type of prostaglandins and thromboxanes will cause the arteries to constrict and the platelets to be sticky.[15] Meat, milk, and eggs are a source of preformed arachidonic acid, and fish are a source of preformed eicosapentanoic acids.

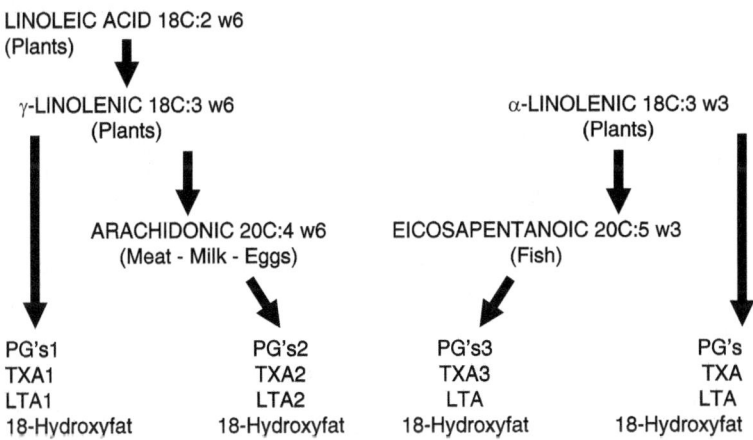

There is much to learn, but available evidence points out that fatty acids in the cell membrane are of great importance in cell chemistry. Just how this is, remains to be worked out; but we know how to get the best source of fatty acids. If we go second hand to the animals, we get an arachidonic acid type of fat in predominance. If we go to the fish, we get an eicosapentanoic type of fat in predominance. If we go to processed oils, the products from omega-6 fats will predominate. If we go to the plants, the body can select a pathway that goes through either of those 20-carbon fats, or else go through pathways entirely different, starting from the 18C:2 w6 or 18C:3 w3 source chemicals. Who among us can say that that is not important? In one study "a 1% absolute increase in a-linolenic acid (adipose stores) was associated with a decrease of 5 mm Hg in systolic blood pressure."[16] A vegetarian diet has been shown to dramatically change platelet fatty acids and platelet function.[17]

Proper Fats Needed For The Immune System:[18-20] In the body certain lymphocytes, called T-cells, use the leukotrienes from fats to communicate with other lymphocytes, called B-cells, and polymorphonuclear (polys) cells. Thus, the type of fats that we eat affects how our body responds to infectious agents that can cause disease whether it be a common cold or a cancer. For example, in rheumatoid arthritis the body appears to respond to the infectious agent in this way.[21] The T-lymphocytes direct the B-lymphocytes, with a leukotriene, to make antibodies against the arthritis germ. The T-lymphocytes also direct the polys by a leukotriene to search out the germ-antibody complex, engulf it, and digest it. It the wrong fat is in the diet, the system fails to do its job, and the germ continues to cause distress. If the person has an intake of sweets of refined sugar, the polys are blinded and have difficulty finding the germ-antibody complex, so that defense system does not work.[22]

Fat and Oxygen Transport: Diets that are high in free or visible fats raise the blood fat level and cause the red blood cells to stick together in what is called "rouleau formation." This situation may last as long as twelve hours after a fatty meal.[23] So long as they are in this condition they cannot take on oxygen readily in the lung, nor can they pass freely into the very small capillaries and give up their oxygen readily.

Balls of Fat (Micelles) Damage Tissue: Other authors have described a situation in which little balls of fat, called micelles, get in high concentrations in the tissues on a high fat diet. These can disrupt cell membranes, like miniscule buzz saws. If this should occur in a critical cell like the conducting nerve bundle in the heart, it can cause a "bundle branch block" or an arrhythmia.[24]

High Fat Diet And Toxic Radicals:[25-26] The high fat diet contributes in yet another way to cause cancer of the skin, cancer of the colon, and diverticulosis of the colon. The unsaturated double bonds are protected from the attack of oxygen so long as they are within the plant cell structure. From the moment that the grains or other plant material are ground or the oil is pressed out of the produce, oxygen begins to attack the double bonds. The more double bonds that there are in the oil, the greater will be the number of oxidized double bonds. These oxidized fats then make up the cell membranes, a dangerous place for them to be.

When there is a high concentration of polyunsaturated triglycerides or cholesterol in the blood and skin, these may be irradiated by sunlight and changed into toxic radicals. These toxic radicals damage the skin cells so that they become cancerous. A somewhat similar situation occurs in the large bowel. When a person is on a diet that is low in fiber and high in polyunsaturated fats, the double bonds of the fat, the bile salts, and cholesterol can be attacked by bacteria in the colon with the formation of poisonous toxic radicals. These toxic radicals can cause damage to the lining of the large bowel so that little diverticuli, out pouching, of the colon develop or cancer of the colon starts. Cancers of the skin, breast, ovaries, pancreas, prostate, and colon have all been attributed to a diet high in polyunsaturated oils or animal fats.[27] To make things worse, these toxic radicals from fat and rancid cholesterol increase the risk of coronary heart disease.

1. D. Sgantas and F.A. Kummerow: Am J Clin Nutr 23:1111-1119, l975.
2. R.L. Anderson, C.S. Fullmer, Jr., and E.J. Hollenback: J of Nutr 105:393-400, l975.
3. L. Anderson, M.V. Dibble, P.R. Turkki, H.S. Mitchell, and H.J. Rynbergen: Nutrition in Health and Disease, 17ed. J.B. Lippincott Co., Philadelphia, 1982, p. 44.
4. R.J. Holman and S.B. Johnson: In Dietary Fats and Health, eds. E.G. Perkins and W.J. Visek, Am Oil Chemists' Society, Champaign, Illinois, 1983, pp 247-266.
5. F.N. Hepburn, J. Exler, J.L. Weihrauch: JADA 86:788-793, 1987.
6. D.L. Carpenter and H.T. Stover: J Amer Oil Chem Soc 50:372-376, 1973
7. J.N. Hunt and D.F. Stubbs: J Physiol 245:209-225, 1975.
8. R. Jian, N. Vigernon, Y. Najean, and J.J. Bernier: Digestive Diseases and Science 27:705-711, 1982.
9. C.M. Surawicz, D.R. Saunders, J. Sillery, C.E. Rubins: Am J Physiol 240:G157-162, 1981.
10. W.A. Boyd: A Textbook of Pathology. Lea & Febiger, Philadelphia, PA, 1943, p. 395.
11. R. Aloia: Loma Linda VAH, Loma Linda, CA., Personal communication.
12. M.G. Crane, R. Zielinski, and R. Aloia: Am J Clin Nutr S48:920, 1988.
13. J.E. Kinsella, G. Bruchner, J. Mai, and J. Shimp: Am J Clin Nutr 34:2307-18, 1981.
14. Marshall, LA, A Szczesniewski, and PV Johnston: Am J Clin Nutr 38:895-900, l983.

15. S. Moncada and J.R. Vane: *NEJMed* 300:1142-1147, 1979.
16. E.M. Berry and J. Hirsch: *Am J Clin Nutr* 44:336-340, 1986.
17. M. Fisher, P.H. Levine, B. Weiner, I.S. Ockene, B. Johnson, M.H. Johnson, A.M. Natale, C.H. Vanderil, J Hoosgasian: *Arch Int Med* 146:1193, 1986.
18. P.V. Johnston: In *Advances in Lipid Research*, Vol 21, ed. R. Paoletti and D. Kritchevsky, Academic Press, Orlando, 1985, pp. 103-141.
19. J. Merten: *Prog. Lipid Res.* 20:851-856, 1981.
20. F.V. Chisari, L.K. Curtiss, and F.C. Jensen: *J Clin Invest* 68:329-336, 1981.
21. J.H. Vauhan: *Hospital Practice* 19:101-107, 1984
22. E. Kijak, G. Foust, and R. Steinman: *Calif. State Dental Assoc.* 32:349, 1964.
23. M. Friedman, S.O. Byers, and R.H. Rosenman: *JAMA* 193: 882-86, 1965.
24. A.M. Katz and F.C. Messineo: *Hospital Practice*, July, 1981, pp. 49-59.
25. H.S. Black, J.T. Chan, and G.E. Brown: *Cancer Res.* 38:1384, 1978.
26. F.A. Kummerow: *Amer. J. Clin. Nutr.* 32:58-83, 1979.
27. E. Wynder: *J Amer Diet Assoc* 71:385-392, 1977.

Chapter 23

GOD'S TRUE REMEDIES = THE SECRET OF SUCCESS

God's True Remedies: In the search for health there are many voices. Every month brings to my attention new drugs or treatments which offer a measure of relief of the symptoms of disease. Not all of these are wrong in and of themselves. Patients are provided a means of immediate relief or temporary correction, but the tragedy is that little, if anything, is done to point out the cause and the true remedy. Many vitamin preparations, herb potions, and secret formulas are touted as the elixirs of life. These may be helpful under some circumstances; but, here too, unless the root cause of the ailment is corrected, the patient will continue to suffer the results of continued disobedience to the laws of health.

For example, coronary by-pass surgery or gallstone removal may be necessary, sometimes under life threatening circumstances, but those two operations do not tackle the cause of the build-up of cholesterol in the body and the plugged arteries. They only temporize, and unless the physician and the patient set out to correct the cause of the disease, a worse condition soon follows. What are the "true remedies" that should serve as the foundation of every therapeutic approach?

When we study Scripture, we find that God introduced Israel to laws of health which were far ahead of their time. On their gigantic camping trip, two million Israelites were faced with a sanitation problem. How do you keep down an epidemic of dysentery, cholera, or intestinal parasites? They were to designate a place to defecate.

They were to wear a paddle on their belt, to dig a hole, relieve themselves, and cover up the excrement (Deut. 23:13). Before they ate, they were to wash their hands up to the elbow. One of the reasons was that they used their left hand to clean themselves after a bowel movement. Remember, the germ theory was not accepted until the time of Koch and Pasteur in the 1860's. Israel was given the principles of cleanliness by washing and quarantine to prevent the spread of infectious agents (Lev. 11, 13-15). The mother and newborn were given a simple way for protection against infection. They were to be treated as though "unclean" for several weeks after delivery (Lev. 12).

In our time, after over three thousand more years of degeneration of the race, God has given us even more specific information about His true, hygienic remedies. These include the following:

> A clear conscience (2SM281).
> Cleanliness, purity of life, clean, sweet premises (2SM287).
> Simple herbs (2SM289,293-4).
> Fomentations and hot and cold compresses (2SM290).
> Cheerfulness (2SM298).
> Charcoal (2SM298-9).

We emphasize a special list which includes seven **natural** remedies and one **supernatural** remedy. "Pure air, sunlight, abstemiousness, rest, exercise, proper diet, the use of water, trust in divine power,— these are the true remedies. Every person should have a knowledge of nature's remedial agencies and how to apply them" (MH127). These were made into the acronym, NEWSTART, to helps us remember them.

NUTRITION: A most healthful diet can be obtained if you (a) avoid all refined foods; (b) select proper, preferably organically grown, farm produce that will give an adequate, balanced intake of amino acids, essential oils, vitamins, minerals, and trace elements; (c) choose the types of nutrients which will help you lose or gain weight as needed, strengthen the immune system, and clear the body of excess cholesterol and fat which impairs circulation and causes degeneration.

The following guiding principles are recommended:
1. Select luscious, tasty foods from items listed below:
   All fruit, **unsweetened**, preferably fresh, but also frozen or canned in fruit juice or water packed
   All greens, especially turnip greens, broccoli, collards, kale, mustard greens, cabbage, and radish greens, etc.
   Use sparingly high oxalate foods such as spinach, chard, beet greens, peanuts, or rhubarb
   All herbs that are mild
   All legumes (beans, peas, lentils, and garbanzos)
   All whole grains. You need two kinds daily plus a legume or greens to get optimal balance of amino acids
   Nuts in moderation; the better ones are almonds, filberts, pecans, and walnuts. **Peanut butter or peanuts not advised.**

2. Eat no animal products: No flesh foods
                              No egg yolks
                              No milk products

3. Eat no refined foods: No oil, margarine, shortening
                             No sugar, syrup, or free starch
                             No white bread, white rice
                             No degerminated corn meal
                             No gluten or soy meat substitutes

4. All nutritional needs on a "proper" **PREVENTIVE** diet can be secured from a **daily** serving of the foods listed below:
A citrus fruit or an alternate source of vitamin C
An additional serving of fruit
A yellow vegetable such as carrots, squashes, etc.
A green vegetable, low oxalate greens, -2 cups (cooked vol.)
A legume, such as beans, peas, lentils, garbanzos, etc.
Two to three different of whole grains
Tubers, nuts, olives, and avocados may be eaten as desired

5. Those on a "proper" **THERAPEUTIC** diet for coronary heart disease, diabetes, hypertension, degenerative arthritis, or other conditions related to plugged arteries would be wise to restrict the high-fat foods from the preventive diet (see above) as follows:

   No olives, avocados, nuts, or high-fat seeds
   No soybeans or tofu

6. Food supplements:
Vitamin B-12 – take 50-500 micrograms once weekly, **chewed** in the food. (Vitamin B-12 is made only by germs or yeast)
Iodized salt. –**IF** salt is restricted, two kelp pills daily
Vitamin D (400 IU daily) –**IF** unable to get adequate sunshine
Fluoride – fluorinated water except in high fluoride areas
Calcium and magnesium – **IF** unable to get good greens on a daily basis

SOME GENERAL RULES FOR GOOD DIGESTION ARE:

Eat slowly, chew the food thoroughly to allow the saliva to mix with the food. Count 30 to 40 chomps with each mouthful.

Avoid liquids with meals. These decrease the flow of saliva with its digestive enzymes.

Two meals a day is better than three. The evening meal, if eaten at all, should be fruit and/or dry toasted bread.

Eat a variety of fruits, vegetables, whole grains, tubers, and legumes during the week from different growing areas, but a limited variety of four or five at any one meal.

Sufficient sodium (salt) is usually available in the foods in their natural state. Flavor your food with lemon, onion, and safe herbs. If you tolerate salt, use iodized seasalt. If you restrict salt, take two kelp pills daily for iodine.

Avoid losses of the essential minerals, vitamins, and trace elements from copious washing, excessive peeling, or faulty cooking. Cook or steam the vegetables or fruit with a minimum of water. Add the cooking juice to food. Do not overcook.

EXERCISE: "Conditioning" exercise is what is needed. Here are three guides to help you exercise at the optimum level safely:
1. The ten-second pulse rate during exercise. Learn how to count your ten-second pulse beat accurately and then use it. Exercise, stop, count your pulse ten seconds, restart exercise. Object: To keep pulse rate during exercise in your range for 20-30 minutes daily.

Ten Second Pulse Rate (approx. guide)
50-60 yr old = 23-22 beats/10 sec.
60-70 yr old = 21-20 beats/10 sec.
70-80 yr old = 19-18 beats/10 sec.

2. Exercise to the intensity that you are barely able to carry on a conversation with someone as you exercise.
3. If you develop chest, left arm, or throat pain or heaviness during exercise, stop and rest. Consult your physician.

Goal: Exercise a minimum of 20-30 minutes at the optimum level of endurance at least five day a week. The body tends to "escape" from conditioning easily. Walking is good exercise. Use a walking stick. Gardening or stationary bike riding are good alternate exercise methods.

WATER: The body needs water for internal and external cleansing. Drink six to eight glasses of pure water daily, more if you sweat much. Drink water on arising, between meals, but early enough before bedtime to avoid interruption of sleep for urination. Drinking water during exercise increases endurance. You need enough water to give you from a half to a gallon of urine in a 24 hour period.

SUNSHINE: Sunshine has several benefits for the body. It furnishes the natural Vitamin D as it lowers cholesterol. Get all that you can modestly, yet avoid burning. You need exposure for at lease ten minutes daily to half your face for sufficient Vitamin D. Vitamin D can be stored for weeks in fat. Adequate vitamin C and E from citrus and whole grains along with correction of the high cholesterol and triglyceride levels in the blood and tissues can help protect against skin cancers.

TEMPERANCE: We need help to get away from all harmful drugs. We should eliminate all tea, coffee, soft-drinks, and alcoholic beverages from our diet. Use plain, pure water instead. Even good things should be used in moderation.

AIR: Pure, fresh air is needed. This means no tobacco smoke or smog. It means good air with negatively ionized particles like those present in the air near forests, lakes, and oceans. Breathe deeply as part of exercises.

REST: Get adequate restful sleep. A light supper, not too close to retiring, is of help. Try to avoid stressful circumstances. Establish good habits, and this will help. "Jet lag" teaches us that the body works best with habits. A relaxing soak in warm water may help you unwind enough after a stressful day so that you will not need that sleeping pill.

TRUST IN GOD: Rest your life in God's hands. An abiding faith in a loving God will help you rest physically and mentally. He is all ready to forgive all of our past mistake, however dreadful they may be. He has promised to take our guilt from us and cleanse us as though we had never sinned. Ask Him. He promises to renew the mind, even to blot out all those mental records of our sins (Cf. 1 John 1:9; Psalm 103:12; Romans 12:1,2; Psalm 51:1-13).

If we are only "willing to be made willing" (2 Cor 8:12; Phil 2:5) He will work in our minds so that we **will want** to do right, and with His power **enable** us to obey Him (Heb. 8:10-12; Phil 2:13; Col 1:11,12,29). All His laws are really promises. Every promise that He has made by way of a law, is **part of our inheritance** (Deut. 33:4; Galatians 3:17-19). We can start **now** to obtain our inheritance from the heavenly Father (Ephesians 1). When Christ died, His will and testament had come into full force (Heb 9:15-17). We can be adopted into His family, "born again" (John 3:3-13; Col 1:12). We then have the right to go by prayer to His throne in the courts of heaven and present our request to Jesus, the Executor-Mediator, of the estate (Heb. 8:1-6; 4:16). If we go by faith, after repentance and dedication to Him, we receive the promised blessing if we ask according to the *will* of God (James 4:3).

Jesus said in His prayer for the disciples: "Thy kingdom come; Thy *will* be done in earth [in us] as it is in heaven...."(Matt. 6:9-13).

We are to put our name in the promise, our own name in the will, when we read it. For example, "For God so loved [insert your name] that He gave His only begotten Son, that if [insert your name] believeth in Him [insert your name] should not perish, but have everlasting life" John 3:16.

"That He would grant [your name], according to the riches of his glory, to be strengthened with might by His Spirit in the inner man.... That Christ may dwell in [your name] hearts by faith, etc." Ephesians 3:16-20.

Chapter 24

THE BENEFITS OF GOD'S TRUE REMEDIES

Over the past decade the health team at Weimar Institute has observed dramatic benefit for many patients who came, learned, and then applied the NEWSTART true remedies. We can give you averages and percentages of changes, but these do not adequately portray the increase in sense of well-being and the remarkable results in relief of pain and suffering. The following summary presents the major results that we have seen.

Serum Lipids: The following changes occured in serum lipids in two weeks in those with abnormal levels on entry into the sessions:

>19.4% drop in Cholesterol, if initial value was 180 mg% or more.
>31.3% drop in Triglyceride, if initial value was 150 mg% or more.
>22.3% increase in HDL-Chol., if initial value was below 30 mg%

Work-Exercise Capacity: The ability of the patients to perform their work improved by an average of 40% within twenty-five days as measured by the treadmill test (Bruce protocol).

Weight Control:
Overweight (10 to 19% over ideal weight) Avo. loss = 4.2 lbs.
Obese (20% or more over ideal weight) Ave. loss = 10.8 lbs.
And all this within 25 days without feeling hungry!

Coronary Heart Disease: Those who entered with angina as a symptom had the following changes: Fifty-three percent became asymptomatic and an additional 26 percent were definitely improved by the eighteenth day. Twenty-one percent had no change in that time period. We have longer range studies in a few patients which indicate definite regression of atherosclerosis as evidenced by improvement in exercise treadmill testing and/or other tests. We are currently setting up to obtain follow-up data on all those with coronary heart disease. Watch for the results of this study.

Hypertension: Of those who entered with the diagnosis of hypertension, 50 percent were normotensive (below 140/90) after two weeks and 65 percent were) normotensive after three weeks on the program **without medication**.

Diabetes: Ten percent of the juvenile type and 33 percent of the adult onset type (AODM) maintained a fasting blood sugar of 120 mg % or below **without** insulin or oral hypoglycemics. Those who continued to require insulin or medication needed only half their previous dose to maintain the blood sugar in better control.

Eighty percent of 21 diabetics with diabetic neuropathy were free of their burning, shooting, painful distress after four to seventeen days on the NEWSTART program. Their numbness persisted, but even this was noticeably improved. Follow-up for two or more years has shown that the improvement continued at home.

Degenerative Disc Disease and Arthritis: There was symptomatic improvement in over half of the patients by the 18th day. Joint distress improved further slowly over a matter of months and years. Some persons have mentioned a worsening of joint pain if they used a "little" sugar or a "little" oil in the diet.

One 29-year-old physician has remained essentially free of pain for the past six years and has had complete disappearance of his herniated lumbar disc by computerized axial tomography (CAT) scan. (See illustrative cases below).

Rheumatoid Arthritis: During 1988, two of six patients with this condition no longer required medication for pain and swelling, and four of the six patients had marked improvement by the eighteenth day. Although the damaged joints remained deformed, the basic disease process had gone into remission.

Other Diseases: A number of other ailments show promise over a period of months of being benefited in the few cases that we have had. These include Chronic Fatigue Syndrome (E.B. Viral syndrome), multiple sclerosis, allergic states, polymyalgia rheumatica (needs several months), and lupus erythematosis.

CASES WHICH ILLUSTRATE THE BENEFITS OF GOD'S TRUE REMEDIES

The following individual results illustrate the type of improvement that we have observed.

Coronary Heart Disease: Patient D.C. was a 62-year-old manufacturer from Michigan who developed intense anginal pain while jogging in mid January, 1984. When he consulted his physician, he was able to go only four minutes of the (Bruce) treadmill exercise test before he had signs on his EKG of inadequate circulation to the heart. Coronary angiograms demonstrated 75% narrowing of the right coronary artery and several areas of comparable narrowing of branches of the left coronary artery. His serum cholesterol was 220 mg% and his HDL cholesterol was about 25 mg%. He was advised to have coronary artery bypass surgery, but he elected to follow the Weimar NEWSTART program. When he called from home, he was given preliminary instructions to start on our therapeutic diet immediately.

By April, 1984, after three weeks at home and twenty days at Weimar Institute on the therapeutic low fat diet, he was able to hike ten miles a day without chest distress. His cholesterol had declined to 141 mg%, and his HDL was 27mg%. His time on the treadmill had increased from six up to nine minutes before comparable changes in his EKG occurred. The patient has stayed on the diet and exercise program faithfully, even on his hunting safaris. After one year on the program, he could go twelve minutes of the Bruce treadmill before having 2-3 mm ST depression. After two years he could go 12 minutes of the Bruce protocol with only minimal EKG changes, and the treadmill test was discontinued because he had reached a pulse rate of 150 (85% of his maximum heart rate).

Without asking medical advice, he returned to his hobby of high altitude hunting. The summer of 1986 he camped and hunted in Tibet at an elevation of 12,000 to 16,000 feet without anginal pain. The following year he made a similar hunting trip in Nepal at about the same elevation. He has since been on similar excursions at like altitudes in the Andes of South America. His serum cholesterol has leveled off at about 170 with an HDL of 34 mg%.

Patient M.H. was a 61-year-old Seventh-day Adventist hospital administrator. Since his serum cholesterol was always in the 130-160 range over the years, he felt fairly safe from a heart attack. His typical breakfast consisted of Mocha Mix and cereal, two fried eggs, fried potatoes and pancakes or French toast. His favorite lunch was a sandwich of peanut butter and mayonnaise on white bread. His favorite between meal snack was potato chips. He exercised sporadically. During one morning walk he developed chest pain which led him to consult a cardiologist. He was found to have severe CHD by angiography and evidence by Thallium Heart Scan of a myocardial infarction with marked thinning of the left ventricle. He chose the plan to change his lifestyle instead of the recommended coronary bypass surgery. His initial cholesterol at Weimar Institute after two weeks on the diet at home was 120 mg% with a Cholesterol/HDL risk ratio of 5.2 because of a low HDL (23 mg%). His risk ratio remained elevated at 4.8* after two weeks on the NEWSTART program. We added chromium GTF (Glucose Tolerance Factor) and niacin food supplements to lower his cholesterol synthesis and increase his HDL synthesis. On this program his cholesterol dropped to 95, his HDL increased to 60, and he had a risk ratio of 1.5. After eight months on the program his repeat Thallium Heart Scan was entirely normal. All previous evidence of poor circulation to the heart was gone. He has continued wholeheartedly on the program. (*We like the risk ratio to be at or below 3.5.)

Hypertension: R.M. was a 57-year-old truck driver from Pennsylvania. He had had anxiety tension syndrome since his service with the Army in the World War II Normandy invasion. Over the past twenty year he gradually gained in weight up to 257 lbs. (70 inches tall). For eight years he had had hypertension and, on entry, was on full doses of three medications for that. In addition to these main problems, he also had arthritis of the neck, attacks of gouty arthritis, and was confused and forgetful at times. He entered the program taking 43 pills a day of eleven different medications. The comparative results of observations at the start of the program and at the end of the twenty-five days are tabulated below.

Item	On entry	Day 14	Day 21
Weight	257	238	235
Blood Pressure	176/108	148/96	130/90
Blood sugar mg%(fasting)	127	127	156
Triglyceride mg%	500+	239	217
Cholesterol mg%	307	289	296
HDL Cholesterol mg%	18		

Bruce Treadmill (METS)	5		12
Total No. Pills/day	43	0	0

His mental confusion cleared after the medications were stopped, and he felt much improved. By the end of one week he no longer had arthritic pain in his neck nor angina on exertion. When he returned to his physician at the Veterans Hospital in Pennsylvania, his physician urged him, "Whatever you are doing, please keep it up."

R.K. was a 54-year-old salesman who had been overweight for 25 years, had hypertension for 20 years with pressures over 200 without medication, and for seven years suffered from easy fatiguability. He developed angina five years previously, had coronary artery bypass surgery three years previously, and had cholesterol deposits removed by surgery from both carotid arteries two years previously. On entry to the 25-day program he was exercising very little because of anginal pain. By the end of the program, he was walking 14 miles a day and required fewer than two pills of nitroglycerin a day. The table below presents his results.

Item	On entry	Day 14	Day 21
Weight	226	200	194
Blood Pressure	160/104	148/90	138/90
Blood sugar mg%(fasting)	103	92	
Triglyceride mg%	183	102	
Cholesterol mg%	451	152	
HDL Cholesterol mg%	35	52	
Chol/HDL Risk Ratio	12.8	2.9	
Bruce Treadmill (METS)	8		9
Total No. Pills/day	24	5	7

At the end of the session he was using half as much antihypertensive medication as on entry.

Diabetes Mellitus: H.J. was a 62-year-old Caucasian male when I first met him at Nameless Valley Conditioning Program near Austin, Texas. Over the years he had gradually gained until his weight was 240 pounds. He had developed diabetes and was checking his blood sugar three times a day. On a dose of 180 to 200 units of insulin daily, he was able to control his fasting blood sugar (FBS) in the 140 to 160 mg% range without insulin reactions.

He entered wholeheartedly into the 25-day program and lost 35 pounds during that period. By the fifth day he was having insulin reactions and his insulin had to be completely discontinued. Five units a day from the same bottle of NPH insulin caused hypoglycemia. From that time forward for the following fourteen months, his fasting glucose remained below 120 mg%. His weight stabilized at about 190 pounds.

He then went on a cruise ship vacation to New Zealand. While on the trip, he gained ten pounds and had to restart insulin. Over the following ten months his weight increased to 223 pounds. His insulin needs built up to 60 units a day to keep the blood sugar in the 140 to 160 range. Once again, this time at Weimar Institute, on a low fat, high fiber diet and a six mile a day walking program, he began to lose weight. By the fifth day he no longer needed insulin to keep his FBS in the 90 to 117 range. During this 25-day session he lost 24 pounds, his blood pressure declined from 138/78 to 106/54, his cholesterol decreased by 22%, and his Chol/HDL risk ratio declined from 12.6 to 7.4. He resolved to stay on the program henceforth.

Diabetic Neuropathy: K.M. was a 58-year-old nurse when she first came to the conditioning center for help. Over the last 25 years, her weight had gradually climbed to her admission weight of 190 pounds (height 61 inches). She had known high blood pressure for 15 years and was taking two different medicines for that. For ten years she had had diabetes mellitus and had been taking chlorpropamide for that. For five years she had had feelings of numbness and tingling and "crawly" sensations in her feet and legs. For three years the pains in her feet had been so very severe that she had to take codeine-containing pain medicine nightly to sleep. When she first came to my office, she stated that her feet and ankles felt as though they were sunburned. When she walked, it felt as though she was walking on razor blades, even on a carpet in her softest slippers.

By the tenth day she was free of the burning shooting pains in the feet and legs. The numbness remained but was subsiding. Her blood pressure was controlled below 138/88 without medication. Since maximal doses of chlorpropamide did not control the blood sugar, she started lente and regular insulin in a total dose of 30 to 35 units per day. She has continued to recover from the neuropathy over the subsequent four years in spite of a critical nonsupportive attitude of her family.

Carotid Artery Stenosis: J.L. was a 49-year-old man in the importing business. He was characterized as a workaholic, long-time smoker, and heavy coffee drinker. For twenty-five years he had had hypertension, indigestion, and insomnia. Shortly before he came into the NEWSTART program, he began to have episodes of blurred vision and transitory weakness of the right upper extremity. Physicians detected a readily audible bruit over the left carotid artery. Ultrasonic examination at two different laboratories revealed 70% stenosis of the left carotid artery.

He remained faithfully on the program for over a year. When he sought reexamination, his physicians noted that there were no signs of carotid artery stenosis. His repeat ultrasonic examination revealed no evidence of obstruction of the carotid arteries. The conclusion of his physician was that the initial ultrasonic examination was in error, but he reminded them that he had had the tests done in two different laboratories.

Because of his occupation which required visits to mainland China, he became careless on his program. His symptoms of transitory ischemia of the brain returned after a year. Once again he sought the help of the team at Weimar Institute and was reestablished on the program. The table below reveals some of his results.

Item	2-3-87	2-17-87	2-26-87	2-9-89
Weight	152		145	172
Blood Pressure	120/80	115/80	100/70	170/100
Triglyceride mg%	219	156		200
Cholesterol mg%	218	167		241
HDL Cholesterol mg%	33	41		40
Chol/HDL Risk Ratio	6.6	4.0		6.6
Bruce Treadmill (METS)	10		11.3	
Total No. Pills/day	5	0	0	0

Degenerative Disc Disease: D.E. was a 31-year-old third year male medical student when he began to have low back pain that radiated into the right buttock. The pain reached such an intensity that he could no longer perform his duties. Computer Axial Tomography (CAT) scan of the lumbar spine verified what his consultant suspected, a herniated disc. When he called me by telephone, he told me his story and lamented, "Is there anything that can be done with diet and exercise?" He feared that he must give up his ambition to become a physician.

I told him of my studies that showed that of all the factors that caused herniated discs, the most important nontraumatic factors were a gradual loss of blood flow to the backbone while the person continued heavy use of the back. I told him that of 170 hypertensive patients between the ages of 35 and 69 years whom I had followed in my practice at the Loma Linda VA Hospital, 25 percent had bothersome degenerative disc disease (DDD), 44 percent had degenerative joint disease (DJD) of the knees, hips, and/or back. One third had had to give up gainful employment prematurely because of back problems. By plain X-ray examination more than 75 percent of the 170 had either DDD, or DJD, or both, of the lumbar spine of moderate to severe degree.

Half of all persons in civilized countries over 50 years of age show x-ray changes characteristic of DJD of the hips, knees, and/or back. Half of the people with X-ray changes will also have the cluster of symptoms that go along with the disease. On the other hand, this disease is relatively rare in aboriginal or native societies. But this is not a new problem. Nearly all of the mummies of elderly Egyptians of long ago had osteoarthritis of the spine from mild to severe degree.[1]

A recent textbook of orthopedics makes this comment about DJD. "The causes for the degeneration [of weight-bearing joints] are apparently numerous and varied, but the commonest type of the disease is the result of continued demand for excessive function [excessive joint use] in the face of a decreasing efficiency [plugging] of blood supply."[2]

Pathologists tell us that the arteries most severely involved with athero-arteriosclerosis are the arteries to the backbone, particularly to the lumbar spine.[3]

Silberberg[4] reported that mice who were fed a standard mouse diet with added cholesterol, developed spondylosis (stiffening) of the spine, and some of them had herniated discs.

With this information in mind the young medical student began a program of low fat, therapeutic, natural foods diet, combined with a traction system using a simple slant board.[5] He promptly implemented these and included a back strengthening exercise program.[6]

Within a month of instituting these simple means, he was essentially free of back pain. He has since remained on the diet and back exercises. He finds that if he works excessively long hours for several days, without adequate sleep, he will have return of the back pain. This can be promptly corrected by a more temperate lifestyle. A repeat CAT scan of the lumbar spine after nearly six years on the regimen showed only marginal protrusion of the disc.

Patient M.G. was a 57-year-old physician when he developed a herniated disc in the lumbar spine after heavy manual work. Surgery was performed on the disc in 1977 after months of progressive worsening pain. He had been a lactoovo-vegetarian all his life, but in 1980 he began to eliminate all refined foods and animal products. I quote from that physician-patient.

"When I learned that poor circulation to the backbone was a major cause of herniated discs (see above), I took one good long look at my lifestyle. I realized that I had some changes to make in my way of living if I was going to be healthier and avoid dying prematurely. You see, I was a pasteurized milk drinking, cheese and ice cream eating, a 'little' oil and sugar using, meat substitute and peanut-butter loving, fried egg relishing, lacto-ovo- vegetarian. I was a weekend athlete, health reform teaching, Adventist physician.

"So I cut out my cow's milk and switched to Mocha-Mix. After reading the Mocha-Mix label, I thought, 'This stuff is mostly oil. I am nowhere near the center of the target for a proper diet for plugged arteries.'

"Only one conclusion seemed right; cut out all refined foods and animal products. No eggs, milk, cheese, butter, oil, margarine, shortening, sugar, or syrup. No more white bread or white rice. I changed from peanuts and peanut butter to almonds and other nuts. I began to walk two miles a day briskly on a regular daily basis. Since I was normal weight for my height, I did not have to eliminate olives or avocados. Of course, I continued to trust in divine power for God to give me the desire and the power to follow His health laws at all times.

"What have been the results? My back has gradually become stronger. I am now able to carry the groceries in from the car for my wife. I can carry my suitcase when I go on a speaking trip. I can even carry a 100 pound sack of cement for a short distance with proper back posture. After the surgery and before the diet, I was unable to do all those things without suffering persistent pain down the right leg for several hours. Lifting 30 pounds was the near maximum that I could do without distress. The improvement has been gradual and steady, noticeably evident after about two years on the program and progressively better for the five years thereafter."

Rheumatoid Arthritis: J.S. was a 30-year-old crippled young lady when she entered the NEWSTART session in 1987. She was born in New England and raised there on a heavy meat and shellfish diet. At the age of 18 months she developed rheumatic fever. One year later she had juvenile (rheumatoid) arthritis. This condition gradually damaged various joints in her body, including the shoulders, spine, wrists, hands, feet, knees, fingers, and toes. Altogether she had had twenty operations on ten joints.

When she arrived in the program, she needed the nurses to give her first dose of pain medication in the morning. After the pain was controlled enough, she could get up, dress, and shuffle over to breakfast. After five days on the preventive diet NEWSTART program, she no longer required any pain medication. On the tenth day she requested permission to go with the walking group to the regular picnic near the Bear River. She hiked the six miles without difficulty or untoward after effects. While at the Institute her weight remained about 114 pounds, her blood pressure remained unchanged at 100/60, and her serum lipid levels remained unchanged. One of the results that she was most grateful for was the ability to kneel and pray for the first time.

She returned to her home in Colorado, and went back to her work of selling religious books. Needless to say she stayed on the program. A year and a half later, she and her husband decided to take a vacation. They drove by the Grand Canyon in Arizona. While there, they hiked the seven and a half miles from the rim down to the Colorado River, spent the night, and hike out the next day. They returned to Weimar Institute to tell us the good news. She had not had to take any pain medication since starting the program and was overjoyed with the ability to see the Grand Canyon in that way.

Multiple Sclerosis: C.H. was a 37-year-old happy energetic young salesperson when she developed progressively worsening fatigue, stabbing pains, blurred vision, numbness and tingling of the lower limbs, urinary urgency and incontinence, and mental confusion. Within six months of the onset of the ailment, she could barely get about. She expected that soon she would be in a wheelchair. By her own statement she rated her health at that time at "5" on a scale of 0 to 100 (with zero being dead and 100 as perfect health). After many tests from several consultants she learned the diagnosis was multiple sclerosis. As if that was not enough, she also had multiple allergies.

An Adventist church friend of hers persuaded her to go on the NEWSTART therapeutic diet. Within a month on this diet she had made definite improvement, but she still had some numbness and fatigue. She was better at times and worse again. She began to keep a record of what she ate, how she felt, and what she did. A study of this indicated that there were some foods that brought on her symptoms of multiple sclerosis in a matter of hours.

By the help of a combination of a rotation diet and diversification of foods, she was able to determine the type of foods that she could tolerate. If she omitted all refined foods (particularly sugar), animal products, food additives, yeast and other fermented products, and eliminated the natural foods to which she was sensitive, she made steady improvement.

On that diet she gradually regained her health until by the end of three months, the numbness was gone. By the end of ten months she was able to go back to work, but required a couple of rest periods during the day. After fourteen months, she was able to return to full-time employment. She then rated her health at 95 on her zero to 100 scale.

Her dietary staples are selected whole grains, greens, and legumes. She cannot handle certain food combinations at the same meal. She has now recovered enough so that she can eat an occassional piece of low sugar fresh fruit. She finds that salads and a special no yeast bread give her more energy. Her exercise consists of walking two miles a day or an equivalent amount of stationary biking. She arranges to get adequate rest. Specially selected purified water for cooking and drinking is important. If she diverges from this simple program, numbness and fatigue alerts her of the danger in a matter of hours.

Although not a regular church member, she depends upon God to give her the desire and power to live correctly. She has utilized the "Twelve Suggested Steps" from the Alcoholics Anonymous World Services for her own problem. I have paraphrased them as below:

1. I admit that I am powerless over my faulty diet and lifestyle — that my life had become unmanageable.
2. I came to believe that a Power greater than myself could restore me to sanity.
3. I make a decision to turn my will and my life over to the care of God as I understand Him.
4. I make a searching and fearless moral inventory of myself.
5. Admit to God, to myself, and to another human being the exact nature of my wrongs.
6. I am entirely ready to have God remove all these defects of character.
7. I humbly ask Him to remove my shortcomings.

8. Make a list of all persons I have harmed, and became willing to make amends to them all.
9. I make direct amends to such people wherever possible, except when to do so would injure them or others.
10. I continue to take personal inventory, and when I am wrong, promptly admit it.
11. I seek through prayer and meditation [upon His Word] to improve my conscious contact with God as I understand Him, praying [and searching His Word] only for knowledge of His will for myself the and power to carry that out.
12. I have a spiritual awakening as the result of these steps, I try to carry this message to alcoholics [and others bound by faulty habits], and to practice these principles in all my affairs.

Author Ellen White puts it this way:

1. You desire to give yourself to God, but you are weak in moral power, in slavery to doubt, and controlled by wrong habits.
2. Your promises and resolutions are like ropes of sand.
3. You cannot control your thoughts, your impulses, your affections.
4. The knowledge of your broken promises and forfeited pledges weakens your confidence in your own sincerity.
5. The knowledge of your broken promises causes you to feel that God cannot accept you; but you need not despair.
6. What you need to understand is the true force of the will.
7. The will is the governing power in the nature of man, the power of decision, or of choice.
8. Everything depends on the right action of the will.
9. The power of choice God has given to men; it is theirs to exercise.
10. You cannot change your heart, you cannot of yourself give to God its affections; but you can choose to serve Him.
11. You can give Him your will. He will take your will, cleanse it, and return it to you.
12. He will then work in you both to will (to desire) and to do (to live) according to His good pleasure.

13. Thus your whole nature will be brought under the control of the Spirit of Christ.
14. Your affections will be centered upon Him, and your thoughts will be in harmony with Him.

1. D. Brothwell and A.T. Sandison: *Diseases of Antiquity*, Charles Thomas, Springfield, Illinois, 1967, p. 363.
2. E. Aegeter and J.A. Kirkpatrick, Jr.: *Orthopedic Diseases*, 4th Ed., W. B. Saunders Co., 1975, p. 639.
3. W. Boyd: *A Textbook of Pathology*, 4th Ed., Lea & Febiger, 1943, pp. 390-1
4. R. Silberberg; *Pathol Microbiol* (Basil), 43:265-75, 1975.
5. C.V. Burton: *Postgraduate Medicine* 70:168-183, 1981.
6. R. McKenzie: *Treat Your Own Back*, Spinal Publications, LTD, P.O. Box 93, Waikanae, New Zealand.
7. E.G. White: *Steps to Christ*, Pacific Press Pub. Assoc., 1956, page 47.

If you would like more details on the treatment of multiple sclerosis, you may contact the patient at P.O. Box 3076, Redwood City, CA. 94064 For more information on the overall health program, contact the author at Weimar Institute, Weimar, CA, 95736.

Chapter 25

DEVELOPMENT OF THE "OMEGA" OF DECEPTION

The pantheistic ideas regarding God in nature were originated by Lucifer (SPT #B7:49). Why? With such ideas, nature is exalted above God (MM91). Satan has used these ideas through the ages to downgrade God. It is his subtle attempt to do away with God and His government. Should we expect him to change at the very end of time?

Ellen White was called upon to rebuke erroneous doctrines such as an "impersonal God pervading all nature" shortly after 1844 (8T292). In 1890, she had been warned that from that time onward there would be a "constant contest" between science, so-called, and religion (MM98). In a letter in 1903 to the leaders in the medical missionary work, she commented in regard to theories which deal with the nature of God and His prerogatives as follows: "The church is now engaged in a warfare that will increase in intensity on the point on which you have been misled" (MM96). Later she wrote, "Again and again we shall be called to meet the influence of men who are studying sciences of satanic origin, through which Satan is working to make a nonentity of God and Christ" (9T68.5). We have been warned that the sentiments in *Living Temple* had been prepared by Satan as a snare for the last days (1SM202).

Ellen White indicated in connection with the discussion of the "alpha of deadly heresies" that there would be another heresy in this connection which she called "the omega" (1SM202-3). The omega was described as of "a most startling nature" (1SM197). It was predicted that it would "follow in a little while," and "will be received by those who are not willing to heed the warning God has given" (1SM200).

As we shall see in the following chapter, there is a struggle over ideologies in the world between the adherents of atheistic pantheism who consider the whole universe as material in nature and those who espouse the supernaturalistic form of pantheism who consider the whole universe to be spiritual in nature. Within the Christian churches it appears that the contest will be between deism on one extreme, the spiritualistic form of pantheism on the other extreme, and the straight Biblical truth about God in between.

Deism should pose no threat to the doctrines of Adventism. Deism would be the extreme that emphasizes God's transcendence and downplays His immanence, which is in contrast with pantheism that would make an impersonal God immanent without maintaining His transcendence.

If we study the sections in the Spirit of Prophecy that deal with the fanciful, spiritualistic theories of the nature of God, we find several results mentioned that would ensue from acceptance of such false theories. Belief in such theories would result in the following:

1. Tend to cause controversy over the presence and personality of God (1SM202-3).
2. Remove God from His position of sovereignty (8T292).
3. Sweep away the whole Christian and gospel economy (1SM204; 8T291).
4. Result in a change in our religion, giving up the doctrines which stand as pillars of our faith, and engaging in a process of reorganization (1SM204, 205, 208; STB #B7:40).
5. Do away with the necessity for the atonement, downgrade the sanctuary service and the ministry of Christ before God, and make man his own saviour (8T291; STB #B7:17).
6. Cause the believer to put dependence on human power rather than on Divine power (8T292).
7. Estimate as nothing the light that Christ gave John in Revelation and make of non-effect the truths of heavenly origin (1SM204).
8. Rob the people of God of their past experience (1SM204).

9. Teach that the scenes just before us are not of sufficient importance to be given special attention (1SM204).
10. A system of intellectual philosophy would be introduced (1SM204).
11. Books of a new order would be introduced (1SM204).
12. The sentiments would be looked upon by some as grand truths. (1SM204).
13. Virtue would be considered to be better than vice (8T291).
14. The sentiments would contain both true and false (1SM199).
15. The founders would go into the cities and do a wonderful work (1SM204-5).
16. The Sabbath would be lightly regarded (1SM204-5).
17. Nothing would be allowed to stand in the way of the new movement (1SM205).
18. Those who continue to believe those false theories will spoil their Christian experience, sever their connection with God, be led eventually to look upon the Bible as fiction (a myth), and lose their eternal life (8T291-3).
19. Result in free-lovism,–concealed at first as "unholy spiritual love", – apostasy, and spiritualism (8T292).

It should be noted that it was distrust between the workers in medical lines and the ministry over their respective attitudes about health reform that played an important role in the development of the pantheistic theories at Battle Creek. (STB #B7:48; MS-15-01). Could it be that distrust and animosity between some the ministry or the educational work and those in the medical work over similar issues will contribute to the development of the omega?

In an unpublished manuscript Elder Julius White, a Bible teacher at the College of Medical Evangelists several decades ago, proposed that the marked concern and fear engendered in the ministry over the heresy of Dr. J. H. Kellogg and those at Battle Creek had left a most unhealthy attitude in the ministry toward the medical workers. He reasoned that this would set the background for the development of the omega; and unless this breach was removed, there would be those in the ministry who would overly emphasize the spiritual and bring into the church another heresy based upon pantheism.

It matters little by which person or group the omega enters the church. Neither the ministry nor the medical workers were immune from the deceptions of the alpha. Should not the same hold true for the omega? From the personal experience of this author, serious inroads have already been made in the doctrines of Protestantism and are gnawing on the pillars of faith in the Adventist Church. It now appears that while our eyes have been searching the ministry and the medical work for the upcoming "Omega," it has stolen into camp through the EDUCATIONAL work. In the schools of America, these teachings have been foisted upon the youth of our land. Under the influence of our public schools our nation has drifted away from a Christian-oriented, sovereign people toward a Humanist/Socialist society (for more information, see Barabara M. Morris, *Change Agents in the Schools*, Barbara M. Morris Report, Upland, CA.). And these humanistic teachings have spread into the camp of Israel.

WILL THE REAL OMEGA PLEASE STAND UP AND BE IDENTIFIED!

Chapter 26

THE MODERN-DAY INROADS OF PANTHEISM

Introduction:

Quite frequently one reads in ecumenical literature and even in evangelical publications phrases which, even though they appear high-sounding and harmless, originate from and are based upon pantheistic concepts. These phrases have cropped up even in Seventh-day Adventist literature. Many of these phrases have been lifted entirely from the writings of philosophers who are proponents of pantheism.

What must one outside our ranks, who may have been steeped in the terminology and beliefs of pantheism, think that we believe, when by our selection of phrases, we use pantheistic ideas to present the gospel? Is it fair for an author to leave it up to his reader to decide "by the context" just what the beliefs of the author are? Are we not obligated to close doors to false theories rather than to open them a crack for deception?

Doctrinal Forms of Pantheism:

The concepts of pantheism have been with us for centuries. When we examine the artifacts of archeology, we find that the god of the pantheists was depicted as grotesque and commonly associated with sun worship. Campbell Bonner[1] describes several of these, Egyptian in origin, in his book about magical amulets. One such elaborate being has three heads. One head is a bearded man, one is bald with a bearded chin, and the third is youthful in character. This figure has four wings and four arms holding objects. The figure has a bird tail from which a snake issues, growing out of the lower back. It has lion's heads on the knees and jackal heads for feet. Such monstrosities remind us of the Hindu representation for Siva and other of their gods. Indeed, the beasts of Daniel and Revelation that fight against God, such as presented in Daniel 7 and Revelation 13 and 17, resemble such monstrosities.

Pantheism implies unity of natures even though it may deny unity of natures. Very often pantheism, in contradiction with its own principles, falls far short of what is required for a consistent assertion of transcendence. Immanence is not a vague intermeshing of the Divine Being with created beings.[2] Pantheism speculates in regard to the nature of the universe. Certain phrases of pantheism speculate as the the nature of God, and it is this speculation which represents, in my opinion, the main harm of the phrases themselves.

The usual respondent defines pantheism to be a theory that considers God's presence to be in nature, in the tree, or in the flower. There is more involved than just that concept. Pantheism by the mental gymnastics of redefinition of words attempts to consolidate the threefold nature of man into one nature. Pantheism, for this reason, is evident in three forms; the first two of which are the most widely propagated.

(1) One form, in effect, **Physicalizes** the Spiritual and Mental natures, and in final analysis considers all three natures to be all **Physical**. Proponents of this form make such statements as, "The worlds alone are real; God is only the sum of all that exists." Other advocates say, "God is merely man's necessities and as soon as his necessities are satisfied, there is no further need for God." Marxist communism represents the current major proponent of this form. When the Russian cosmonaut circled the earth, Khruschev taunted Western ideology by saying, "They were up there for hours and never saw an angel or the Garden of Eden."

(2) The second form, in effect, **Spiritualizes** the Physical and Mental natures so that the universe is **Spiritual** only. It says essentially that, "God alone is real; the world is only a collection of manifestations or emanations from Him having neither reality nor distinct substance." This form is represented by the doctrines of such authors as Plotinus, Spinoza, or Hegel. From this form we get such phrases as "God is ultimate reality," or "Ultimate reality is will," or

"God's will is ultimate being and absolute reality." According to the *Encyclopedia Britannica* (1952) this form is the one most widely held by the western philosophers.

(3) The third form **Mentalizes** the Physical and Spiritual things of the universe and calls the entire universe **Mental** nature. Logically this form, too, would have to exist since it has been revealed to us that the nature of man is threefold (FCE57). The Christian Scientist Church propounds this form. They conclude, "Mind is all that exists," that "Matter is an unreal illusion subject to decay and dissolution," and that, "Mind is synonymous with Spirit."

As one considers the writings of pantheists, he realizes that such authors do not always present the concepts so that they can be distinctly categorized into one of the three forms; and they may even profess to believe in a personal "Divine Being."[3] Words may be redefined by usage, and the reasoning gets involved and confusing. Basically, each form does away with belief in three personal beings of the Godhead and their capacity to create things and have interpersonal relationships with beings created in their image. To the avowed pantheist there is no law of God, no sin, no redemption. All things continue evolving as they have been.

1. C. Brown: *Studies in Magical Amulets Chiefly Graeco-Egyptian.* The University of Michigan Press, Ann Arbor, Michigan, 1950, p.317.
2. See, Regis Jovilet: *The God of Reason.* Burns & Oates, London, 1958
3. A. W. Spalding: *Origin & History of Seventh-day Adventists*, Vol. 3. Review & Herald Pub. Co., Maryland, 1962, p. 138.

Chapter 27

SOME THEORIES AND MANIFESTATIONS OF PANTHEISM

Common Things and Sacred Things:

Pantheism would make no distinction between sacred things and common things; they would be considered as one in nature. Scientific discussions that deal with the physical or mental sciences become proper for presentation on the Sabbath day. No distinction is made between Scriptural spiritual discourses or sermons on healthful living on the one hand and expositions on anatomy and physiology of the body or causes and prevention of disease on the other hand.

It is true that the health message and the tidings of salvation are to be blended; they are not to be divorced (MM250; 1SM112; Ev519). And yet we realize that the gospel of soul salvation and the instruction in health reform are to be one in purpose, one in character, and one in mind, but **not** one in nature. We cannot equate the "gospel" of cholesterol and heart disease (as it has been called by some Adventists) with the gospel of Calvary. We cannot convert a good common topic into a holy one merely by combining or interspersing it with a Bible study part of an evangelistic series. If we present both on the Sabbath day, we may leave the impression with the audience that there is no difference between good common things and sacred things (1SM39.1).

If one does not clearly understand the distinctness between spiritual things and material things, then it will be difficult for him to perceive and separate in his thinking the difference between sacred and common things.

Good common things and activities are proper in their place. It is good to be a carpenter, but it is not proper for a carpenter to set up his work bench in the sanctuary of God on the Sabbath to do routine hammering, sawing, and fitting on that day whether he himself is consecrated to God or not. In the realm of the physical and mental we have six working days of the week designated for common labor and the elective care of the sick. We recognize that there are occasions when some common activities are right and proper even mandatory to be done for suitable reasons on the Sabbath.

Sacred things are proper in their place. They should be handled in God's prescribed way with due respect. In the realm of sacred things we have the holy hours of the Sabbath and the science of salvation that deals with the soul. Of course, spiritual things need not be restricted to the Sabbath. The sacred hours of the Sabbath are designated by God to be a period of time for special emphasis upon spiritual matters while only those physical things which minister to spiritual attainment of God's people are to occupy our time and attention on that day.

It is written of Jesus that, "He was doing God's service just as much when laboring at the carpenter's bench as when working miracles for the multitudes" (DA74). And yet, we all realize that He would not have moved His carpenter's bench and tools into the sanctuary of God and build furniture on the Sabbath. We may worship God at all times while we are about our common tasks, but the performance of these tasks are not acts of worship.

The lawn of the church may need to be mowed, but not on the Sabbath day. This is true even in light of the statement, "Everything connected with the cause of God is sacred, and is to be thus regarded by His people" (2SM160).

Recently there has been a trend in various of our churches to present lectures or seminars that deal with the care of the body or the care of the mind during the holy hours of the Sabbath. At this juncture we should make a clear distinction between three types of lectures that may be involved in this issue of church services or evangelistic series.

(1) **Scriptural spiritual discussions**: —These are sermons traditionally given in evangelistic series or in a church. They deal directly with topics of eternal salvation. Pertinent illustrations from the world of nature may be used to clarify the understanding of

things of spiritual interest just as Jesus did when He talked of a sower who went forth to sow, but the thrust of the message should be spiritual matters (Matt.13:3-13).

(2) **Sermons on healthful living**: —These should be Bible based. They are appeals based on Scripture urging healthful living, calling attention to the Creator's directions for a happy healthy life. Examples of such sermons have been given to us in the book, *Ministry of Healing*, by E. G. White.

(3) **Scientific discussions of health topics**: —By including the word "scientific" I am not implying that numbers 1 and 2 above are not scientific for there is a science of salvation. Scientific discussions here considered, in contrast with the other two, deal primarily with the physical and/or the mental nature of man. These would expound on the anatomy, physiology, or chemistry of the body or on causes and treatment of diseases of the body or mind. **Any** good physician, whether a Christian or an atheist, could give such a discussion. An Adventist physician might use the added knowledge of medicine as enlightened by the Bible and the Spirit of Prophecy in his presentation, but usually they would not refer directly to quotations of them when prejudice might close the ears. Christian physicians realize that good health of body and of mind is conducive to better spiritual understanding; but they recognize that the ailing can be saved and the robust can be lost.

The body is the "habitation for the mind" (FCE426). It is to be the "temple of the Holy Ghost," but such a relationship does not make the flesh holy. The physical is inferior to the spiritual just as human nature is inferior to divine nature. (1SM247). This is independent of sin.

The body is to be set aside for holy use (sanctified) yet the building up of and care for the body and/or the mind is common in nature. Just as the dedicated church environs may need certain alterations or repairs, some even on the Sabbath, so may the physical body. We should not fall into the trap of withholding care for the mental or physical needs of our bodies on the Sabbath, but taking that into consideration should not blind us as to the difference between a sermon on healthful living and a scientific discussion of health reform.

I would not quibble over the precise categorization of an indivudual health lecture, but I do believe that we cannot take a talk on arthritis or peptic ulcers, for example, and equate that with the gospel of the cross in so far as category is concerned. One health educator physician put it this way, "I could talk about health for arthritis sufferers and make suggestions in regard to medical treatment and physical therapy on any of the six working days of the week, but on Sabbath my 'arthritis' talk would be about stiff-necked Christians."

Is it proper to present on the hours of the Sabbath that good Mormon film of the physiology and benefits of exercise called, "Run Dick: Run Jane," as has been done in our churches? Does the motive of health education supercede and sanctify the film? Does prayer at the beginning and end of a volleyball game change it into a religious exercise? Would it help to have the players yell, "hallelujah," whenever they hit the ball?

This blending of medical topics with a spiritual message for Sabbath presentation may be so artfully done that the scientific information is barely discernable from the spiritual message. Let us say that the speaker designs his talk so that he presents clearly scientific material on cell membranes, the anatomy of the mitochondria, or the metabolism of cholesterol, and then uses that background information to develop some applicable spiritual lesson. Is such a talk about the material things, is it on spiritual matters, or is it an alternating mixture of the two, or does the speaker consider that the two are but one in nature?

If we present medical information in our Sabbath talks closely intermingled with the spiritual message, will that clean it up sufficiently to justify giving the medical information on the Sabbath? I just cannot see how it can be. It seems to me that such a way is unfair to God-given principles of Sabbath keeping. It appears to be an attempt to justify giving the medical information on Sabbath. When Jesus referred to sowing grain in His parables, He did it so that He might draw a spiritual message from the work, but He did not have a secondary motive to teach agriculture. He used that common work as an illustration in passing. "Be not deceived, God is not mocked."

But I hear some say, "We have always done it this way." Or, "That is the best time to get an audience." Or, "Everyone is doing it." Tradition has never sanctified anything. Our consciences need to be educated upon this matter. Pray for the Holy Spirit to enlighten us.

I attended a Friday night meeting at Loma Linda University in which the subject was, "Oil in the Bible." During the question and answer period afterwards, the discussion delved into several common medical topics such as, the milk fat problem, does cows milk spread cancer virus, does pasteurization destroy cancer viruses, etc. Someone in the audience eventually protested by quoting, "For the kingdom of heaven is not food and drink; but righteousness and peace and joy in the Holy Ghost" (Rom. 14:17 NKJV).

Can a good motive justify the methods used? At one of our colleges the students offered their services on Sabbath afternoon to tutor "disadvantaged" students in a neighboring city with their mathematics, reading, and geography. This would have been a noble deed for a Sunday. Think, why was it not done on that day? Was it done on Sabbath because they had to work on the other days? Strange things are done when we make no distinction between the sacred and the common. Yet, disobedience from *agape* even is still presumption.

Making God a Non-Entity:

Pantheism may develop from one or the other of two directions. On the one hand, proponents may attempt to make a unity of the three-fold nature of things in the universe or remove the distinction between the sacred and the common, and from that concept make a non-entity of God. On the other hand, proponents may assume that God is a non-entity and from there derive the pantheistic philosophy of the unity of the three-fold natures.

A variation of the above would be the assumption that only one Person of the Godhead is a non-entity. Because of the unique role of the Holy Spirit, pantheistic reasoning could theorize that He is an all-pervading influence rather than a Person with powers of authority and a special function in the plan of salvation. Such reasoning could be done while at the same time maintaining the personalities of the Father and the Son. The plan of the devil seems to be this: if a person cannot overcome Them in the great controversy, then try to convince the world that one or more of the three Persons in the Godhead does not exist. It appears that he is trying to avoid their authority. (GC498.8).

The Bible and the Spirit of Prophecy are too specific to be misled. "There are three living persons of the heavenly trio; in the name of these three great powers – the Father, the Son, and the Holy Spirit – those who receive Christ by living faith are baptized..." (Ev615).

Naturalism versus Supernaturalism:

Some philosophers teach that we have to believe in either "supernaturalism" or "naturalism." I contend that there is a third alternative. The Spirit of Prophecy plainly states that God made both spiritual, or supernatural, things and material, or natural, things (MH414). We as Seventh-day Adventists can subscribe neither to the supernaturalistic philosophy of the nature of the universe nor to the naturalistic philosophy.

Plainly, supernaturalists believe that God alone is real and everything else is merely an emanation or a manifestation of Him; whereas, the naturalists believe that the universe consist only of matter and that there is no supernatural. Now, the true alternative is to believe in the three Persons of the Godhead who made both spiritual things and material things and sustain them by spiritual and physical power.

Evolution:

If by your reasoning, you have determined that there is no God; then the things of nature and life have to be explained on some basis other than creation. Most readers are well familiar with the evolutionary theory for the origin of life. Philosophers have a theory, based upon the second form of pantheism, which speculates that **matter**, itself, is evolving. According to the "Theory of Actuality" "the real" is not a "thing" or a "state at rest," but an "activity or a process," an "incessant becoming," if you please. This idea is termed "dialectical evolution." Those authors state further, "Indeed the whole drift of present-day science is to regard 'events' rather than 'things' as the ultimate components of the world of reality,"[1]

This can be illustrated as follows: Those who accept dialectical evolution would look at a table or a chair and say, "That is not a real thing; it is merely an event. Before its present form it was a tree and iron ore; next, it will be ashes and rust." That theory attempts to take away God's ability to make atoms and let them become constituents of objects with various shapes and functions separate from Himself.

The late Dr. A. W. Truman reports attending a Bible class on the Los Angeles campus of the College of Medical Evangelists. He stated that much of the class period centered around a discussion of whether a table and chair in the room was a "thing" or not.

"God is Ultimate Reality"

This phrase, "God is ultimate reality," originated from those who believe in the supernaturalistic form of pantheism. They coined the phrase and gave it their meaning. **The Phrase itself speculates as to the nature of God.** It goes beyond what has been revealed to us in the Bible and the Spirit of Prophecy. The various words that have been used in the Bible and Spirit of Prophecy that name or identify God are, almost without exception, descriptive of what He has done or is capable of doing. They do not try to describe His nature. For example, God is called "the Creator," "our King," "Ruler of the universe," "the Omnipotent." Is it not of more than passing significance that the names of God used by the prophets fail to speculate in regard to His essence?

The phrase, God is ultimate reality, is really saying that nothing is real nor does anything exist apart from God. Some may wish to put a different definition on this; but if one analyzes the phrase to its logical endpoint, the most reasonable conclusion that one can sensibly make out of that phrase is this:–when one finally finds something that is real, that thing is God. The phrase is, in effect, saying that God is unable to create a world or a person or to make a law or to love and yet have these entities real and detached from Himself.

The phrase appears to be good theology to the Hindu, to the Catholic, and to others. "Hinduism teaches that the essence of every living thing is atman, its spirit or soul, which comes from Brahman," Further, it teaches, "Brahman forms the inmost essence of everything,"[2] When the pope visited New Delhi in 1964, one of the phrases that he emphasized by repetition as he stepped off the plane was this, "God is ultimate reality." One of the Catholic doctrines is that by miraculous transubstantiation the wafer and the wine becomes the flesh and blood of Christ.

Unbalancing the Attributes of God:

Why should these false concepts that challenge God's system of dealing with guilt of sin and the destruction of the wicked at the end of the millennium be linked with this pantheistic philosophy? This question has been dealt with elsewhere, but we can summarize some thoughts at this point.

If we accept a god to worship, a god which differs in important ways from that described in Scripture, that is idolatry (RH12-03-08).

If we set up a material object or thing and deny the supernatural, that is **materialistic pantheism**.

If we set up the mind as the universe and deny the physical and the supernatural, that is **Christian Science pantheism**.

If by reason and/or speculation we decide on spiritual attributes of God which differ from that revealed in Scripture, we set up a god that differs from the true God. Thus, law or love or faith may be the new god.

If that god is a god of justice, without love, "LAW" is the god.

If that god is a god of love, without justice, "LOVE" is the god.

If that god is a god of reason, without revelation, "REASON" is the god.

If you believe, as some do, that the only penalty for transgression is the natural cause-and-effect consequences and nothing more, then you are, in effect, believing that the only relationship that you have is with law, and not the God of law. Such a belief leads one into worshiping an idea which is false, and that is a "Baal" worship (RH12-03-08). In final analysis such a concept leads to the removal of God from the position of being the only lawmaker, and places man in position of being a legislator.

The true God may exist in a person's own thinking, but if that person superimposes upon the true God, a god of sentimental love without Scripturally defined justice, he is, in reality, a follower of that form of pantheism which makes the whole universe spiritual in nature. This is attempting to make God after our own image.

God is Love; Love is God:

In a sermon presented on *The Adventist Hour* television program over fifteen years ago it was stated by the minister that "God is love; Love is God," "God is law; Law is God," etc. God was pictured as one who did not judge; and if He were to destroy the wicked by fire, He would be labelled a sadist by the speaker.

To clarify what the above phrases about God are trying to get across, let us illustrate it with a more familiar situation. The phrase, "I see God in the sunflower", can be taken in two ways. First, in a pantheistic sense, one can understand this statement to mean that a thing such as a flower would be an actual physical part of God. Second, in a **nonpantheistic** sense, the phrase means that we can perceive what God is like by looking at what He has made. This latter concept maintains the creatorship and transcendence of God.

Similarly, when I say, "God is love," Scripture is quoted; but it, too, can be taken in two ways. First, in a pantheistic sense, one can regard that God is some all-pervading influence such as love; therefore, wherever one sees love, he sees God. One who holds such a concept could just as well state that love is God as to say that God is love. Second, in a **nonpantheistic** sense, the phrase means that God is a person who originates love. Just as He can make a flower or a tree, He can also make spiritual things such as law, love, faith, and wisdom. By the context of 1 John 4:8, we can tell that the phrase, "God is love," should be taken to describe a personal God who originates love. It is interesting to note that the writings of Ellen G. White in regard to pantheism deal almost entirely with this spiritualistic form of pantheism. "The mighty power that works through all nature and sustains all things is not, as some men of science represent, merely an all-pervading principle, and actuating energy. God is a Spirit; yet He is a personal Being; for so He has revealed Himself:" (MH413.2).

The Adventist preacher who gave the above mentioned television sermon and similar sermons became entangled with free lovism and lost his way.

The Light of the World:

Pantheism misinterprets John 1:9 in such a way that Christ is an all-pervading light. They say, there is a "spark of divinity" in every person (cf. 8T291.8).

A number of years ago a few Adventist physicians in the school of medicine of Loma Linda University began to tell the medical students that there was no reason for them to go to foreign fields or to their neighbor with the gospel as far as that person was concerned. When I inquired of one of them why they made such statements, the answer was, "God is in every one. Nothing that you do will result in their salvation or cause them to be lost."

Such a philosophy, if believed, would do away with the missionary program that God has designed for the salvation of mankind. Jesus is the "Light of the world" (DA463, 475). We are to be lower lights to lead the indifferent and unconcerned "lost coins" to Christ (COL194-6; 9T171). We are to search for the "lost sheep" (COL192). We are to welcome the prodigal sons and daughters as they return to their Saviour and Father. (COL209-10). This "Light" that lighteth every man must be taken to them, or they may not see Him (COL413-21). God has put Himself under obligation to use His church to spread the message of salvation (4BC1151; cf. COL79; 1SM99; DA297).

Partaking of Divinity:

I have heard it proposed that the analogies and symbols that Christ used to describe the interrelationship between Himself and His followers should be interpreted to mean that in partaking of divinity we would then be divine as Christ was divine. The idea is of a pantheistic "spark of divinity" in every one.

Jesus said, "I am the vine, ye are the branches" (John 15:5). Also, "Except ye eat the flesh of the Son of man, and drink His blood, ye have no life in you" (John 6:53). The apostle Paul wrote, "for we are members of His body, of His flesh, and of His bones" (Eph. 5:30).

Since the Lord is transcendent, how are we to partake of divinity? Is it by eating God? At the Lord's supper was He performing transubstantiation? How could Jesus say, "I am in the Father, and the Father [is] in me," and still teach that He and the Father were two different Persons (see John 14:10, 20; Ev614)? Just how are we to "abide in Christ," and how does He "abide [remain] in us" (John 15:4)?

Jesus discussed these important points with His disciples just before His death. He stated that His **words** and the example of His life, "They are spirit, and they are life" (John 6:63; cf. Ev614). "If ye continue in my word, then are ye my disciples indeed" (John 8:31).

Jesus said in regard to **His abiding in us**, "If ye abide in Me, and my words abide in you, ye shall ask...," and ye shall "bear much fruit¤" John15:7, 8).

In regard to **our abiding in Christ**, He said, "If ye keep my commandments, ye shall abide in my love,..." (John 15:10 New KJV).

The gist of Christ's statements need not and does not connote a mystical pantheistic union of divinity and humanity. It is spiritualism that teaches, "'...it is his [man's] destiny... to progress, even to eternity, toward the Godhead'." (GC554).

God makes a human being, a separate free moral person, detached from Himself and capable of independent thought and action (Ed17.5). God expresses words; He acts, and these have meaning. We partake of divinity by receiving these expressions into our minds in the right spirit, by receiving Christ as our Saviour (DA389.6, 675.8), and by taking part of His proffered power to think and to act in accordance with His will (DA676.4). This is essentially the new covenant relationship (Jeremiah 31:33, 34).

Unity of Nature and Wholeness:

In the use of these two words "unity" and "whole" as applied to man, we come into an area of pantheism which is quite subtle. These words may best be recognized as used in a pantheistic sense by the manner in which they are fitted into the context of other pantheistic phrases and terminology of certain authors.

The pantheist looks at man as a "unity" and, by implication or by outright meaning, presents the concept that the nature of man is one. In their thinking, the other two natures of man are, in "ultimate" definition, really the same as the nature which they consider that constitutes the whole. For example, the pantheist would say that the nature of man is spiritual and nothing more. He might also use the terms "mental" and "physical," but he would change the meaning of mental and physical by the redefinition of words and treat those two as though they were spiritual.

When the pantheistic theologians looks on "wholeness" in the sense of unity, oneness of nature, the science of salvation that deals with sin, atonement, and redemption needs to be revamped. From their standpoint sin is defined as "the cleaving asunder of the unity of man and the production of civil war within, warfare among the parts of life." I gather from their writings that sin would be a war between the three natures of man, such as war between the spiritual nature and the mental nature or war between the physical and spiritual natures. In the thinking of the pantheist, redemption would merely consist of reasoning with the person to stop, by some means, this intrapersonal internature conflict.

Those concepts need to be resisted. Man was created as a **unit** with a physical, a spiritual, and a mental nature. Each of these suffer the effects of sin. The sinner is at war with a personal God, not at war with himself. The spiritual nature has love of sin and guilt of transgression. The mental nature has the propensities and tendencies from the remembrance, the "record," of sin. The physical body suffers the damage to genes from the disobedience of his ancestors and the disease and debility to his body that have resulted from his own misdeeds. Redemption corrects the effects of sin on the person. The love for sin and the guilt are removed at conversion and repentance, the record of sin will be "blotting out" time at the "times of refreshing," and the physical defects will be removed at the Second Coming by God through the ministry of Christ and the Holy Spirit.

The devil has tried to cloud our understanding of this restoration of sinners from the effects of sin and of the state of the dead by the doctrines of pantheism and dualism. When a person is physically and mentally dead, there is no life as far as that creature is concerned. Nothing is left over except the constituents that were used by God (Psalm 146:4; Eccl. 12:7). There is no physical, nor mental, nor spiritual essence which continues to "live" past death. Existence of the "born again" person requires the presence of the three-fold nature as a unit. God has a record of the memory pathways of the mind, called the "spirit" or "character" (cf. 6BC1093; 5T310.3; COL356.6, 332.7; 4T606.8), as well as a record of our physical characteristics, and with these He can reproduce the same person at the resurrection. The mental record, the feelings and thoughts combined, are there as "records" in heaven but are not "alive" after mental death of the person (cf. 5T310.3; CG562).

Loma Linda University has an aim which is "To Make Man Whole." In recent years the meaning of this motto has been debated, hinging upon the word "whole." Some consider man as a whole already and speak of "treating the whole man." When "whole" is equated with the word, "entire," then there is no problem; but this is not always the case. Some want to use it in the sense of unity of natures.

The use of the word "whole" in connection with the motto, I feel, is taken from the words of Christ (Matt. 9:12, Mark 2:17, or

Luke 5:31). These texts refer to our commission to work with God to correct the effects of sin on the physical, mental and moral natures of sinners. In other words, we are to cooperate with God to make man as healthy (whole) physically as possible here and now through knowledge of and obedience to God's physical laws; to make man healthy (whole) mentally through knowledge of and obedience to God's laws of the mind; and to make man healthy (whole) spiritually through knowledge of and obedience to God's spiritual laws. We are to introduce men to the forgiving grace of God for spiritual rebirth and to the enabling grace, so they may experience the joy of obedience to all God's laws by His power.

Holistic Medicine:

God has revealed that the nature of man is three-fold. Man is a **unit not a unity**. Man is in rebellion against God spiritually, mentally, and physically. Pantheism would look at man as a unity and, by implication or by outright meaning, present the concept that the nature of man is one. We hear and read of "Holistic" medicine. Some speak of treating the "whole man."

As mentioned in the previous section some quite correctly equate "whole" with the word, "entire," but this is not the intent of all speakers and authors. Some consider man to be unity, of one nature. The approach to the sick and the religious ministry is different if you consider a person as a unity instead of one with a three-fold nature.

Examples of unitarian holistic medicine are evident in a brochure describing a workshop by the Mandeville Center of the University of California at San Diego. It is touted as "The Medical Model of the Future – An in-depth Survey of Holistic Health."

In the symposium scheduled for September, 1977, we see a mixture, of oriental healing arts such as Jin Shin Jyutsu, "the ancient art...concerned with a process of channeling energy flow within the body to establish balance." There is a session on "Tibetan Gong Meditation" and another entitled "Laying on of Lighted Hands." An examination of the course descriptions indicates that much of it is spiritualistic-pantheistic in nature. The session, "Integral Psychology and Esoteric Healing" by Robert Gerard, Ph.D., President of the International Foundation for Integral Psychology, is described to "share how to contact and channel psycho-spiritual energies for the benefit of individuals and groups. The presentation will include a meditative experience in order to contribute as a group to a planetary process of renewal."

What can be the meaning of this sudden emphasis on "holistic medicine?" We know that Satan plans to sweep the whole world into the ranks of spiritualism (GC588). Can this be one way?

Those who are ill are more likely to be receptive to religious things. Those who are seriously ill or have a medically incurable ailment tend to grasp at miracle cures and such treatments almost regardless of expense.

God chose to use miracles at the time of Christ to demonstrate the goodness and power of divinity (DA368, 406). Satan has endeavored to imitate and counterfeit miracle working (5T696-7). An example is the workings of Pharaoh's magicians against Moses (PP264-5).

What will be the status of miracles in our time? A study of available writings indicates that God plans a different emphasis now (2SM54; CH469). Satan and his agents will be allowed to perform actual miracles (1T302; 5T698). In addition to these he will perform deceptions, imitation miracles (MM110; 5T698; 9T16). He may cast a spell over a person, cause them to be ill, and then propitiously "heal" the person by removing the spell (GC588-9; 2SM53).

Let us consider how "Holistic Medicine" fits into the picture. A person becomes ill from ignoring the laws of health. He seeks the advice of a good Adventist physician who outlines the needed change in life style for the patient so that he may recover a measure of his lost health. The patient objects to this change in his way of eating, drinking, and sedentary life. He wants a pill to cure him. If he refuses to change his life style, and the pills are ineffective, what is he left to do? (CH458). He hears of a "Holistic physician" who has good results with his patients. He goes to him. Through the "laying on of lighted hands," he is healed by a miracle of spiritualism. (CH455-61). Will he later turn from such a practitioner? Not likely.

God says that the message of health reform is **not** the third angel's message (CDF77), but that the presentation of health principles must be united with this message. "Health reform is to be made a part of the third angel's message," as an "entering wedge" or a "right hand" to lessen suffering in the world and to purify the church (CDF77). "The body is the only medium through which the mind and the soul are developed for the upbuilding of character" (CDF73). Ill health is not conducive to mental effort or spiritual growth.

In addition, the advantages that a healthy body offers–health reform through God's true remedies–brings the appetites and passions into subjection to the higher powers of the mind (AA311; 3T491-2). When appetite holds sway over reason, the person is not free as God intends. God plans that our reason, directed by His word and the Holy Spirit, shall have mastery in our lives (MH130-1). Such a preparation is needful to be ready to participate in the loud cry of the third angel's message (CDF32, 69).

When God says, "Gluttony is the prevailing sin of this age," we should praise God (CDF32). We can now go to Him with full confidence for sufficient wisdom and power to control our appetites (CDF17; MH130-1). Daniel prayed three times a day for control of appetite and passions even with the threat of the lion's den (MM144). Should we do less?

God has laws that deal with mental and physical health as well as with soul salvation (MM10; CDF69; 6T306). In the last remnant of time, will God wink at disobedience to His laws for body care so long as we acknowledge the Sabbath and do not receive the mark of the beast? Evidence seems clear that we cannot ignore His natural laws (CDF17, 118, 120). Disobedience to natural laws results in disease and premature death, but there is more to it than that. Can we show belief in God if we continue to use flesh foods which He states is one cause of cancer (CDF388)? And what about tea and coffee and rich foods (CDF123-4, 425)? Either we do not believe, or we do not care what happens to our health! Both positions show serious disregard for the Creator.

In regard to miraculous healings, what will be God's emphasis in the last remnant of time? First, God does not want us to pray for healing of those who plan to disregard His laws of health (CDF26, 401). Second, He does not propose to use the working of miracles as a test of His participation in the care of the patient (2SM55). Third, He wants His people to combine the message of healthful living by natural means with the teaching of the Scriptures (MH127; 1T486, 559; CDF75; 6T301). This is "genuine medical missionary work." Fourth, the last generation will glorify God by obeying His will in the physical, mental, and spiritual realms by faith in Christ. His ways of health are vindicated. He can heal them through obedience to just and perfect laws or by a miracle, whatever He chooses (MM15-6; CDF26, 49).

The warning against spiritualistic physicians, given in 1882, seems more timely now (CH458-9). Like the word "gay," the word "holistic" is now polluted. A new word must be selected to convey our approach to the care of the patient physically, mentally, and morally.

Eight Natural versus Eight True Remedies:

Closely related to the problem of "natural versus supernaturalism" is the problem of natural remedies versus the supernatural working of God for humanity. Some who work in health education have slipped into a habit of calling the remedies that are presented by Ellen White (see MH127) the "eight natural remedies." Almost invariably "trust in divine power" is included amongst the eight. Yet "trust in divine power" is a supernatural remedy. Ellen White is precise in her language in this reference. She says, "...–these are the **true** remedies." In the next paragraph she states, "The use of natural remedies requires an amount of care, etc.," but she does not call trust in divine power a natural remedy. Further on, on page 130, she states, "Apart from divine power, no genuine reform can be effected.... Not until the life of Christ becomes a vitalizing power in our lives can we resist the temptations that assail us from within and from without."

I need supernatural help from God. My patients need God's help; but if I call "trust in divine power" a "natural remedy," then I will get only what help I can get for my patients and friends from pure air, sunlight, abstemiousness, rest, exercise, proper diet, and the use of water. Why? I have, by default, excluded the supernatural workings of God. Furthermore, I have treated the situation as do the pantheists as though there was no difference between the natural and the supernatural.

Those seven natural remedies are very good. God has arranged it so that all can have those bounties. Those all come from a beneficient God. Yet, they are as effectual in the hands of an atheist as they are in the hands of a Christian. But what I need most of all is the desire **to want to change** my life style and the enabling **power to change**. I need this steadily and permanently. True enough, there are strong willed people who can stop smoking and put into practice a good diet and exercise plan, but it is a mental task and a drudgery. There is a better way. This is where "trust in divine power" enters into the program.

Those of us on this earth are mentally wrestling, not only with our old habits and propensities that have accumulated in our minds in our lifetime, but also we westle with supernatural powers, "the rulers of the darkness of this world." Thanks be to God who has included the promise of help by His divine power. We are not left to do battle with only the natural weapons and our own reason and will power. We have the assurance of His supernatural help if we acknowledge our need and ask.

Chapter 28

PANTHEISTIC CONCEPTS STEALTHILY ENTER THE CHURCH

For centuries the enemy of souls has propagated pantheistic ideas, sometimes subtly and at other times blatantly, through philosophers and infidel authors. For example, if one critically examines the early works of Wordsworth and of his contemporaries, one finds a thread of pantheistic ideas through them.

The ideas of pantheism may be detected in the writings of some current ecumenical authors, certain evangelical Protestants, and some Catholics. For over thirty years, our denomination has advised our ministers to go to other institutions of learning outside of our faith for further training. In these institutions of "higher" learning they were exposed to this supernaturalist philosophy of the nature of man and the universe. And why not? It is the prevailing philosophy in America and Western Europe by which their teachers explain the nature of the universe. Why should not those men teach what they believe?

No doubt these Seventh-day Adventist students went there with the idea in mind that they would not accept any erroneous theories. However, not one of us knows all truth or understands all error. The sifting process for truth and error requires a most excellent screen. The false concepts that they rejected were the ones that **they knew** were wrong. They accepted what they did not determine was false. It is difficult to immerse yourself in varying percentages of sludge and come out smelling like a rose. As a result we have bits and pieces of the error of Babylon and her daughters accepted by Adventist students and brought back into our churches and schools to be mixed with Seventh-day Adventist theology. It is made all the more subtle in this way because error enters couched in Adventist terminology and only those tenets closest to truth are initially introduced.

We would react with consternation if we were to read in the Bible that Elisha had sent the young sons of the prophets to Nineveh for further learning after they had graduated from the schools of the prophets. If the young priests of Israel had been sent to Babylon to study and "upgrade" their education in various things, including the things of God, it would seem odd to us through our retrospectoscope. Yet, is this not essentially what is done now, when we advise young minsters fresh out of SDA colleges to go to the universities of the land which are run by churches of various persuasions or by atheistic organizations for further study along theological or literary lines? Is it any wonder then that we find various phrases or concepts of ill repute entering into the sermons and literature of our denomination?

We have warnings which discourage further training in institutions of "higher" learning of the world (MM62; FCE98-99, 470, 535-6; CPT15, 45, 497; COL41). Of course, these admonitions have to be balanced with the statement to follow by the same writer. "We would that there were strong young men, rooted and grounded in the faith, who had such a living connection with God that they could, if so counseled by our leading brethren, enter the higher colleges in our land, where they would have a wider field for study and observation" (5T583-4). Unfortunately, we have used the above statement to make such activities a routine, almost mandatory thing by peer pressure and financial inducements.

Several reasons are given for considering further training in the institutuions not of our faith, These include: to associate with different classes of people, to obtain a wider field for study and observations, to become acquainted with the workings and methods of others, to obtain a knowledge of theology as taught in that institution, to be better prepared to labor for the educated class, and to meet the prevailing error as did the Waldensian scholars (GC70).

It is interesting to note that the Waldenses took the calculated risk of exposure to the temptations, the unavoidable witnessing of vice, for the purpose of making converts there. Perhaps their greatest danger was the encounter with "Satan's wily agents" who urged upon these scholars "subtle heresies and dangerous deceptions" (GC70).

Have we been as successful as the Waldenses, or have we lost more to the enemy than we have gained?

God's Answer to Pantheism:

Three Persons, the Father, the Son, and the Holy Spirit, act as one in whatever they do. They are one in purpose, one in character, one in mind, but are three Persons (MH422; Ev615). Repentant sinners are baptized into the names of these three personal Beings (Matt. 28:19). On the other hand the ungodly, "thinks, in his insolence, 'God never punishes'; his thoughts amount to this, there is no God at all...'" (Psalm 10:4, Moffatt).

Inspiration also consistently maintains that the universe consists of a physical (material) realm and a spiritual (moral) realm. God made both; they coexist and yet are distinct in nature (cf. CPT16.8; AA284; MH414). "In the creation of the earth, God was not indebted to pre-existing matter. 'He spake, and it was;... He commanded, and it stood fast.' All things, material or spiritual, stood up before the Lord Jehovah at His voice,..." (MH414.9).

When God created man, He made him a unit with a three-fold nature,- a physical, a mental, and a spiritual nature (see PP46.9; FCE57.3). The three-fold nature of man is maintained in the description of his creation (Genesis 2:7), and in the dissolution of man at the time of his death (Psalm 146:4; 6:5; Eccl. 12:7). Man is under law in these three realms. "To transgress His law, physical, mental, or moral, is to place one's self out of harmony with the universe, to introduce discord, anarchy, ruin" (Ed100.1). These three natures are sustained by God. "All who consecrate **body**, **soul**, and **spirit** to His service will be constantly receiving a new endowment of **physical**, **mental**, and **spiritual power**" (MH159.8 emphasis supplied; see also DA390.7; Ed123, 171; AA284).

> "He has prepared this living habitation for the mind; it is 'curiously wrought,' a temple which the Lord Himself has fitted up for the indwelling of His Holy Spirit. The mind controls the whole man.... All the physical organs are the servants of the mind,..." (FCE426.1).

The physical organs may be kept living in the hospital by mechanical and chemical means for many months after mental life has ceased. The body of a mother may be kept alive for weeks after her mind is dead, to preserve the life of her baby in the womb.

Scripture teaches us that spiritual and mental life depends upon a living physical body for existence. Nicodemas needed to be "born of the Spirit" before he was spiritually alive (John 3:3-6).

What Is To Be Done?

Some way modern pantheism must be counteracted. Some one must gather up these bits of Babylonish theology, point them out for what they are, and refer them back to those who can use them. These subtle pantheistic phrases are a curse to the religious world. They are as much a curse as the doctrines of Sunday sacredness, the immortality of the soul, and the multitude of other errors.

The prophet Zechariah has shown us how to dispose of them. It would be good, figuratively speaking, to write these on a scroll, place the scroll in an ephah, set a lid of lead on the top, and send the container with the scroll back to the land of Shinar (Zech. 5), back to Babylon and the daughters of Babylon who originated them. There they will be cherished and made use of.

Concluding Remarks:

This discussion was not prepared so that one would have a label to attach upon some one, Adventist or otherwise.

Those who reiterate pantheistic phrases or are involved in those doctrines fall into at least three categories. Some are, through ignorance, remouthing the phrases without understanding their meaning or are unthinkingly participating with others more deeply involved in the doctrines. Some are more entangled, so that the fundamentals of pantheism have altered their presentation of Seventh-day Adventist doctrines or have caused them to make no distinction between the sacred and the common. Such may have a heart perfect toward God, but they have a blind spot in their spiritual visual field. They need our special prayers. Some are out and out avowed pantheists. Their doctrines need to be opposed, but treat them as you would want to be treated. The ramifications of pantheism are so subtle and so deceptive, take heed lest you yourself should fall.

Some say that it is "speculation to think that pantheism will once again be a problem to us." Friends, pantheism has been with us a long time. The doctrines upon which the spiritualistic form are based are with us now. I have not presented any that I have not seen and heard myself.

Ellen White penned these words, "*Living Temple* contains the alpha of these theories. I knew that the omega would follow in a little while; and I trembled for our people" (1SM203.5).

She voices the reason for her concern, "I have seen the results of these fanciful views of God, in apostasy, spiritualism, and free-lovism" (Ev602.8). Apostasy, because they develop a whole new science of salvation (1SM204.2); spiritualism, because the whole universe is considered supernatural; and free-lovism, because "love is God" and the body is considered holy.

In regard to discussions about Pantheism, several points in the book, *Evangelism* pages 623-25 deserve special emphasis.

(1) It is best not to preach on the subject of pantheism.

(2) It is not good to read quotations from authors who write these errors.

(3) Repetition of these errors helps Satan present his false theories to the people.

(4) Controversy over these spiritualistic theories will only confuse minds.

(5) Ministers and teachers who give themselves to the study of these pantheistic teachings run the risk of departing from the faith.

(6) Unmask these falsehoods by holding up and magnifying the truth.

On the other hand, we have been admonished to, "Let every man arouse, and work as he has opportunity. Let him speak words in season and out of season, and look to Christ for encouragement and strength in welldoing" (1SM195). Physicians have been chided for listening to fanciful, spiritualistic interpretations of Scripture and for remaining silent (1SM195-7). We are told to, "Unmask the pretentious sophistries" (1SM196). Angels of God have been delegated to come to our aid in this conflict (1SM196).

In the study for these few pages the author has endeavored to restrict his research to only enough reading to verify that these sentiments are indeed as stated. He has endeavored to restrict repetition of the erroneous phrases to only enough to unmask the situation. He is not interested in entering controversy on the subject for the reasons mentioned above.

Chapter 29

THOSE DRAMATIC CHANGES IN EUROPE - THE PANTHEISM COMPONENT

On December 3, 1989, George Bush was unable to meet with Mikhial Gorbachev on the Russian battleship at Malta because of high winds. It led one American general to comment words that were loaded with prophetic meaning. "There is another wind blowing over Europe that is influencing world events."

Perhaps you have wondered what is the meaning of the dramatic political and religious changes in the past year in Europe, Russia, and more recently in the Middle East. Why have the communist-dominated countries changed their ruthless will to rule and permitted these changes to occur? **What "other wind blowing over Europe" could bring all this about?** Can you imagine what the present conditions would be in the Middle East if Saddam Hussein of Iraq had decided to invade Kuwait a year or two ago when Russia was supplying arms to him? All of this has been most startling and rapid. Many have repeated the phrase, "The final movements will be rapid ones" (9T11).

What does the Bible in prophecy have to say, if anything, about the influence of communistic atheism against the Lord's work? What will be the next great events? Our main study will concentrate on the last five verses of Daniel 11, parts of Revelation 11, and of Revelation 13 and 17.

To grasp the prophecies we need some definitions. Here are some needed ones that are accepted by students of Bible prophecy.

Time of the end: The time period from the end of the 1260 year time prophecy in 1798 until Jesus comes. Dan 12:4.

King of the south: Egypt, atheism, whose modern major proponent is atheistic communism.

King of the north: Babylon, profligate woman, union of church and state, the papacy. Jere. 25:12;46:13,20,24; Rev. 17:1-5

Usurper king of the north: Lucifer — Satan. Isaiah 14:12-14.

True King of the north: Jesus. Psalm 48:1,2.

Edom: Descendents of Esau
Moab: Descendents of Lot
Ammon: Descendents of Lot
} *[Islam came from Mohammed, a descendent of Ishmael]*

Tents of his palace: Tent headquarters of a king when he went forth to war. Another interpretation of palace is "idol"

Seas: People, nations, and tongues. Rev. 17:15.

Glorious holy mountain: House of God. Isaiah 2:2-4; Psalm 48:2; Daniel 2:34,35,44,45; Micah 4:1-3.

Harlot Woman: Apostate church and her daughters who follow her teachings, Babylon. Rev 17:5.

Pure Virgin: True church, Lord's bride, Holy Jerusalem. Rev. 21:9-10.

Horns: Political forces or powers or kings. Rev. 17:12.16

Beasts: Special political governments that work against God.

Fornication: Illicit coworking between church and state.

Background Information: All heaven is working to prepare God's church for its role in the "final atonement" for the world, especially for the closing hours. God has given us considerable historical background and prophetic guidance to assist us in the great controversy between good and evil.

From the time of the call of Abraham to the first coming of Jesus, Palestine was a geographic location for Israel under the special protection of God. The enemies of Israel under the leadership of Satan were Egypt from the south, Assyria or Babylon from the north (Jere. 50:17), and the Moabite, Edomite, and Ammonite neighbors to the east.

At that time Egypt and Babylon were the two great centers of civilization, one along the Nile and the other along the Tigris-Euphrates. The Egyptians believed in many gods of **nature**, the cobra, the Nile, frogs, cattle, etc.; whereas the Babylonians believed in many gods of the **supernatural**. Both worshiped the sun. Both considered their kings to be gods.[1] These were pantheistic.[2] Edomites were descendents of Esau. Moabites and Ammonites were descendents of Lot.

We speak of the "Spirit of 1776" in connection with the founding of the United States of America. Similarly, while Israel was the **chosen nation**, the people themselves and their guiding principle (or spirit) could be geographically located. Likewise, the three main enemies of Israel had their characteristic principles (or spirit) and could be located geographically. We recognize a "spiritual" Israel, a "spiritual" Egypt, (king of the south), a "spiritual" Babylon, (king of the north), and a "spiritual" Edom and Moab.[3]

After the Messiah came, and Israel, as a nation, had rejected Him, the "kingdom of God" was taken from Israel and given to others (Jer. 31:35-37; Matt. 21:43) "until the times of the Gentiles be fulfilled" (Luke 21:24). Israel **as a chosen people** was no more in a geographic location. Yet the "spirit" of true Israel would be perpetuated throughout the world by converted Jews and Gentiles alike. The message of Paul and the other apostles was, "If ye be Christ's, then are ye Abraham's seed" (Gal. 3:29; Acts 15:6-29). Just so, the "spirit" of Egypt and the "spirit" of Babylon and the "spirit" of all the desert neighbors of Israel were dispersed throughout the world.

Now, wherever in the world there are true followers of Christ, we find "spiritual Israel." Wherever there are followers of the atheistic-pantheistic principles of Egypt, we find "spiritual Egyptians." Wherever there are followers of the spiritual-pantheistic teachings of Babylon, we find "spiritual Babylonians." If we grasp this premise, we will not make the mistake in the "time of the end," of localizing last day Israel or their enemies to a specific, geographic area. The final conflict between the principles of God's kingdom, the tenets of Egyptian atheism, and the coercive religion of Babylon will be going on worldwide within the mind of each person, within the family, within the neighborhood, and within nations. To be in the right army, we must understand the guiding principles of true Christianity, of the spirit of Egypt, and the spirit of Babylon.

Parenthetically, we should be on guard against another major error. The Jewish people at the time of Christ had misinterpreted the prophecies of the coming Messiah. The prophecies that applied to the second coming of the Messiah as King, they had applied to His first coming as servant and sacrifice. Just so in our time, some may misinterpret the statements that apply to His coming to cleanse the earth at the end of the thousand years (Rev. 20:7 to 22:5), and apply them to the time before the thousand years, when He comes to take His people to heaven (Rev. 19:11 to 20:6; 1Thess. 4:16,17).

In Ellen White's discussion of the French Revolution, in *The Great Controversy*, we have important clues which unfold a key segment of prophecy. When God saw fit to prepare this world for the closing events just before the time of the end, He opened up special insights to the reformers into the Scriptures. "The spirit of liberty went with the Bible" (GC277). This spirit of liberty would open the way for the spread of the gospel; it would reveal the tenets of the true faith and contrast them with those of coercive religion. In the process, it would tear down monarchical despotism. Satan saw the need to combat the Reformation and this spirit of liberty by bringing up another power to fight against God. This new "manifestation of satanic power" was atheism, "spiritually Egypt" with the "spirit of unbelief and defiance" against God like the Pharaohs of old (GC269). It also had the licentious "spirit" of Sodom (ibid).

This manifestation of satanic power developed right on time shortly before 1798, the Biblical "time of the end." At the beginning of "the time of the end," this atheistic power working in the French government attacked, not only the monarchy, but also the papal church. The pope was taken prisoner. By this maneuver Satan made it appear as if something bad (French atheism) was attacking something good (papal religion). The one head of the beast of Rev. 13 that was in power at that time received a deadly wound. Rev. 13:3.

Daniel and The "Time Of The End": First, please read Daniel 11:40 to 12:1 in the King James Version and then read the paraphrased version below in which the definition of the words or phrases have been transposed for the original word.

> (40) About 1798 shall atheism push at the papacy: and the papacy shall come against atheism like a whirlwind, with chariots, and with horsemen, and with may ships; and he

shall enter into the countries, and shall overflow and pass over.

(41) The papacy shall enter also into the glorious land, and many [countries] shall be overthrown: but these shall escape out of his hand, even Edom, and Moab, and the chief of the children of Ammon.

(42) The papacy shall stretch forth his hand also upon the countries: and atheism shall not escape.

(43) But the papacy shall have power over the treasures of gold and silver, and over all the precious things of atheism: and the Libyans and Ethiopians shall be at his steps.

(44) But tidings out of the east and out of the north shall trouble the papacy and Satan: therefore the papacy and Satan shall go forth with great fury to destroy, and utterly to make away many.

(45) And the papacy and Satan shall plant the tabernacle of his palace or idol between the people on this earth and God's sanctuary in heaven; yet the papacy and Satan shall come to his end, and none shall help him.

(1) And at that time shall Michael [Jesus] stand up, the great prince which standeth for the children of thy people: [probation will close] and there shall be a time of trouble, such as never was since there was a nation even to that same time: and at that time thy people shall be delivered.

In this prophecy we see that atheism will develop and work against God, but it will also be opposed to the apostate church-state power, Satan's other major force. Next we see a time when this apostate church-state power, Babylon, will make an overwhelming resurgence. It will overcome that atheistic power. Yet some powers, such as Edom, Moab, and Ammon will not be overcome by the papacy.

We see that an apostate church shall set up a tabernacle of ministry for the usurper king of the north between the people in the world and the heavenly sanctuary where Jesus ministers (cf. 2 Thess. 2:4 and EW55-56). The papacy has done this by placing their priests between the ministry of Christ for sinners when they hear their confession and "absolves" them without the blood of Jesus. The papacy has done this when they interpose the mediation of dead Mary, the mother of Jesus, between sinners and the mediatorial work of Christ in the heavenly sanctuary. They have placed several idols in Satan's tabernacle (tent). Among these are the idol wafer, the idol sabbath (Sunday), and tradition (7BC977).

According to the *New Catholic Encyclopedia*[4] under the topic, "Assumption of Mary" and her proposed mediatorial work, we find that there has been a gradual building up of the belief in the "coredemptive" work of the "Mediatrix" Mary. Pope Sergius I (circa 687 A.D.) seems to have started this when he paid tribute to the anniversary of the death of Mary and later commemorated her "assumption." By 733 to 740 A.D. she was referred to as "Mediatrix." By the seventeenth century the concept of the "coredemptive" work of Mary, the mother of Jesus, was "generally accepted."

The Bible teaches that death is a sleep (Luke 11:11-14). The dead know not anything (Eccl. 9:5; Psalm 115:17); and yet, we see the "king of the north" propagating the dogma that not only is Mary, the mother of Jesus, alive, but that she has also been taken to heaven and is serving as a mediator between the people on this earth and the God of heaven. In fact, the Roman Catholic church has conferred upon Mary the authority to grant pardon to Satan himself if he should repent.[5]

The Bible teaches that "We have a great High Priest who has passed through the heavens, Jesus the Son of God..."(Hebrews 4:14). No man [or woman] can take this position. It has to be given Him of God (Hebrews 5:4). Jesus said, "I am the way, the truth, and the life: No man cometh unto the Father, but by me" (John 14:6). Peter himself said, "Neither is there salvation in any other: for there is none other name under heaven given unto men, whereby we must be saved" (Acts 4:12).

Not only does Satan set out to place his usurper ministry in his headquarters tent, but he attacks the doctrinal truths of Christ's ministry in the heavenly sanctuary. We can see this from what has happened within the Seventh-day Adventist Church.

Since 1955 in connection with the Walter Martin/Donald Barnhouse issue, the book *Questions on Doctrine* and the "New Theology," tenets we can see his vicious attacks against two major pillars of the Adventist faith – the Investigative Judgement and the Final Attonement. Instead of these truths, Satan offers the false doctrines that "the attonement was completed at the cross" and that "Jesus took not upon himself the seed of Abraham, but He took the flesh of Adam before the fall." Thus, neither victory over sinning nor the final cleansing from the guilt of sin will be accomplished for humanity by the ministry of Christ in the heavenly sanctuary.[6]

Daniel prophesied that the king of the north would "regard not the God of his fathers nor the desire of women, nor regard any god; for he shall magnify himself above them all. But in their place he shall honor a god of fortresses; and a god which his fathers did not know..." (Daniel 11:37-38).

The attempted assassination of Pope John Paul on May 13, 1981, the anniversary of the Fatima prophecies, caused him to look into the Fatima prophecies more diligently. This led him to take seriously the "Third Secret" of the Fatima apparition that Russia and the world were to be dedicated to the Virgin Mary. It has led him to set out on his "new world order agenda."[7] According to Malachi Martin, "He [Pope John Paul] is waiting, rather, for an event that will fission human history, splitting the immediate past from the oncoming future. It will be an event on public view in the skies, in the oceans, and on the continental landmasses of this planet. It will particularly involve our human sun.... But on the day of this event, it will not appear merely as the master star of our so-called solar system. Rather, it will be seen as the circumambient glory of the Woman [Virgin Mary]...."[8]

Tidings "out of the east and out of the north" will cause him (Satan) to go forth to overcome many (Cf. Rev. 12:17; 1 Peter 5:8). Satan will take the field of battle in person, personating Christ, performing miracles and imitation miracles to deceive (2 Cor. 11:14; GC612, 624). He will be supporting the harlot woman (Rev. 17:8-11; 12:17). He will pretend to be the "great medical missionary" (MM87-8). Yet he will be brought to an end. Christ, Michael, will stand up, throw down His censer of priestly ministry, close probation for all, and come to take His people home (Daniel 12:1; Rev. 18:8-24).

The Beast From the Bottomless Pit: In Rev. 11 John relates a vision of this same time period and identifies the beast "out of the bottomless pit" to be an atheistic power, "spiritually Egypt." We see this same beast next in Rev. 17. In chapter 17, though, the profligate woman Babylon, the great apostate church, is seated upon the **beast from the bottomless pit.**

How does the papacy arrive in that position of dominance above atheism? By having, **for the final phase of Satan's rebellion,** an ideology of deception that is superior to that of atheistic communism! It is in this aspect of the study that an understanding of the theories of pantheism is of special help. The king of the south and the king of the north represent the two major forms of pantheism in Satan's armamentarium. Both forms consider the universe to be of one nature, a unity, and deny the truth of the personhood of God.

Communistic-atheistic pantheism considers the universe to be all physical or material. It denies God, miracles, and supernatural events. Catholicism, on the other hand, considers the universe to be all spiritual. With this tenet it teaches that "God is ultimate reality." They believe that a priest can convert the bread and wine into the actual flesh and blood of Christ. They maintain that the ability to work miracles is a sign of the true church. When Catholicism unites with spiritualism and with the false prophet (apostate protestantism) to work miracles, Rev 13:1-14; 16:13,14), all the strength of atheistic pantheism will crumble. The church "sits" upon many waters which in prophetic language means "peoples." Adherents of atheism will switch their allegiance almost en masse and do the biddings of the apostate church, the type that considers the universe to be supernatural.

With atheistic pantheism at work as the "king of the south" and the spiritualistic pantheism at work as the "king of the north," we can see the great conflict against the God of heaven, as pictured symbolically in Daniel 11:40-45. God's people, spiritual Israel, wherever they are, will be caught between these enemy forces, as Israel of old was caught between their geographic enemies from the south (Egypt), their enemies from the north (Assyria or Babylon), and their Edomite and Moabite neighbors.

For over forty years this globe has lived under the shadow of hydrogen bomb clouds and rocket trails. The guns, rockets, and rhetoric have been pointed in two main directions, at each other. But neither the western civilization nor the communist dominated nations have dared do anything that would jar the trigger of the other. The iron and bamboo curtains have been maintained. Occasional risks have been taken very cautiously by communism to test the will of the opponent, but the conflict stops short of using the final weapons. Both factions fear that the next world war, if it were to come, would end civilization for all. Thus, the world has been in a kind of stalemate in so far as **physical arms** are concerned. Governments can no longer use their most deadly weapons to settle their differences or to dominate. So they turn to spiritual weapons.

In Daniel 11:41 we see another group in the battle. We see, "Edom and Moab and the main part of the Ammonites" that shall be "delivered out of his hand." Who are these? These are Arabs, most of whom hold to Islam, the one other main ideology that dominates the economy and thinking of the world. Islam was founded by a descendent of Ishmael. Where does it stand in regard to so-called "Christianity" and to communism? They reject both. Proud, coercive Islam dominates its adherents by cruelty (Isaiah 16:6; Jere. 48:6 to 49:33).

Even though "Edom, Moab, and Ammon" do escape the king of the north, Egypt (atheism) shall not escape out of the hand of the king of the north. As we see in Revelation 17, Babylon (the papacy and her daughters) will yet sit astride the beast out of the bottomless pit (communism). How does this happen? We see a great resurgence of interest in spiritual, religious, things in the communistic world in spite of every effort to shut it out of the minds of the millions for the past seventy years. Churches may have been shut down and made into museums; their ministers and priests may have been imprisoned and slaughtered; their schools have been used to drill into the minds of a generation that there is no god, no life after death, no spiritual things; but when the time comes for the final showdown between Christ (the real King of the North) and Satan (the usurper king of the north), Satan must have as his dominant deception those who believe strongly in supernatural manifestations.

"The agencies of evil are combining their forces and consolidating. They are strengthening for the last great crisis. Great changes are soon to take place in our world, and **the final movements will be rapid ones**" (9T11).

"Those who hold the reins of government are not able to solve the problem of moral corruption, poverty, pauperism, and increasing crime. They are struggling in vain to place business operations on a more secure basis" (9T13).

The boast of Nicolae Ceausescu, hard-line communist ruler of Roumania, that he would crush any attempt to change the type of government. What happened to him should serve as a signal to other atheistic leaders that their days are limited unless they, too, change.

What Brings About The Final "Rapid Movements"?: In Daniel 11, verses 44 and 45 (R.S.V.), we read in reference to the king of the north that "tidings from the east and the north shall alarm him." These tidings will cause him to "go forth with great fury to destroy, and utterly make away many," to "pitch his palatial tents between the seas and the glorious holy mountain...." The next scene is, "he shall come to his end, with none to help him." Michael,

Christ, the true King of the north, "[shall] stand up..., and there shall be a time of trouble, such as never was...." (Daniel 12:1).

Who is the true "King of the north"? Who is behind the "king of the south" and the "king of the north"? Could it be that one person, the usurper king of the north, is masquerading as both the king of the south and the king of the north? This is potentially confusing, but we see the usurper king of the north in Rev 12 as the great red dragon.

Isaiah tells us about the usurper king of the north in the "proverb" against the "spiritual" king of Babylon. Lucifer, "son of the morning," said in his heart, "I will ascend into heaven, I will exalt my throne above the stars of God; I will sit upon the mount of the congregation, in the **sides of the north**" (Isa 14:13).

The psalmist tells us of the true King of the north. "Great is the Lord, and greatly to be praised in the city of our God, in the mountain of his holiness. Beautiful for situation, the joy of the whole earth, is mount Zion, on the sides of the north, the city of the great King" (Psalm 48:1,2; See also Ezekiel 8:14).

What are the "tidings out of the east" and the tidings "out of the north" that are so important? What does God plan to do to prepare the church for the final phases of the controversy between Christ and Satan? The history of ancient Babylon helps us grasp the picture and understand the answer.

In ancient time Babylon was destroyed by the armies of Media-Persia under Cyrus who came from the north and east (Isaiah 41:25 to 42:4; 46:11; Jere. 50:9; 51:11). Belshazzar and his cohorts were having a great feast and drank out of the vessels from the temple of God (Daniel 5:1-4). In the prophecy of these events, Isaiah cites Cyrus by name and quotes the Lord as saying of Cyrus, he is "My shepherd" and "His [God's] anointed" Isaiah 44:28-45:1. Cyrus and the historical destruction of ancient Babylon and restoration of Israel to their heritage was so arranged by God to foreshadow the destruction of modern spiritual Babylon and deliverance of modern Israel by Christ, the true King of the north (and east), at His second coming (Cf. Rev. 16:12; Isaiah 41:2,25,26; 46:1; Rev. 19).

In our time Babylon, the apostate church, will be "drunken with the blood of the saints," and will be offering "a golden cup in her hand full of abominations...," to the whole world. These abominations are her false doctrines that nearly all in the world will receive to their own damnation (Rev. 17:2-4; 18:3). But there will be a remnant group of believers who reject these, who will choose God's way, and who will be delivered to return to their inheritance, the heavenly Canaan.

What are some of these "abominations" in the cup?[9]

Tradition over a "Thus saith the Lord."
Infant baptism instead of immersion of a thinking adult.
Auricular confession with blasphemous forgiveness by a man.
Penance - man works to be accepted by God, not by faith alone.
Transubstantiation (the mass) - bread and wine created into God.
"God is ultimate reality" - phrase that makes God a nonentity,
Peter becomes the "rock" for the church instead of Christ.
Peter and the priests have the "keys" instead of Scriptures.
Immaculate conception - dead Mary becomes the mediator.
Invocation of the saints - dead Saints become mediators.
Immortality of the soul - souls can be bought out of purgatory.
Eternal torment of the wicked - God's justice impugned.
Extreme unction - man saved by ceremony.
Sunday sacredness instead of the seventh-day Sabbath of the Lord.

In olden times a king was "married" to his kingdom (cf. Isaiah 54:5-7). When Jesus (Michael) gives up His work as High Priest and becomes King of kings, He "marries", Zion, His bride, the true church. However, just before the "Bridegroom comes to the wedding," He comes to His temple as the "Messenger of the covenant" to purify His people (Malachi 3:1-5).

He performs a work for His people to prepare them for heaven and for the time of trouble that is coming upon the earth (see GC426). This work of preparation of His people will include (1) the removal of the "northern army" and (2) the outpouring of "the early and the latter rain" of Joel 2:20-32, (3) the refining and purifying described in Malachi 3:1-5, (4) the sealing of Ezekiel 9, and (5) the "final atonement" with the blotting out of sin described in Zechariah 3:1-5 and Acts 3:19. It will include the messages to the world portrayed by the three angels of Revelation 14 and the repeat call of the mighty angel of Revelation 18.

Thus, two great messages or movements will be sent from heaven and directed by God for the preparation of the church and the world for the coming of Christ in the clouds of heaven. (1) the "sealing message" for God's people and (2) the "loud cry" for the honest in heart to come out of Babylon, the fallen churches, and worship the true God. In Revelation 7, the sealing angel is seen flying in **from the east** and speaking with a **"loud voice."** In Revelation 18, another angel from God's throne on the sides of the north adds his "mighty voice" to the messages of the three angels of Revelation 14. These messages urge all to take advantage of the plan of salvation. In addition to the call of these angel messengers, "**another voice out of heaven**" emphasizes this final invitation (Rev. 18:1,4).

Since sin entered this world, our Lord has offered unlimited mercy to His enemies in the world. At the end of time in a more emphatic way, God's government and all His ways of dealing with His followers as well as His dealings with sin and sinners will be vindicated. His justice as well as His love and mercy will stand clear before the universe. All will be given sufficient information with which to make an intelligent decision.

"Holy angels have been employed in directing this work, they have in charge the **great movements** for the salvation of men; but the **actual proclamation** of the gospel is performed by the servants of Christ upon the earth" (GC312). Angels came to Mary, Joseph, the shepherds, and men and women were prepared for their part to announce various events involved in the first coming of the "Messiah." Likewise, the messages that have to do with the preparation of a people for the judgment of the living and Christ's second coming must be clearly understood and given. The rapidity and the world-wide extent of this message is represented by angels "**flying**" in the midst of heaven" (Rev. 14:6-12; GC355-6). What tidings do God's messengers bring?

1. G.S. Goodspeed: *History of the Ancient World,* Charles Scribner's Sons, New York, 1904, pp. 17, 27.
2. C. Bonner: *Studies in Magical Amulets Chiefly Graeco-Egyptians,* Univ. of Michigan Press, Ann Arbor, MI, 1950. p. 317.
3. J.C. Haussler: *Syllabus and Guide to Study for Prophetic Interpretation I,* La Sierra College, Arlington, CA, 1959, pp. 38-53.
4. *New Catholic Encyclopedia,* McGraw-Hill, Washington, D.C., 1967, Vol 1:971ff and Vol 9:356.
5. Alfonsus M. de Liguori, *The Glories of Mary.* Quoted in, M.E. Walsh, *The Wine of Roman Babylon,* Leaves of Autumn Books, Payson, AZ, 1981, p. 143.
6. J. Reich: *The M L Andreason File,* LMN Publishing, St. Maries, ID, 1988

7. M. Martin: *The Keys of This Blood*, Simon and Schuster, New York, 1990, pp. 46-50.
8. ibid. pp. 639-657.
9. M.E. Walsh: *The Wine of Roman Babylon,* Leaves of Autumn Books, Paysons, AZ; 1981.

Chapter 30

TIDINGS OUT OF THE EAST AND OF THE NORTH

"Tidings Out Of The East" As we study the prophecies of Daniel and Revelation that apply to the final movements, we are told that the "kings of the east" are coming (Rev. 16:12) and that an angel "ascending from the east" comes to "seal" the servants of God in their forehead (Rev 7:1-3). The angel of Ezekiel nine was to put a mark on the forehead of those who mourn for the prevailing sinfulness and who do not participate in the sin. This work of sealing refers to examination of the character and starts with the characters of the "ancient men" in God's sanctuary (church). It is like the King that prepared a wedding for His Son. He furnished a wedding wardrobe for us, the guests. Just before the wedding, the king comes to examine, to investigate, the guests to see whether they are wearing the robe (Matt. 22:2-14). God has given us another example which foreshadows this work.

At the time of deliverance from Egyptian slavery, the Israelites had a sign on the lintel and on the door posts. Angels of God were directed to slay those who did not have the mark. In Egypt, the mark of the Passover blood and the slaughter of the unbelieving Egyptians was literal. A condition of Israel's deliverance from Egyptian bondage was that they must keep the Sabbath, the memorial of God's creative ability, and they were to remain under the cloud that guided their deliverance. In this way, they showed their trust in Jehovah to protect them from all their enemies and supply all their needs.

In the closing scenes of this world's history there will also be a mark, but it will be in the mind, "a settling into the truth, both intellectually and spiritually, so they cannot be moved" (4BC1161). The outward visible "mark" of this work of grace will be the observance of the true Sabbath of the Lord (Exodus 31:13). The slaughter will be the loss of spiritual life at the close of probation and loss of physical life (Ezekiel 9:5-9).

There will be a people who will choose to let "God work in them both **to will** [desire to do] and **to do** [be empowered to do] His good pleasure" (MB142; SC47). God's people will be pleading with Him for a perfect heart toward Him (PK591.1; 2T505-6). As they live trustingly in this relationship, God pours out His Spirit in the "early rain" to enable them to perform **righteous acts** (TM507). Righteous acts repeated become **righteous habits** (COL356). All the righteous habits together make up the **righteous character** (COL356). This is the **"imparted robe of righteousness"** that God weaves in them by the "loom of heaven" while they are covered by the "imputed robe of righteousness" which they obtain from Christ through faith in His merits (COL311-2; AA483.2; DA312.5; #1SM366.8). This **imparted righteous character** is the "oil" that the wise virgins had, but the foolish did not have (COL407-8; CG173.3; TM234.1). It is the "white raiment" which Laodicea needs (4T88.8). It is the "gold tried in the fire" that the sons of Levi will have (5T129; 4T89). God calls it, "the righteousness of the saints" (Rev. 19:8); but the saints refuse to take credit to themselves (Matt. 25:37,38). They call it "the righteousness of Christ" (PK591). You see, all glory for our deliverance goes to the Father, Son, and Holy Spirit (Jude 25; 2BC1035).

It is interesting how God has chosen a **time of worship** rather than an **object of worship** as a sign of loving obedience and allegiance to the Creator God. He chose and sanctified the seventh-day as the Sabbath at creation (Genesis 2:2,3). He has never changed it (Mal. 3:6; Matt. 5:17,18). He designated that it was to begin and end at sundown when mankind is awake and active rather than at midnight when most people are asleep. A conscious decision is to be made to "guard well the edges of the Sabbath" (6T356). There are no "natural consequences" involved if one is off the time of keeping the Sabbath by an hour or so, but there is a violation of committment to the Lord of the universe. Insofar as the followers of God are concerned, what we think and do on the Sabbath and when we keep His day gives our answer to the number one question in the great controversy, Does God alone have the right to decide what is right in all things, or can each person follow his own will as Satan would have it? Does the beast have the right to pick the day?

The mighty shaking of God's people and the sealing will start with those long in the way in God's church (1 Peter 4:17) and will continue until the first fruits of the living, the 144,000, are all sealed (Rev 7:1-8; 14:1-5; 3SM158). When these are sealed, they will add their voices to "the loud cry of the third angel," and the message will extend throughout the world to everyone (EW271-2). A great unnumbered multitude will also join the Lord, be sealed, and be translated (Rev 7:9-17; 3SM429). That latter group, the main harvest of the living, will remain unnumbered until all have decided, because all are invited from the least to the greatest. There is no limit to the number that could be saved (Joel 2:20-32; Matt 22:1-14).

"Tidings Out Of The North": Immediately after the portrayal in Revelation 17 of the woman Babylon (apostate religion, particularly, papal Rome) sitting upon the beast out of the bottomless pit (atheistic powers), we read these words. "I saw another angel coming down from heaven, having great authority, and the earth was illuminated with his glory. And he cried mightily with a loud voice, saying, 'Babylon the great is fallen'.... And I heard another voice from heaven saying, 'Come out of her, my people'" (Rev. 18:1,2,4). This mighty angel unites his voice with the three angels of Revelation 14 in the climactic call for all the honest in heart on the earth to be saved. His message is a reiteration of the message of the second angel (Rev. 14:8). The voice of this mighty angel when added with to that of the remnant church and the angels giving the three angels' messages, produces "the loud cry." **All of this proceeds from heaven, the sides of the north.**

What is embodied in these "tidings from the north"?

Message of the First Angel: This angel has the "everlasting gospel to preach" in all the world. Every inhabitant of the earth is called to "fear" God and give "glory" to Him. They are told that "the hour of His judgment [the investigation of the guests] has come," and to worship the Creator of heaven and earth (Rev. 14:6,7).

What is the "everlasting gospel"? It was first stated to Adam and Eve in Eden when the promise was given of forgiveness and cleansing from sin (Genesis 3:15). God promised to "write" hatred for sin and love of righteousness within the heart of all those who desire it and ask for it. He promised to write the knowledge of His law in the mind of those who ask for that (Hebrews 8:10-12). These promises represent the "new covenant" or agreement for our salvation (Hebrews 8:8; Jer. 31:31-34). It includes restoration of communication, through Christ, between God and man (Isaiah 59:1-3; 15-21). It includes transfer of guilt and blotting out of the remembrance of sin from the heart (Heb. 8:12; Acts 3:19). It includes being "strengthened with might through His Spirit in the inner man," working in us "exceedingly abundantly above all that we ask or think, according to the power that works in us" (Ephesians 3:15-20). In other words, it includes the **two free gifts:** justification by faith in Jesus, and obedience by faith in Jesus (Romans 5:1,2). It even includes the pleading, drawing power of the Holy Spirit, even while we are sinners (Romans 5:6-11; MB150).

What does it mean to "fear" God? It means to reverence, to stand in awe of, to worship Him. Why? He is our Creator, our loving King, and our Redeemer. He is entitled to this because of what He is like as portrayed in His laws for governance of His subjects and because of what He has done for us.

What does it mean to "give glory to Him?" Like Jesus, our example, we define it. "To give glory to God is to reveal His character in our own, and thus make Him known. And in whatever way we make known the Father or the Son, we glorify God" (7BC979). This is what Jesus did for His Father while He was here (John 17:1-4). This is what Jesus meant in His answer to the question of Thomas and Philip shortly before Gethsemane (John 14:5-11). God intends to shew the world what the members of the Godhead are like by working mightily through His followers on earth who "are willing to be made willing" (Phil. 2:5,13; Romans 12:1,2; Eph. 5:25-27).

To "give glory to God" also means to ascribe all of what we are and every good and righteous deed to Him. Elijah on Mt. Carmel had to pray seven times for the rain to come. Why? He was in danger of taking credit for the great revival that was wrought in Israel that day. Between the seven prayers he was examining himself to see wherein he was likely to take glory to himself. When he reached the conclusion that God was everything and he was nothing in his own eyes and in the eyes of God, then God answered his prayers for rain (2BC1035). Not long afterwards in the cave, he ascribed credit to himself when he mentioned to God how much he had done (1 Kings 19:10-14).

What is the meaning of the phrase, "the hour of His judgment is come"? To grasp this, we will need to study the sanctuary service in Exodus, Leviticus, and Numbers. As we do, we will understand the cleansing of the sanctuary, comprehend more of what the Messiah did on earth, and be better able to follow His ministry as High Priest in the heavenly sanctuary (Hebrews 2:14-18; 4:14-16; 7:27; 8:1 to 9:28).

In the last days, those who follow the ministry of Jesus in the sanctuary above will be pleading for a perfect heart, will be confessing and forsaking every known sin, will be submitting themselves for God to work in them moment by moment, and will be pleading for the God to reveal all their unrecognized sin (PK590-591). All their guilt of every known and unrecognized sin will be transferred from them to the sanctuary above, and their sins will all be pardoned through the merits of Jesus (GC480-5).

At the time of this judgment, the investigative phase, the names of all those who have believed on Jesus will be brought up in the court of heaven (GC483). If all their guilt has been removed, if they have let God work in them as He willed, the commission will go forth, "restore to them their full inheritance" (Hebrews 9:15; GC483-4; Micah 4:8; PK591). Thus, their sins will go beforehand to judgment (1 Timothy 5:24), and the original dominion that Adam lost will be restored to them (Micah 4:8).

This "investigative judgment" and "final atonement" will include four special benefits for the people of God (GC480). First, the everlasting covenant will be fulfilled in them which will give them two things (GC485). God's law will be "put in their mind" so that they will know exactly what God wants them to do under all circumstances without someone having to tell them. Thus they will be enabled to cease unrecognized disobedience, sins of which they had been previously unaware. Second, God's law of love will be "written in their hearts" so that they will just love to live and do everything that God wants them to do (Hebrews 8:10-12). Third, the command will go forth, "blot out their record of sin from their heart" (GC480-3). "Take away the filthy garments" from them (Zech. 3:1-5; GC480-3). And finally, they will receive the "refreshing from the Lord" (Acts 3:19; GC613). The Lord will pour out the full measure of His Holy Spirit upon them (AA54-5; TM506-8).

With these advantages, - the work of God in character development of the early rain, the full knowledge of God's will, the perfect love for God, the removal of all guilt and record of sin from their heart, and the full indwelling of the Holy Spirit, - they will be enabled to stand through the time of trouble without a mediator.

They will be permitted to go directly to the Father or to their Lord for full guidance and the enabling power of the Spirit (GC613-4).

The soul temple will be cleansed for this last generation, those that will be translated without seeing death while they are alive (GC490; Lev. 23:27-32). They have sent their sins "before hand to judgment." The final act of the High Priest to cleanse the sanctuary in heaven will be to take upon Himself the guilt of every sin of every person who has accepted His sacrifice, and then place them upon Satan" (GC422; Lev. 16:20- 24). By virture of His own blood He can do this for each person who believes in Him (Heb. 9:7, 14, 20-28).

The Message of the Second Angel: When the nominal Christian churches spurned the message of the first angel, God rejected them. In the summer of 1844, the second angel's message was given, "Babylon (the false and apostate religions) is fallen" (Rev. 14:8; GC380-90). This call was heeded as about fifty thousand withdrew from those churches (SR364-6). Those two messages for that time fulfilled the purpose that the Lord had in mind, but God's followers had more work to do before they would be ready to give the message of that third angel (Rev. 10:8-11; GC424-25). They needed to understand the sanctuary service and to apply it to the prophetic messages and their understanding of the gospel. They should have heeded the message to "measure the temple of God, and the altar, and them that worship therein" (Rev. 11:1,2). Few, if any, of those who were giving the advent message were worshiping God on His holy day. How could they give the warning message of the third angel about worshiping the beast and about receiving the mark of the beast (Rev. 14:9-11)?

The Message of the Third Angel: After telling the people on this earth about the plan of salvation and how to obtain their inheritance from the Father, and after the call is delivered by the second angel to separate from the false, apostate churches, God reveals why they are to come out. He must deal with the rebellion against His authority and clean up every vestige of sin from this earth. Those who refuse the offer of pardon and cleansing from Christ, must be sentenced to execution when the earth is to be made new. This is no arbitrary decision on God's part. Those who worship the beast and do his bidding, have chosen the beast to be their king. This beast (of Rev. 13:1-10) is none other than the earthly agent of the usurper king of the north. "This symbol, as most Protestants have believed, represents the papacy, which succeeded to the power and seat and authority once held by the ancient Roman empire"

(GC439). This is the head that received the "deadly wound" when, in 1798, the French army placed the pope into captivity, the power that "leadeth into captivity shall go into captivity" (Rev. 13:10).

In the last half of Revelation 13 we read of another beast power who comes up out of the earth. The other beast came up out of the sea. Seas in Bible prophecy represent people or a populous area (Rev. 17:15). This second beast comes up about the time that the leopard beast gets the deadly wound and has its activities curtailed. The United States of America is the one major nation which arose at about 1798 from an area relatively uninhabited. Its two powerful characteristic principles which has given it power to accomplish its role in the nations of earth are Republicanism and Protestantism. It speaks by the action of its legislative and judicial authorities (GC 442).

At its inception our country exhibited lamblike treatment of the downtrodden masses of the world who sought religious freedom with separation of church and state. But, after a period of time this two horned lamblike beast will change its characteristics and begin to speak like a dragon and start to exercise the authority of the leopard-like beast (Rev. 13:11,12). Thus, both the leopard-like beast, whereever he is in dominance, and the two horned beast, to all who are under his influence, begin to act alike and force their religious tenets upon "every tribe, tongue, and nation on earth" (Rev. 14:7-12,15,16). Provisons will be made for Sunday exaltation and enforcement of other tradional religious tenets on penalty of economic boycott and finally death. Such actions by the legislative and judicial authorities of the United States repudiates the principle of our constitution which provides for separation of church and state. That is what will restore the workings of churchcraft and statecraft, heal the deadly wound, and make the "**image** of the beast who was wounded by the sword and lived" (Rev. 13:14,15).

> "Romanism in the Old World and apostate Protestantism in the New will pursue a similar course toward those who honor all the divine precepts" (GC616).

What will be the sign or "mark" that "those who dwell on the earth make an image to the beast" and worship it? It will be the honoring "the venerable day of the sun" as the day of worship in direct conflict with the day that the Lord has given mankind which is the Seventh day sabbath. Not only has the day of worship been changed, an occurrence predicted in Daniel 7:25, but the time of worship has been changed from even, to even as God directed, to midnight to midnight.

This time of worship is like a national flag. In the recent news we have observed people living under the protection of "the stars and stripes," show their disdain of the United States by stamping its flag in the dust and burning it. Those who do such are not deserving of citizenship in this nation. Similarly, God has established a specific day and time of worship as evidence of love of and obedience to His government. Anyone who tramples upon that day or changes the day and time is in rebellion against the God of heaven (Isaiah 58:12-14). He is pledging allegiance to the government whose sign he honors. By observing Sunday, which has no authority higher than the leopard beast, instead of the seventh-day Sabbath, he is showing disdain for the Lord of the seventh-day Sabbath (Exodus 20:10; Mark 2:28) showing preference for the government established by Satan, the usurper king of the north. The "man of sin," who claims to have changed the time and day of worship from Sabbath of the Lord to Sunday, and calls that a sign or mark of its authority, is the papacy. Therefore, all those who understand this and knowingly do this receive "a mark on their right hand [working force] or on their forehead [mental assent]" (Rev 13:16; GC578-9). Those who worship the Lord, the Creator of heaven and earth, in the true spirit at the time He specifies will receive the seal of God in their foreheads (Rev. 7:2,3; GC640).

Chapter 31

THE FINAL MOVEMENTS WILL BE RAPID ONES

These two movements, the coming of the angel of Revelation 18 (verses 2 and 4) from the true King of the north in heaven and this sealing angel of Revelation 7 from the east for the closing up of God's work on the earth, will "alarm him [the usurper king of the north]"? Satan will go forth with "great fury" to deceive and to destroy, even coming in different places on the earth "as an angel of light," "personating Christ," saying smooth things, working miracles, and starting false religious revivals, even bringing down fire from heaven in the sight of men (2 Cor 11:14; 6BC1105-6; Rev 13:13; GC624).

There will be a "little time of trouble" that will come upon the earth just before probation closes for all (EW85). It is during this time that the "loud cry" will be given, when trouble of drought, flood, tornado, earthquake, anarchy, crimes of various sorts, and financial difficulties will grip the world. We can see how easily and quickly financial distress can come upon the whole world by the recent events stemming from the Iraqi invasion of Kuwait. There does not need to be actual combat of troops, but only a stalemate. Economists realize how devastating it would be if the standoff between the Iraqi leaders and the rest of the world for only one year. Is this the time when "national apostacy" will end "only in national ruin," or will it be later? (Ev235); yet holy angels will be holding back the "four winds of strife." Not only will political and military strife be restrained, but also the elements of nature, earthquakes and tempests, will be held under control until the servants of God are sealed Rev. 7:1; TM444.

A few phrases from Ellen White (9T11-17) give us a glimpse of this time:

"The Spirit of God is gradually but surely being withdrawn from the earth."

"The calamities by land and sea, the unsettled state of society, the alarms of war, are portentous."

"The agencies of evil are combining their forces and consolidating. They are strengthening for the last great crisis. Great changes are soon to take place in our world, and the final movements will be rapid ones."

"Bold robberies are of frequent occurrence.... Thefts and murders are committed on every hand. Men possessed of demons are taking the lives of men, women, and little children."

"In the great cities there are multitudes living in poverty and wretchedness, well-nigh destitute of food, shelter, and clothing...."

"[Others] in the same cities..., are spending their money on... liquor, tobacco, and other things [like drugs] that destroy the powers of the brain, unbalance the mind, and debase the soul."

"Those who hold the reins of government are not able to solve the problem of moral corruption, poverty, pauperism, and increasing crime. They struggle in vain to place business operations on a more secure basis."

How much clearer could any one describe the weekly news headlines in the last few months. As these conditions build up in severity, they will arouse the religionists to persuade governments to pass moral laws. This will mean the union of church and state. Their cause may be good, but their means of obtaining it are wrong. The traditions and laws of men will supercede the laws of God. Revelations 13 shows us that Protestantism in America (the two horned beast) will unite with the Papacy (seven headed beast) in the old world to force all people to conform on penalty of economic sanctions and finally death (GC615-6). The great focal point will be the Sabbath, the sign of God's authority (GC615). This image of the beast and this mark of the beast, the Sunday law, will be formed before probation closes (7BC976).

Satan has tried to confuse the world by working in disguise and changing the powers with which he works. The church is really dominant over "the beast that was, and is not, and yet is" (Rev 17:8). We do not have to name all the seven (or eight) forms of kingdoms that Satan has dominated by the Babylonish woman. Atheism, the beast that "once was, and is not [in John's time], and that will ascend out of the bottomless pit" at the time of the end, has been used by Satan to fight against God and His true followers as did ancient Egypt (GC273). But the spiritually Egypt, king of the south power, also wages war against the Babylonish woman (the church aspect), even to give the papal power (governmental aspect) a deadly wound. This atheistic, governmental head will continue for a short time (Rev. 17:10).

We note further that all those on the earth, whose names are not in the Book of Life, will "marvel" when they see "the beast that was, is not, and yet shall be present [margin]." These descriptive phrases fit the description of the beast of Revelation 13:1-10. This beast "was" as Babylon. It was not in John's time, and yet "shall be present" as the papal political power from 538 to 1798 A.D. Those will marvel when they see it reemerge after the deadly wound is healed.

One similar statement needs to be considered in this context. The "beast that was, and is not, is himself the eighth, and is of the seven, and is going into perdition" (Rev. 17:11). What looks like a new (the eighth) beast, is not really a new beast at all. It is one in which the spiritually atheistic power is merged into the reemerged "king of the north" papal power.

Whatever the form, whether beast or Babylonish woman, it will go into perdition as described in Rev 17:8; and 18:8.

It is probably not wise to be dogmatic about the identification of the seven governmental phases of the beast with the seven heads. However, my first choice for the eight beasts mentioned in Revelation 17:11 with their heads, respectively is as shown below. My strongest reason for including Egypt is that the king of the south (Egyptian atheism) plays a most important role in the last six verses of Daniel 11.

"Fallen"	1.	Egypt "was" - atheistic-pantheistic slave masters of Israel
"Fallen"	2.	Assyria took the ten tribes into captivity
"Fallen"	3.	Babylon took Judah into captivity, but many of these returned
"Fallen"	4.	Media-Persia - Satan through Haman nearly destroyed Israel
"Fallen"		

	5. Greece - humanism infiltrated Israel's priesthood from Alexandria
"Is"	6. Pagan Rome - brought in Mithraism and persecuted the Christians
"Is not"	7. Papal Rome – coercive religion dominated the civilized world ...
"and yet is"	...and martyred Christians. Received a deadly wound at the hand of the eighth beast, atheism; but then remerges after wound heals.
"was,"	8. Atheistic "spiritual" Egypt – brought back into
"is not"	power to work against God and the Bible for a
"ascends"	"short time" in the time of the end. This power gives the
from	deadly wound to the seventh beast, but while the deadly
the pit"	wound steadily heals, the beast "is" for a "short time."

The stage is all set up. The main actors are in place. As of this writing, the papacy dominates the situation in Poland, Czechoslovakia, East Germany, and Roumania. The Polish communist leaders foresaw this coming about four years ago. When they looked about for some weapon to counteract the burgeoning of the papal power, they offered to print at government expense about 200,000 copies of the book, *The Great Controversy* by Ellen White. They perceived that that book taught powerful doctrines against their number one enemy, the papacy; but that plan did not save their cause.

The papal heirarchy has always voiced objection to democracy because the rulers derive their laws from the governed. Their preference has been for the rule of "kings" and dictators. The masses are forced to obey the rules from the higher powers. Currently, we hear many voices in the recently liberated nations in Europe which call for a "democracy." It remains to be seen just how and by whom the ruling will be done in these new "democracies."

In this study the Biblical evidence indicates that the final persecuting forces will be dominated by an apostate church power, the harlot woman. In the European scene ten "horn" political forces will receive power and authority and, in turn, give these to the leopard-like beast of Revelation 13. The leopard-like beast of Revelation 13 will also receive political support, as shown in Revelation 17, from the atheistic beast power that comes out of the bottomless pit. The two-horned beast of Revelation 13 will exercise all the power of the leopard-like beast of Revelation 13, give breath to that beast, and cause the whole world to make an image to it (Rev. 13:12-16).

In short, the powers in Europe will support the papacy. The communistic forces will be "converted to religion" and support the papacy. The United States of America will give its economic and political support to the papacy. Thus we have a thumbnail sketch of what Satan uses to wage war against our Lord and the remnant church.

What is the next scenario for God's people and the World? "The final movements will be rapid ones" (9T11). The remnant church will go through the "mighty shaking" (1T179-84). False theories and the rejection of the Laodicean message will cause the shaking (TM112; EW270). **Be prepared for "every wind of doctrine" that could deceive the very elect (RH01-11-87).** Study the Word of God as you have never studied before (Ed126). "Since we are surrounded with so great a cloud of witnesses, let us lay aside every weight, and the sin that easily ensares us, and let us run with endurance the race that is set before us, looking unto Jesus...." (Hebrews 12:1,2). Now is the time to awaken out of sleep and let the Holy Spirit fill "our lamps" and build a righteous character within us (COL411-2).

> "It is in a crisis that character is revealed.... So now, a sudden and unlooked-for calamity, something that brings the soul face to face with death, will show whether there is any real faith in the promises of God.... The great final test comes at the close of human probation, when it will be too late for the soul's needs to be supplied" (COL412).

As God's Spirit is withdrawn from those who reject God's merciful plan for salvation, the wicked will wax worse and worse (MH142-3; 5T208-213;9T11-18). Satan and his forces of evil will be released. Not only will his influence over mankind be released, but his control over the natural forces be greater so that there will be increases in floods and droughts, hurricanes and earthquakes, and disasters of various sorts (9T13; GC590). God's people will be looked upon as the cause, "a Mordecai in the gate," for all these calamities (5T450; EW85; 9T13). The early phase of God's final retributive judgments will begin on this earth. These culminate in the seven last plagues. A call will be made for a national Sunday law (GC604-12).

God's people will be "sighing and crying" because of the conditions in the church and because of the wickedness of mankind

(GC611; 5T209-13). They will be giving the "loud cry" of the third angel (GC609-612). Also, "The fearful results of enforcing the observances of the church by civil authority, the inroads of spiritualism, the stealthy but rapid progress of the papal power—all will be unmasked" (GC606). While many will leave the church during the mighty shaking (EW270-1; 4T89), a "large number [will] take their stand upon the Lord's side" (GC612). All this will only enrage the enemies of righteousness (GC614), yet they will be held in check until the last message of warning is completed (GC611).

"By thousands of voices, all over the world, the warning will be given. Miracles will be wrought, the sick will be healed, and signs and wonders will follow the believers. Satan also works with lying wonders, even bringing down fire from heaven in the sight of men (Revelation 13:13). Thus the inhabitants of the earth will be brought to take their stand" (GC612).

"Fearful sights of a supernatural character will soon be revealed in the heavens, in token of the power of miracle-working demons.... Persons will arise pretending to be Christ Himself, and claiming the title and worship which belong to the world's Redeemer. They will perform wonderful miracles of healing and will profess to have revelations from heaven contradicting the testimony of the Scriptures "(GC624).

"As the crowning act in the great drama of deception, Satan himself will personate Christ. The church has long professed to look to the Saviour's advent as the consummation of her hopes. Now the deceiver will make it appear that Christ has come. In different parts of the earth, Satan will manifest himself among men as a majestic being of dazzling brightness, resembling the description of the Son of God given by John in the Revelation. Revelation 1:13-15." (GC624).

Several groups are working for political or economic reasons for a "New World Order" under some central control. These include such organizations as the Trilateral Commission, the Council of Foreign Relations, the World Future Society, and the Aspen Institute for Humanistic Studies, Transnationalists, Internationists, as well as Marxist-Leninist Communism.

It is astonishing how many of the major religions of the world are looking for the coming of a world leader. All expect their "saviour" to set up his dominion on this earth based upon their religion. Most Protestants and Catholics expect to see "Jesus" return and set up His kingdom on this earth. The Jews are looking for the Messiah. Moslems, Hindus, and Buddhists are expecting the return or reincarnation of a prophet. The New Agers are looking for Maitreya, their "christ."

The Seventh-day Adventist church is unique in teaching that at the second coming of Christ, He will not set foot upon this earth, but will come in the clouds of heaven, destroy the wicked by the brightness of His coming, raise the righteous dead, and take all His saints with Him to heaven (1 Thess 4:15-18; Revelation 19). Then, after a thousand years in heaven, Christ and the saints will return to this earth, bring down the New Jerusalem, and raise the wicked for their final judgment; and then Christ will recreate the earth (Revelation 20 and 21).

Satan desires to make it appear that even the Seventh-day Adventist church is expecting Christ to set up His kingdom on this earth when He comes next. In April, 1959, a Shepherd Rod group who claim earnestly that they are Seventh-day Adventists, met in Waco, Texas, waiting for Christ to return, open the way for them to return to Palestine, and enable them to proclaim "the loud cry". About fifteen families of an offshoot group, called the Davidian Seventh-day Adventists, actually moved to Palestine in anticipation of these events. The special artists painting of Christ's second coming printed on the cover of the August, 1990, issue of Ministry Magazine was also to lead people to think Seventh-day Adventist have changed their theology and now believe that Jesus is coming next time to set up His kingdom on this earth.

Let us pray fervently that God will raise up the workers needed around the world in this time of relative peace, to teach the special truths for this time. We have a little time left in which to finish this work before the "terrible crisis" which is soon to follow (5T463).

When the third angel's message closes, and the sealing angel returns and announces that his work is done, then Jesus stands up and ceases His work of mediation. He lifts His hands and says, "It is done" (GC613). God's people may then go directly to the Father as well as to Jesus for light, guidance, and power (GC614). God's people will suffer temptation and trials, but God will keep them free from sinning, perfectly (GC620). The righteous will not sin, not even by a thought, because God has prepared them by the final atonement to stand as Jesus stood (GC623).

Satan will bring on the "great, final" time of trouble (Daniel 12:1; GC614). The apostate church will be all decked out (Rev. 17:4-6) and will work (fornicate) with the governments of earth to get her will done. She will do this through whatever governmental systems that she can. She will do this by controlling the citizens of those governments, that is, by "sitting upon many waters" (Rev. 17:1,15). When the ten horn powers had crowns on their heads, their rulers were monarchies, yet subject to the power of the church (Rev. 13:1). In the time of the end phase, the ten horn (powers) will receive authority for a short while and will give their power and authority to work the will of the church until they see the harlot for what she is (Rev. 17:12-16). During this final phase, "until the words of God are fulfilled," the horns are without crowns, non- monarchical in character (Rev. 17:17).

In the eyes of many, the king of the south, atheistic communism has been shown to be unable to provide the comforts and necessities of life, the utopia. Edom, Moab, and Ammon, representing Islam, will be shown to trust in their cruel god and will be unable to help the world without a Saviour. In the last remnant of time the king of the north, Babylon [the papacy] and her daughters [apostate protestantism], will be unable to provide the spiritual needs of the world. Satan and his agents will crumble before the great mountain of the Lord (Daniel 2:44,45). He and all his helpers "will come to his end, and none shall help him" (Dan. 11:45; Rev. 18:8-24).

Notice that it is during this "great time of trouble", brought on by Satan, after probation closes, that God will pour out the seven last plagues (Rev. 15:5 to 16:21; GC627-32).

Then, glory, hallelujah, God's people will be delivered (GC634-52). When they see their Messiah, their Christ, their King coming in the clouds of heaven with the myriads of holy angels, they will say, "Lo, **THIS** is **OUR** God; we have waited for Him, and He will save us: THIS is the Lord; we have waited for him, we will be glad and rejoice in his salvation" (Isaiah 25:9).

Chapter 32

GOD'S HARVEST SEQUENCE

The kingdom of Christ was represented in miniature at the mount of transfiguration (DA422). Moses represented all those who will die and will be resurrected. Elijah represented all those who will be translated without seeing death even once. If we can keep these two main groups distinct in our thinking, we can better understand the harvest of the saints as it is further divided into the first fruits and main harvest subgroups. Jesus is the representative and first fruits of all of the saved because of the uniqueness of His Divine-human nature (1 Cor. 15:23). He suffered the second death for everyone; a thing that no one else in the universe will have done.

The First Fruit Ceremony: The description of the first fruit ceremony in Leviticus divides the ceremony into two parts. The first part took place at the time of the Passover, and the second part fifty days later at Pentecost.

On the 14th of Abib, the Passover lamb was slain and a portion of a field of barley was marked off, but the grain was not cut. In olden times the grain was tied in bundles and left standing to ripen further. On the morning before the Sabbath, on the 16th day of Abib, three select men cut the tied sheaves of barley in the presence of witnesses and combined them into one large sheaf. This was waved before the Lord as the "sheaf of the first fruits" on the morning after the Sabbath (Lev. 23:9-11). Along with this waving, a one-year old lamb was offered with its meal and drink offering (Lev. 23:12, 13). The rest of the harvest, the main harvest was not to be used for food until this was done (Lev. 23:14).

The second phase of the first fruit ceremony took place fifty days later. At that time the "new meat offering" was performed. In that ceremony two loaves of bread, made from the first fruit grain, were waved before the Lord along with the prescribed animals for a burnt offering, a sin offering, and a peace offering (Lev. 23:15-21).

The Harvest of Those Who Die in the Lord: When we consider the above services for those who die in the Lord, we can see more clearly what will happen to those saints. When Jesus died, the graves of the first fruits of the sleeping saints were opened. On the morning of the first day, Christ arose, the antitype of the first fruits. He then called the first fruits of his sleeping saints forth from the grave (1SM:304). They were "waved before the Lord," as it were, on this earth when they went into the city and appeared to many (Matt. 27:53) and proclaimed, "Christ has risen from the dead, and we are risen with Him" (1SM305). These had been "colaborers with God, and who at the cost of their lives had borne testimony to the truth" (DA786).

Statements in their context in *Desire of Ages*, pages 786, and again on page 832-33, suggest that the first fruits of the dead ascended with Christ when He did after His resurrection and then again with Him from Olivet. At least we know that they ascended from Olivet with Christ to be presented to the Father as evidence of His victory over death and the grave (1SM306).

It is interesting to follow the scenes in heaven when Jesus ascended after His resurrection. The first request that Christ makes of His Father reveals what is uppermost on His mind. Before He would accept the adoration of the angels, He asks of the Father for us, "If Thy justice is satisfied, 'I will that they also, whom thou hast given me, be with me where I am'" (1SM307). How can you help loving someone like that?

After the ascension from Olivet the ceremony was performed in which Jesus was inaugurated into His office as priest and king. This event is to be compared with the seven day ceremony at which Aaron and his sons were set aside for their priesthood (Exodus 28 and 29). At the end of the ceremony in heaven, Christ "received all authority in heaven and on earth, and was the Anointed One over His people (AA38-39).

During the time period immediately after Christ left them at Olivet, the disciples were preparing themselves for the coming of the Comforter. They were preparing themselves by praising and blessing God in the temple, bowing in prayer to repeat His assurances, extending higher and higher the hand of faith, humbling their hearts in true repentance, confessing their unbelief, recalling the words that Christ had spoken to them just before His death, praying with intense earnestness for fitness to meet men, putting away all differences between themselves, drawing nearer and nearer to God, searching their hearts deeply, crying to the Lord for the holy unction for soul-saving, and claiming that power which Christ had promised (AA36-37).

With this ceremony in heaven Christ was installed as priest and king and the first fruits of the dead were installed in their positions as priests and kings along with Him (Rev. 1:6; 1 Peter 2:5). Thus the second part of the first fruit ceremony, the "wave offering" of loaves before the Lord was accomplished in heaven. The main harvest of the dead was, thus, assured to occur at the appropriate time, at His second coming (1SM305-6).

The Harvest of Those Who Will Be Translated: In like manner the harvest of those who will be translated without seeing death is defined. We would expect to see a first fruit subgroup and a main harvest subgroup of the saints to be translated. Is there another group which is called the first fruits who will be saved?

The only other group called the first fruits and who fit the description of some who would be translated is the 144,000 (GC649). We read of them in Revelation 7 and 14. In Revelation 7 we read of the 144,000 at the time of the sealing, and in the last half of the chapter we read of a "great multitude, which no man can number" who will also stand before the throne (Rev. 7:9). This Scripture could be referring to all the saved from all ages, those who will be resurrected as well as those who will be translated without seeing death, but the context and description suggests a group which go through the time of trouble at the end of the world. Ellen White refers to them somewhat differently from the "millions, of all ages" around the throne of God (GC665). Furthermore, she uses the texts Revelation 7:14-17 in describing what the 144,000 will go through (GC649).

Since the 144,000 are called the first fruits "from among the living" and will be translated, this "unnumbered multitude" of Revelation 7 must refer to the main harvest of the living. This belief is strengthened by the ceremony of the first fruits which would define the harvest to include some who would be selected earlier than others and serve a special purpose as well as a main harvest company. There is, therefore, a parallel situation between those who will be represented by Moses and by those who will be represented by Elijah.

	Moses Group	Elijah Group
Firstfruits	Were Resurrected Declared a risen Jesus Ascended with Christ Number not given	Never die Give the "loud cry" Translated at 2nd Coming 144,000
Main Harvest	Sleep until 2nd coming Millions of all ages Who joined in God's Work.	Never die "Unnumbered multitude" Witness for God in the Time of Trouble

The first fruits in the Elijah Group in the table above are indicated by the description of Ellen White to be those who go through the mighty shaking (EW270-1). Those who had gone through the mighty shaking were described by several phrases as follows:–

- Had a double company of guardian angels about them,
- were clothed with armor from head to their feet,
- moved in exact order,
- countenances shone with the light and glory of heaven,
- **had obtained the victory,**
- and evil angels could have no power over them.

This group then gave the loud cry of the third angel, and many more joined their ranks.

In the sealing work, the angels were directed to begin their work "at my sanctuary" (Ezekiel 9:6). They started with the "ancient men which were before the house" (See 5T210-4). For the last generation this is a solemn time. God has promised that "every spot or stain" will be removed from our robe of character (5T214). He then promises also to keep that robe pure and spotless for eternity (5T216). We have no promise that those in the church who have had great light will remain in the church, but we are assured that others, who have not had the opportunity to see the truth for our time, will be allowed to join the ranks of those who will be sealed. The first group appears to be a literal number of 144,000, but God has not put a limit to those who will join after the sealing of the first fruits. He leaves that subgroup "unnumbered" so that all who come to Him can be saved.

We can study about the 144,000, but we are not to speculate just which person will be in that group (7BC978). God will do the choosing. Some who have died were seen to be "**with** the 144,000" (2SM263), but that must not be construed to mean that some resurrected people will help make up that number. The first fruit ceremony helps us keep this clearly understood.

Chapter 33

CONCLUSION AND APPEAL

In conclusion let us consider what our study leads us to believe will be the needs of those who will go through the time of trouble. In this book we have looked at the preparation of the saints to stand from several different analogies that the prophets have portrayed in the Scriptures and the Spirit of Prophecy. We shall now summarize this preparation, but not necessarily in the sequence that they occur.

Those who will be translated without seeing death will need:

- To be born again by adoption into the Lord's family. Their names must be written in the Book of Life if they are to obtain their inheritance.
- Full consecration to God; acceptance of the Saviour as the sole Ruler of their heart; all their talents and their earthly goods dedicated to His service; a heart perfectly sanctified.
- A love for God and what He stands for that needs no reward.
- An abhorrence of Satan and what he stands for (GC670.4); a hatred of sin so great that they would rather die than sin.
- All their guilt of sin removed from them to the sanctuary in heaven.
- An experimental knowledge by actual partaking of God's power to keep them from sinning (5T221.4); to know the secret of success by practice (DA667.5;PP509.2); not satisfied with just the theory of truth (GC426.6).

–Habits of thought to overcome evil; a habit of turning to God for strength, by this means habitually overcoming every known propensity and tendency to evil (MH454.1).

–An attitude of guarding the senses, the avenues of the soul; limiting the exposure of the mind to no more temptation than is absolutely necessary to carry out their work for God (3T476.6; 1BC1087-8).

–The mental thought record of sin erased from the heart since these may (1) originate a temptation or (2) be a responsive chord to a temptation from the world via the senses or direct temptations from the devil (MB116.7); all filthy pictures in the "halls of memory" of the heart covered and blotted out; all propensities and tendencies to sin overcome and purged (GC623.1).

–The full outpouring of the Holy Spirit, not just the "earnest" of the Spirit. They must be led continually by the Spirit, which denotes that they must follow the guidance of the Spirit (MB150).

–God's law written in their hearts and put in their minds in its entirety as Adam and Eve had before the fall.

–An intelligent knowledge from the study of the Scriptures and the Spirit of Prophecy of Christ's ministry in heaven, of the prophetic events ahead, and of what God expects of them in cooperation with Him. This is relative to their age, mental capacity, and access to the printed Word.

The children of Israel were slaves in Egypt. They had harsh taskmasters. In addition, Pharaoh was murdering their sons. Yet, shortly after their deliverance, they murmured frequently against God and wanted to go back. *Will God have to permit life on this earth to become as unbearable as that or untenable to that extent before we will want to leave here?* It is fast getting that way!! Every week brings us fresh indications of the inhumanity of man, of famine, and of disasters. How much more pollution of air, water, and food will we have to tolerate?

It was said of Nicodemus, "He was not so much impressed by the necessity of the new birth as by the manner of its accomplishment" (DA173.4). *Now, let us not get so bogged down with argumentation over mechanisms that we fail to realize that we need to be rid of sin and its effects upon us, and every provision has been made for this in God's order.*

Little children and adults went into the Promised Land. Jesus lived from infancy to adulthood without sin. He was born with the full indwelling of the Spirit. He also inherited our infirmities through Mary (DA117.3; RH04-05-06). God's law was written in His heart and mind. Regardless of His age He knew exactly what His Father expected of Him while on this earth. He did the will of His Father through the power that is available to us. "He had kept His Father's commandments, and there was no sin in Him that Satan could use to his advantage" (GC623.4). If the members of God's remnant church will cooperate and be willing to part with every sin when it is revealed to them, God will prepare them and help them to stand through the time of trouble without sinning and without a mediator (Jude 24, 25).

Perhaps we do not believe that Jesus can keep us from sinning. We look across our Jordan and say, "How can we ever overcome those giant Jericho sins? The walls, the standards are too high; we don't see how we can make it! Or perhaps we come up to our little city of Ai temptation and think, "We can conquer this little trial in our own strength. No need to call to God for help."

Why not try God's facilities and depend upon His wisdom? Enoch and Elijah made it without seeing death.

Perhaps we are not sure that heaven is a real place made of real material things and real spiritual things (MH414.9; GC674-5). Maybe we think that life on this planet is not too tough, you just have to get used to it. We act as though we are afraid to let go of the tangible things on this earth until death stares us full in the face. **Then** we know that we lose this life regardless of whether we believe in life eternal or not.

Heaven is made of real spiritual things and real material things, and the Maker, our loving Redeemer, is there (GC674-6). His first request when He ascended to heaven, before He would allow homage from His accompanying angels, tells us what was uppermost on His mind. His first request was, "I will that they also, whom Thou hast given Me, be with Me where I am" (GC501.9; 5BC1150; DA834; 1SM307). Such love as that is nearly beyond comprehension!

By faith there will be some saints who will not taste death, who will be sealed, who will receive all the benefits of the final atonement while they are alive, and who will live by the power of the indwelling Spirit through the great time of trouble without sinning. **By faith alone** they will respond to the pleading of the Holy Spirit, repent, be born again, and receive the benefits of imputed righteousness. **By faith alone** they will set themselves aside for holy use by responding to the Holy Spirit. **By faith alone** they will respond to the Holy Spirit and call for wisdom and power to obey God in every thing. **By faith alone** they will prove that God's laws are just and good and can be kept by the facilities made available through imparted righteousness.

They will agree that God is vindicated (PP68.8). He can point to them and say, "Here are they that keep the commandments of God, and the faith of Jesus" (Rev. 14:12). The saints can say, "**This** is **our** God; we have waited for **Him**, and He will save us" (Isaiah 25:9).

"When the character of Christ shall be perfectly reproduced in His people, then He will come to claim them...." COL69

We invite you to view the complete
selection of titles we publish at:

www.TEACHServices.com

or write or email us your praises,
reactions, or thoughts about this
or any other book we publish at:

TEACH Services, Inc.
P U B L I S H I N G
www.TEACHServices.com
P.O. Box 954
Ringgold, GA 30736

info@TEACHServices.com

TEACH Services, Inc., titles may be purchased in bulk for educational, business, fund-raising, or sales promotional use. For information, please e-mail

BulkSales@TEACHServices.com.

Finally, if you are interested in seeing
your own book in print, please contact us at

publishing@teachservices.com.

We would be happy to review your manuscript for free.

www.ingramcontent.com/pod-product-compliance
Lightning Source LLC
Chambersburg PA
CBHW070547160426
43199CB00014B/2400